John Searle's Philosophy of Language:
Force, Meaning, and Mind

This is a volume of original essays on key aspects of John Searle's philosophy of language. It examines Searle's work in relation to current issues of central significance, including internalism versus externalism about mental and linguistic content, truth conditional versus non-truth conditional conceptions of content, the relative priorities of thought and language in the explanation of intentionality, the status of the distinction between force and sense in the theory of meaning, the issue of meaning skepticism in relation to rule-following, and the proper characterization of "what is said" in relation to the semantics/pragmatics distinction. Written by a distinguished team of contemporary philosophers, and prefaced by an illuminating essay by Searle, the volume aims to contribute to a deeper understanding of Searle's work in philosophy of language, and to suggest innovative approaches to fundamental questions in that area.

SAVAS L. TSOHATZIDIS is Professor of General Linguistics and the Philosophy of Language, Department of Linguistics, Aristotle University of Thessaloniki.

John Searle's Philosophy of Language

Force, Meaning, and Mind

edited by

SAVAS L. TSOHATZIDIS

CAMBRIDGE
UNIVERSITY PRESS

CAMBRIDGE UNIVERSITY PRESS
Cambridge, New York, Melbourne, Madrid, Cape Town, Singapore, São Paulo

Cambridge University Press
The Edinburgh Building, Cambridge CB2 8RU, UK

Published in the United States of America by Cambridge University Press, New York

www.cambridge.org
Information on this title: www.cambridge.org/9780521685344

First published 2007

Printed in the United Kingdom at the University Press, Cambridge

A catalogue record for this publication is available from the British Library

ISBN 978-0-521-86627-9 hardback
ISBN 978-0-521-68534-4 paperback

Contents

Contents

Contributors

NICHOLAS ASHER is Professor of Philosophy and Professor of Linguistics at the University of Texas at Austin

KENT BACH is Professor of Philosophy at San Francisco State University

STEPHEN J. BARKER is Associate Professor and Reader in Philosophy at the University of Nottingham

WAYNE A. DAVIS is Professor of Philosophy at Georgetown University

CHRISTOPHER GAUKER is Professor of Philosophy at the University of Cincinnati

MITCHELL GREEN is Associate Professor of Philosophy at the University of Virginia

ROBIN JESHION is Professor of Philosophy at the University of California, Riverside

KEPA KORTA is Director of the Institute for Logic, Cognition, Language and Information at the University of the Basque Country

MARTIN KUSCH is Professor of Philosophy and Sociology of Science at the University of Cambridge

Contributors

JOHN PERRY is the Henry Waldgrave Stuart Professor of Philosophy at Stanford University

FRANÇOIS RECANATI is Director of Research at the Centre National de la Recherche Scientifique, Paris

JOHN R. SEARLE is the Willis S. and Marion Slusser Professor of the Philosophy of Mind and Language at the University of California, Berkeley

SAVAS L. TSOHATZIDIS is Professor of General Linguistics and the Philosophy of Language at Aristotle University of Thessaloniki

Acknowledgments

The editor wishes to expressed his gratitude to the contributors for their stimulating offerings, to John Searle for his support and participation, to Hilary Gaskin of Cambridge University Press for welcoming and encouraging this project, and to Charis-Olga Papadopoulou for her patience and kindness.

Introduction

SAVAS L. TSOHATZIDIS

This volume presents eleven original essays that critically examine aspects of John Searle's seminal contributions to the philosophy of language, and explore new ways in which some of their themes could be developed. After an opening essay by Searle in which he summarizes the essentials of his conception of language and what he currently takes its most distinctive implications to be, the critical essays are grouped into two interconnected parts – "From mind to meaning" and "From meaning to force" – reflecting Searle's claim that an analysis of meaning would not be adequate if it could not integrate a proper analysis of illocutionary force and if it could not itself be integrated within a satisfactory account of mind.

Searle's views on how force, meaning, and mind are interconnected form part of the general account of intentionality (in the broad sense of an entity's being *about* entities other that itself) that he has developed over the years, and his opening essay includes an outline of that account, emphasizing three of its basic ideas. First, the idea that linguistic intentionality does not merely require the expression of propositions and the existence of conditions under which they might or might not be satisfied, but also the association of those propositions with illocutionary forces of various kinds, which determine the various kinds of acts (asserting, requesting, promising, etc.) that possession of a language characteristically makes possible. Second, the idea that, in a similar way, mental intentionality does not merely require the apprehension of propositions and the existence of conditions under which they might or might not be satisfied, but also the association of those propositions with psychological modes of various kinds, which determine the various kinds of states (believing, desiring, intending, etc.) that possession of a mind characteristically makes possible. And, third, the idea that linguistic meaning derives from the communication-driven installation of conventional procedures whereby the satisfaction conditions that

1

mentally entertained propositions have under various psychological modes become the satisfaction conditions that linguistically expressed propositions have under various kinds of illocutionary forces (procedures, for example, whereby the satisfaction conditions of beliefs become the satisfaction conditions of assertions, the satisfaction conditions of desires become the satisfaction conditions of requests, the satisfaction conditions of intentions become the satisfaction conditions of promises, etc.).

Moving beyond the recapitulation of these basic ideas, Searle's opening essay explores two directions in which the picture of language that they make possible offers, in his view, explanatory advantages. First, by firmly grounding linguistic meaning in pre-linguistically available forms of intentionality (and thus fulfilling the continuity requirement that a naturalistically adequate account of linguistic meaning should, in his view, fulfill), this picture affords, according to Searle, a solution to the problem of the semantic *unity* of the sentence, as well as an explanation of the fundamentally distinct roles of reference and predication within that unity: the semantic unity of the sentence, he suggests, is a consequence of the thesis that the intentionality of sentences derives from the intentionality of mental states, given the independently motivated thesis that a necessary condition of the possession of a mental state is the capacity to recognize when it would and when it would not be satisfied, and given that it is only whole states of affairs, rather than individual constituents of those states of affairs, that are possible mental state satisfiers. And the fundamentally distinct roles of reference and predication within a sentence derives, he argues, from the fact that the most basic kind of conscious mental state is a *perceptual* state, whose possession involves the capacity to recognize salient objects and salient features of objects as constituents of the states of affairs that act as perceptual state satisfiers. The second kind of advantage offered by this conception of language is, Searle suggests, that it can identify and explain the distinctive sense in which linguistic meaning is normative: the fact that a creature happens to be in a mental state with certain satisfaction conditions does not entail that that creature undertakes, by virtue of being in that state, any *commitments* toward other creatures regarding the fulfillment of those satisfaction conditions; however, the fact that a creature produces a linguistic utterance with the same satisfaction conditions as one of its mental states does entail, according to Searle, that that creature undertakes, in producing the utterance, certain *commitments* towards other creatures regarding the fulfillment of those conditions, since the imposition of any satisfaction condition on a not *intrinsically* intentional object like an utterance would be impossible outside a system of *conventions* that a particular group of creatures has adopted for the sole purpose of enabling *communication* between its members about the external world; and it is the existence of those commitments, according to Searle, that confers upon linguistic contents a special normativity that is lacking from the mental contents from which they ultimately derive (and which is the source, in his view, of every other sort of social normativity).

The volume's critical essays do not purport to address all aspects of the multifaceted work that Searle has produced over the past four decades on linguistic intentionality and its mental background, but the aspects of that work that they do address are clearly important, both in terms of their pivotal role within Searle's system of ideas, and in terms of their connections to issues of prominent philosophical interest. It is, therefore, both to a better understanding of Searle's work and to a better understanding of the wider philosophical debates within which that work is embedded that the essays aim to make a contribution.

The volume's first part, "From mind to meaning," contains six essays, of which the first three examine aspects of the account of the intentionality of perceptual experience that Searle places at the foundation of his account of mind (and, as just noted, of language itself). François Recanati acknowledges the significance of the condition of causal self-referentiality that Searle introduces into his analysis of conscious perceptual states, but argues that Searle misconstrues that condition when he assigns it to the propositional content of the perceptual state rather than to its psychological mode: the requirement that, in veridical perception, the perceived scene must be the cause of its own perception, is, Recanati contends, a requirement that concerns not the propositional content of the perceptual state (that is, what the subject perceives) but rather its psychological mode (that is, the fact that the subject is in a state of perception as opposed to, say, a state of expectation). After arguing that similar misallocations occur not only in Searle's analysis of mental states but also in his analysis of speech acts (where conditions that properly concern the illocutionary force of the speech act are misrepresented as concerning its propositional content), Recanati claims that these problems require replacing a basic assumption of Searle's approach to mental and linguistic intentionality with a different one. The assumption to be replaced is the assumption that it is only the content (as distinct from the mode) of a mental state that determines the state's satisfaction conditions, and that it is only the content (as distinct from the force) of a speech act that determines the act's satisfaction conditions. And the alternative assumption Recanati recommends (within a framework whose details he has developed in independent work) is one that allows a mental state's satisfaction conditions to be determined *jointly* by its mode and by its content, and a speech act's satisfaction conditions to be determined *jointly* by its content and by its force. Recanati then applies that idea to the analysis of specific intentional states, noting that its application is capable of doing justice to the fact that, in many cases, the content (as distinct from the mode) of an intentional state is, contrary to what Searle has been assuming, *not* a complete proposition, but rather an entity akin to a propositional function (whose arguments are drawn from elements determined by the state's mode). And he concludes by showing how his approach provides a solution to an important problem in the analysis of the relation between perception and memory: the idea that episodic memories *retain* the content of perceptions naturally leads to the view that a memory and a perception on which the memory is based must have the same content; but that appears to be in conflict with the equally natural view that a memory and a perception on which the memory is based cannot have the same content, since memories concern past experiences whereas perceptions concern present ones; the resolution of that conflict, Recanati argues, requires adopting the view that a perception and a memory deriving from it do have the same content, but that the content in question is *not* a full proposition, but only a propositional schema whose unspecified temporal parameters are set to the present or to the past depending on whether it is associated with the perception mode or with the memory mode.

A main motivation of Searle's analysis of the intentionality of perception was his aim to show that a thoroughly internalist approach to questions of mental and linguistic content can successfully cope with certain facts widely held to be only accountable on the basis of externalist premises. Specifically, the hardly disputable fact that perceptual experiences put perceivers in relation to *particular* objects in the world has seemed to many to preclude an analysis of the intentional content of perceptual experiences as consisting in its entirety of purely conceptual elements supplied by the perceiver's mind. And Searle's analysis was aiming to deflate that so-called *particularity objection* to internalist analyses of mental content (and thus to pave the way for an internalist response to externalist accounts of linguistic reference), by claiming that his own internalist analysis does make room for the particularity of the objects of perceptual experiences because it insists that, when a subject perceives a particular object, it not only judges that there is an object there, but also that the object that is there is the cause of the *particular* experience that the subject is undergoing. The particularity objection, and its implications on Searle's position in the debate between internalism and externalism, is at the center of the essays by Kent Bach and Robin Jeshion. Both Bach and Jeshion argue that Searle's analysis as formulated does not succeed in deflating the particularity objection, but each locates the source of Searle's main difficulty in a different place, and each offers a different appreciation of the significance of the threat that Searle's account thereby faces. According to Bach, Searle cannot meet the particularity objection because the causal self-referentiality condition that he assigns to the content of perceptual states only ensures the particularity of the subject's *experience* of an object of perception, and not the particularity of the *object* itself. (Readers will note that if this criticism is valid, an analogous criticism would be valid against Searle's token-reflexive analysis of indexicals and demonstratives, which is directly inspired from his analysis of perceptual experience: the criticism would in that case be that, though the token-reflexive analysis aims to guarantee the particularity of the *referent* of an indexical or demonstrative, it only guarantees the particularity of the *utterance* containing an indexical or demonstrative token.) Bach's preferred solution to the problem insofar as it concerns the objects of perceptual experiences does not seek to secure the particularity of those objects either by adding to the content of the experiences further general propositions of the sort supplied by Searle or by substituting to those propositions a singular proposition of the sort favored by Searle's externalist opponents; his preferred solution is rather to deny that the particularity of the object of a perceptual experience is a feature determined by its content (which, in Bach's view, is not a complete proposition) and to suggest instead that it is a feature determined by its psychological mode: a perceptual experience, Bach grants, cannot be of a particular object unless that particular object causes the experience; but that requirement, he insists, specifies what it takes for an experience to be perceptual and not what a subject having a perceptual experience experiences. Bach's suggestion, then, is that Searle could and should seek to meet the particularity objection by exploiting his own distinction between the mode and the content of mental states, and by rejecting an assumption that both he and his externalist opponents commonly make, namely, that the content of perceptual experiences is the only terrain in which the particularity of their objects could be captured.

Robin Jeshion's essay argues that the particularity objection is ultimately unavoidable for internalism, and that the extent to which Searle's internalist account of perceptual experience is open to externalist challenges is significantly greater than has so far been appreciated. Reviewing first some common worries to the effect that the causal self-referentiality condition introduced by Searle may be too complicated or too sophisticated to be supposed to be available to the subjects of perceptual experiences, she suggests that these worries are not decisive and that Searle can in fact address them. She next argues, however, that the particularity objection can be raised against Searle on grounds quite different from those that have triggered the introduction of the causal self-referentiality condition, and that the specific form that the particularity objection takes when it is raised on those new grounds cannot be dealt with by Searle unless he abandons either his internalism or his fundamental and widely shared conviction that perceptual experiences put their subjects directly in contact with the external world. Jeshion's principal claim is that perceptual experience of objects through vision necessarily involves conscious identification of the real-world *locations* of objects relative to the experiencing subject, and that, contrary to what Searle's account requires, the subject's awareness of its relation to those external locations cannot be fully specified in purely internal terns – in other words, that the content of the subject's experience cannot contain a fully identifying specification of what the subject is aware of when it judges that an object is *there*, if the specification of the location denoted by "there" is to be couched in purely conceptual terms. (Jeshion notes that a parallel problem arises in the context of Searle's account of linguistic reference: even granting the token-reflexive part of Searle's account of the meaning of indexicals and demonstratives, reference to particular *locations* by means of indexicals and demonstratives cannot be supposed to be enabled, Jeshion contends, by the kind of meaning that Searle ascribes to indexicals and demonstratives, since that meaning fails to be sufficiently specificatory by virtue of being purely conceptual.) Having provided detailed a priori reasons against a purely internalist account of the content of perceptual experience, Jeshion completes her discussion by considering a rich body of recent experimental research that suggests that subjects are able to consciously track the successive locations of multiple moving objects under conditions that preclude the hypothesis that their ability to do so is based on conceptually encoding their changing locational properties. She therefore concludes that there are good empirical and nonempirical reasons for doubting that Searle can deflate the full range of externalist arguments that can be lodged against his internalist account of the content of perceptual experiences, even though the causal self-referentiality condition that he has introduced might well constitute an apt characterization of one aspect of those experiences.

Externalism may not, of course, be the proper alternative to internalism with respect to the analysis of every sort of intentional content, and in the next essay, whose topic is Searle's analysis of the sense and reference of proper names, Wayne A. Davis argues that Searle's internalist analysis of names, assuming that some of its key elements are replaced with certain original elements that Davis recommends, not only can avoid externalist objections that have been widely assumed to be fatal to it, but is clearly superior to its externalist rivals. Davis takes the basic insight of Searle's early discussion of proper names to lie in his insistence that their semantically relevant properties cannot be fully elucidated without reference to the conceptual contents that their users associate with them, and contends that purely referential, externalist accounts of the semantics of names, even though they can be used to raise valid objections against aspects of Searle's account, encounter insuperable difficulties of their own precisely because they ignore the semantic role that these conceptual contents play. Davis next argues, however, that Searle's central assumption that the semantically relevant conceptual content of names is *descriptively* specifiable makes it impossible for him either to avoid externalist objections or to exploit his internalism's real advantages, and should be replaced with the idea that names conventionally express *atomic* concepts, which, precisely because of their atomicity, cannot be reduced to any description or combination of descriptions of their purported referents. Davis then shows how the view that names express atomic concepts accounts for aspects of their semantic behavior that are impossible to explain on externalist premises, how it can explain certain other aspects of their semantic behavior that externalists have rightly drawn attention to (but which they have mistakenly tried to explain by denying that names have semantically relevant senses and not by accepting that they have *non-descriptive* semantically relevant senses), and how it allows the reaffirmation of Searle's basic internalism by removing the real but unnecessary burdens created by his descriptivism.

The last two essays of the first part of the volume discuss certain assumptions about mind and language concerning which Searle is not in dispute with other philosophers, but rather in fundamental agreement with the great majority among them; and they aim to question those widely shared assumptions, in part by scrutinizing Searle's own way of defending them. Christopher Gauker's essay disputes the assumption, which is fundamental to Searle's and to most other contemporary work on mind and language, that conceptual thought has ontological and explanatory priority over language. On Gauker's view, thought processes that are language-independent do exist – *imagistic* thought processes, in particular, are of that kind – but these thought processes are precisely the ones that are *not* conceptual; properly *conceptual* thought, Gauker contends, is essentially linguistic, and so cannot be supposed either to preexist language or to contribute to its non-circular explanation. (Conceptual thought, in Gauker's view, simply consists in the process of *imagining conversations*, with the purpose of preparing oneself to solve problems of the same kind as those that are routinely solved thanks to the coordinating effects of real conversations.) Gauker's essay is primarily devoted not to expounding his positive view, which he has explored at length elsewhere, but to rebutting a representative array of influential arguments that are commonly taken to make such a view untenable, by establishing beyond doubt that conceptual thought is independent of language. Some of the arguments for the language independence of thought that Gauker examines and rejects – for example, the arguments that begin from considerations of language learning and lead to the so-called "language of thought" hypothesis – are ones that, as he notes, Searle himself should repudiate, since they presuppose views – in particular, the computational view of the mind – which Searle has famously attacked on independent grounds. But some others – for example, those that revolve around the idea that the intentionality of mental states is intrinsic whereas the intentionality of linguistic utterances is not intrinsic – are ones that are due specifically to Searle, and determine much of the structure and content of his account of meaning (it is, for example, the idea that mental intentionality is intrinsic whereas linguistic intentionality is not intrinsic that underlies Searle's fundamental claim that linguistic meaning arises out of a process of *transferring* satisfaction conditions from mental states onto linguistic utterances). Gauker argues in detail that all these arguments for the language independence of thought are open to serious empirical, conceptual, and methodological objections, and suggests that appreciation of the force of these objections, even though it might not immediately convert one to the view that all conceptual thought is essentially linguistic, should be enough to make one highly skeptical about the legitimacy of the currently orthodox view, of which Searle is a prominent representative, that conceptual thought has ontological and explanatory priority over language.

Skepticism about the dependence of linguistic contents on mental contents would probably be taken to be mild, if compared to skepticism about the very existence of either mental or linguistic contents as *community independent* properties of individuals' thoughts or utterances. The latter sort of skepticism, together with the suggestion that practices of communal agreement are constitutive of the contents of an individual's thoughts or utterances, is famously associated with Saul Kripke's interpretation of Wittgenstein's rule-following considerations. And Searle, along with most other contemporary philosophers, has sought to resist Kripke's interpretation, by arguing both that it misrepresents Wittgenstein's views and that, independently of its exegetical accuracy, it does not succeed in offering, through the communitarian account of rule-following it recommends, an acceptable solution to the paradox about content attributions that Kripke identifies in the course of his discussion of Wittgenstein. Martin Kusch's essay examines in detail Searle's critique of Kripke, and argues that Kripke's position is defensible against all aspects of Searle's critique: it does not misrepresent Wittgenstein's actual views; it is correct in suggesting that the paradox about content attributions that Kripke identifies is unavoidable for all individualistic views of mental or linguistic content; and it can successfully address all the objections that Searle has taken to be detrimental to communitarian attempts at resolving that paradox. Kusch concludes that Searle has not succeeded in showing that individualistic conceptions of content, such as the one that he espouses, are immune to the challenges posed by Kripke's communitarian interpretation of Wittgenstein, and suggests that what Searle has analyzed as the "background" of intentionality – that is, the set of *pre*-intentional capacities and practices that make mental and linguistic intentionality possible – would be an important element in further developing a communitarian conception of mental and linguistic content, provided that it would not be interpreted in Searle's own characteristically internalist terms.

The volume's second part, "From meaning to force," begins with an essay by Kepa Korta and John Perry in which, after acknowledging (along with Searle and most other philosophers of language) the need for a distinction between propositional content and illocutionary force as two distinct components of meaning, they argue that the standard way of conceptualizing propositional content as corresponding to "what is said" in the utterance of a sentence is seriously inadequate and calls for modifications with important theoretical consequences. The ordinary notion of "what is said," Korta and Perry contend, conflates several different types of information that are normally capable of being imparted through the utterance of a sentence, and these types should be kept strictly separate from each other, not only because they are not necessarily co-instantiated in every utterance event, but also because, even when they are, they play importantly different roles both in the speaker's activity of planning an utterance and in the addressee's activity of interpreting it. Having argued that no single theoretical construct can adequately cover the various phenomena that theoreticians have sought to elucidate by making use of the ordinary notion of "what is said," Korta and Perry propose replacing that ordinary notion, for analytical purposes, with a series of distinct theoretical concepts, each of which determines a different *kind* of propositional content that a *single* utterance is capable of conveying, and show how this multipropositional conception of an utterance's content can be made precise by using the resources of Perry's reflexive-referential theory of meaning and cognitive significance (an outline of which is presented in their essay's appendix). The two most important kinds of propositional content that that theory is in a position to attribute to the utterance of a sentence are its *reflexive* propositional content and its *referential* propositional content, whose main difference is that the former does, whereas the latter does not, construe the utterance itself as a propositional constituent. Korta and Perry then show in detail why both of these kinds of propositional content need to be attributed to an utterance in order for different aspects of its significance to be adequately captured, and argue that one consequence of the multipropositional conception of utterance content they defend is that it motivates an important modification to Searle's and to most other conceptions of illocutionary acts: the various demands that Searle's analysis of illocutionary acts places on what he describes as their "propositional content" cannot, they point out, be satisfied by a single *kind* of propositional content, but are rather such that some among them can *only* be satisfied by an illocutionary act's *reflexive* propositional content, while some others can *only* be satisfied by the same illocutionary act's *referential* propositional content; and since

Korta and Perry agree with Searle that all the demands are legitimate, they conclude that, contrary to what Searle (and, following him, many others) have been assuming, a typical illocutionary act should be represented as consisting not in the application of an illocutionary force to a supposedly unique propositional content, but rather in the simultaneous application of that force to several propositional contents of various different *kinds*, of which the reflexive and the referential kind are the most significant.

A multipropositional conception of propositional content clearly constitutes an important departure from the conception of content that is characteristic of Searle's and of most other accounts of meaning, but it still preserves Searle's fundamental idea, inherited from Frege, that propositional contents are components of meaning of an entirely different nature from the illocutionary forces that apply to them, and that the truth-theoretic apparatus that is appropriate to the analysis of the former is irreducible to the action-theoretic apparatus that is appropriate to the analysis of latter. That fundamental idea comes under attack, from two different angles, in the essays by Stephen J. Barker and Nicholas Asher. Barker's essay identifies five main reasons that Searle and others have given in favour of positing propositions as necessary components of meaning irreducible to illocutionary forces, argues in detail that these reasons are not compelling, and develops, in the course of rejecting them, an alternative, proposition-free, conception of meaning, whose relevant underived concepts are action-theoretic rather than truth-theoretic, and which is claimed to be able to account equally well, and in some cases better, for the phenomena that have been thought to make appeal to propositions indispensable. Barker takes the basic idea motivating the appeal to propositions to be the idea that it is beliefs rather than assertions that are the primary truth-bearers, and builds his alternative proposal around the opposite idea that it is assertions rather than beliefs that are the primary truth-bearers (beliefs being merely dispositions to perform acts of assertion): an assertion, on Barker's analysis, is a speaker's *expressive commitment* to defend a (functionally conceived) state of mind which, as such, is *not* truth-apt, and an assertion is evaluated as *true* if and only if the speaker's hearers expressively commit *themselves* to defending a type-identical (and intrinsically not truth-apt) state of mind in their own case. Barker then shows why his conception of truth-valuation as an outcome of converging acts of expressive commitment is not open to objections that defenders of propositions might be inclined to lodge against it, how the account of assertion that embodies such a conception can be applied to the analysis of a wide variety of logically simple and complex sentences with due attention to compositionality requirements, and how, when that account is supplemented by a parallel account of *proto*-assertion (a proto-assertion is not a commitment to defend a functional state of mind, but an advertisement of an intention to undertake a commitment to defend such a state of mind), it can deflate all remaining reasons (in particular, those related to the proper treatment of sentence-embedding and sentence mood) that have been given for positing propositional content as an irreducible component of sentence meaning independent of illocutionary force.

While Barker's essay aims to motivate the thesis that one *need not* appeal to classically conceived propositions in order to construct an adequate semantic theory, Nicholas Asher's essay aims to motivate the thesis that one *must not* rely on classically conceived propositions if one aims to fully realize that purpose. Asher notes that the standard truth conditional definitions of sentential connectives could be regarded as semantically adequate *only if* the sentences embedded under them were exclusively declarative, but points out that there is considerable evidence that various kinds of non-declarative sentences, in particular imperatives and interrogatives, do semantically embed under these connectives in ways that make a truth conditional account of the latter impossible. He therefore argues that if a *unified* account of the meaning of sentential connectives was to be achieved, it would have to refer to the various illocutionary *forces* that are constitutive of the distinctive meanings of the various sentence types, and not to their allegedly force-independent propositional contents. Asher then proceeds to show that such a unified account is not only theoretically desirable but actually constructible. An essential step toward that construction, in Asher's view, is the adoption of a dynamic semantical framework, which, by virtue of representing sentences of *all* grammatical types as types of *action* affecting input informational contexts in characteristic ways, provides a basis for a unified semantic treatment of the sentential connectives as operators applying to types of action of those various sorts. And since the way in which a sentence, considered as a type of action, affects an input informational context depends not only on the type of action it is, but also on the type and structure of the particular informational context that it modifies, a fully explicit semantic account of sentential connectives also requires, Asher contends, a formal representation of the discourse structures in which sentences embedded under connectives can occur. Asher proposes an original combination of dynamic semantics and discourse representation theory that provides a framework within which these requirements can be met, and then shows how that framework enables a unified and compositionally precise account of the meaning of sentential connectives that would not be possible if force-independent propositional contents were taken to be the uniquely proper targets of semantic analysis.

In my own contribution to the volume, I begin by adopting a weak interpretation of the force-content distinction which, while sensitive to some of the motivations behind the standard one, does not make it a matter of definition, as the standard one does, that the sententially expressible content to which an illocutionary force is applied is propositional, and thus creates space for principled dispute over whether any particular such content can or cannot be properly taken to be propositional. I then examine in detail Searle's Frege-inspired, and widely shared, thesis that a yes–no question and its grammatically corresponding assertion not only have contents that are propositional, but actually have the *same* propositional content, and show that that thesis has a wide range of clearly unacceptable consequences both for Searle's proposed analysis of illocutionary acts and for his proposed classification of them into five jointly exhaustive classes. (In particular, it leads to an analysis of yes–no questions that cannot be preserved unless by assuming either that inconsistent propositions can have the same content or that the identity of an illocutionary act is simultaneously dependent and not dependent on the identity of the proposition to which its force is attached; and, appearances to the contrary notwithstanding, it makes it strictly impossible to include yes–no questions into any of the five categories of illocutionary acts that Searle proposes as jointly exhaustive.) The solution I recommend involves the claim that a yes–no question not only does not have the same propositional content as its grammatically corresponding assertion, but, unlike its grammatically corresponding assertion, does not have a *propositional* content at all (its content being, rather, a set of possible illocutionary acts whose members are such that if one of them were felicitously performable to the exclusion of the others, the question would have been settled). Assuming the weak interpretation of the force-content distinction originally introduced, I then incorporate that claim into a suggested distinction between two fundamental kinds of illocutionary acts: *first-order* ones (for example, assertions), whose forces are applied to propositions, and *higher-order* ones (in particular, questions), whose forces are applied not to propositions, but rather to sets of possible first-order illocutionary acts.

The volume concludes with an essay by Mitchell Green that returns to Searle's favourite theme of the connection between mental and linguistic intentionality by concentrating on Searle's claim that each kind of illocutionary act is an *expression* of a particular kind of mental state, namely, of the state that its speaker must be in if the act is to be sincere. Green doubts that all types of illocutionary acts express mental states (or have sincerity conditions), but accepts that most of them do, and is mainly concerned with showing why Searle's account of the activity of expressing a mental state by an utterance is unsatisfactory, and how a satisfactory account could be developed. Searle's account is unsatisfactory, in Green's view, because, apart from being underspecified in certain crucial respects, it construes the expression of a mental state by an utterance as one of the utterance's *conventional* properties – a construal that, Green argues, cannot be correct, since the expression of a mental state is fundamentally the production of *evidence* for the existence of that state, and since evidential relations cannot be conventional. The alternative account that Green puts forward is inspired from certain concepts developed within the evolutionary biology of communication – in particular, the technical notion of "handicap" as a type of signal that cannot be faked by an organism except at the organism's considerable cost – and analyzes the speaker's expression of a mental state by an utterance as, in effect, the conclusion of a certain kind of *inference* that hearers make in order to preserve the hypothesis that the speaker is sensitive to community norms that have been designed to ensure the reliability of types of linguistic signals by penalizing the production of unreliable tokens thereof: assuming a community norm dictating that any speaker producing utterances of a certain type and lacking a mental state of a certain type is liable to suffer a loss of credibility within the community, hearers will interpret a speaker's deliberate use of an utterance of that type, and so his deliberate exposure to the risk of loss of credibility within the community, as *evidence* that the speaker probably does have the mental state that the norm prescribes as appropriate for utterances of the type the speaker has used; and the production of evidence for a defeasible inference of that sort is precisely, according to Green, what a speaker's expression of a mental state by an utterance consists in.

It is my hope that the essays in this volume will deepen the reader's understanding of key aspects of Searle's philosophy of language, and at the same time will encourage exploration of innovative ways in which some main issues in that field can be approached.

Chapter 1

What is language: some preliminary remarks

JOHN R. SEARLE

1 NATURALIZING LANGUAGE

I believe that the greatest achievements in philosophy over the past hundred or one hundred and twenty-five years have been in the philosophy of language. Beginning with Frege, who invented the subject, and continuing through Russell, Wittgenstein, Quine, Austin, and their successors, right to the present day, there is no branch of philosophy with so much high-quality work as the philosophy of language. In my view, the only achievement comparable to those of the great philosophers of language is Rawls' reinvention of the subject of political philosophy (and therefore implicitly the subject of ethics). But with this one possible exception, I think that work in the philosophy of language is at the top of our achievements.

Having said that, however, I have to record a serious misgiving I have about the subject. The problem is that its practitioners in general do not treat language as a natural phenomenon. This may seem a strange charge to make, given that so many contemporary and recent philosophers of language are anxious to emphasize the empirical character of their theories of language. Quine and Davidson are striking examples of resolute empiricism. My objection is that few contemporary and recent philosophers of language attempt to treat language as a natural extension of non-linguistic biological capacities. Language is not seen as continuous with, nor as an extension of, the rest of our specifically human biological inheritance. I think there is a deep reason, both historically and intellectually, why language has not been treated naturalistically. It is because the philosophy of language went hand in hand with the development of mathematical logic. Indeed, Frege, in effect, invented both the philosophy of language and modern logic. And the growth of the philosophy of language through Russell and the early Wittgenstein was very much seen as an application of mathematical logic. Even later Wittgenstein and Austin, both of whom reacted against the excessive logicism of the philosophy of language, did not see language as a natural biological phenomenon. It is not hard to think of language as an extension of biological capacities, but if by "logic" we mean formal systems of the sort developed by Frege and his successors, then logic is definitely not a biological phenomenon. On the contrary, specifically human biology existed for tens of thousands of years before logic in this sense was ever invented.

What would it be like to try to treat language, in my sense, naturalistically? The first step would be one that many philosophers have resisted and that is to see linguistic meaning, the meaning of sentences and speech acts, as an extension of the more biologically fundamental forms of intentionality that we have in belief, desire, memory, and intention, and to see those in turn as developments of even more fundamental forms of intentionality, especially perception and intentional action. Among the most basic forms of intentionality, the most biologically primitive, along with hunger, thirst, and sexual desire, are perception and intention-in-action. Given perceptions and actions, animals have the capacity to develop memories and prior intentions, as well as beliefs and desires and other forms of intentionality, such as expectation and fear, anger and aggression. I believe we should see the biological foundations of language in prelinguistic intentionality. Our initial question should be, What are the similarities and differences between the prelinguistic forms of consciousness and intentionality and the linguistic forms? We do not know how in fact language evolved, and in the absence of fossil evidence we may never know exactly how it evolved, but we do know that it did evolve, and we ought at least to be able to answer the question, What are the logical, conceptual relations between prelinguistic forms of consciousness and intentionality and the evolved linguistic forms?

I want to emphasize that this approach is quite different from the standard approaches. Davidson, for example, thought that only a being that has a language can have intentional states such as beliefs and desires. I think he had the biology exactly backwards. Many species of animals have perceptions, perform actions and are capable of acquiring beliefs, desires, and intentions, though they have no language. Furthermore, several species are capable of prelinguistic thought processes. I suggest that we think of human language as an extension of these prelinguistic capacities.

The aim of this chapter is to explain some of the essential features of human language, and I will emphasize especially those features of language that relate to human society. Notice I say "What is language?" and not "What is *a* language such as French, German or English?" I will not be interested in what makes one language distinct from others, but in what they all have in common. In addition to the naturalism urged in previous paragraphs, a second main theme of this chapter will be that the standard accounts of language in philosophy of language and linguistics tend to underestimate, and therefore misrepresent, the role of society and of social conventions. The general accounts of society given in such disciplines as sociology tend to underestimate, and therefore misrepresent, the special role of language in society. I will be arguing, among other things, that language is essentially social, but not just in any old way: rather, in a way that makes human society essentially linguistic. The key connecting link between language and society is the notion of *deontology*, a notion involving commitments of various kinds, about which I will say more later. Language, for reasons that I will attempt to state, requires a deontology, and the deontology introduced by language makes specifically human forms of society and human civilization possible.

One of the essential questions addressed in this chapter is this: Since human societies are importantly different from animal societies, which of those differences are accounted for, and how exactly are they accounted for, by the existence of human languages?

2 LANGUAGE AS PHONOLOGY, SYNTAX, AND SEMANTICS

The standard textbook accounts of language say that specific languages such as French or German consist of three components: a phonological component that determines how words and sentences are pronounced, a syntactical component that determines the arrangement of words and morphemes in sentences, and a semantic component that assigns a meaning or interpretation to words and sentences. More sophisticated accounts add that there must also be a pragmatic component that is not a component of specific languages; rather, it sets certain constraints on the *use* of language and is not internal to specific languages in the way that the syntax of French is internal to French and the syntax of German is internal to German. For our purposes we can ignore phonology because it is not essential to language that it be spoken. (It is important, however, that any language, whether spoken or not, must be thinkable.

It is sometimes said that people think in words. Unless they are talking out loud to themselves, that is not true. They think in *images* of words.) The relation of syntax to semantics is, however, crucial. Syntax organizes semantics according to three principles: discreteness, compositionality, and generativity. Discreteness is that feature by which syntactical elements retain their identity under the various syntactical operations. So, for example, when you change a sentence around, the words (and morphemes) do not lose their identity. Unlike baking a cake where the ingredients are changed by being mixed together, forming a sentence does not change the words and morphemes that are being mixed together; and you can have a sentence containing eight words or twelve words, but you cannot have a sentence containing nine and a half words. Compositionality is both a syntactic and a semantic property. Syntactically, a complex element such as a sentence is built up out of simple elements, words and morphemes, according to the formation rules of the language. Semantically, the meaning of the whole sentence is determined by the meanings of the simple elements together with the syntactical structure of the sentence. For example, we understand the sentence "John loves Mary" differently from the sentence "Mary loves John," even though they both have the same elements, because the elements are arranged differently. Generativity, as I am using the term, implies that the syntactical operations of the language allow the speakers to generate an indefinite number of new sentences. There is, strictly speaking, no upper limit to the number of sentences in any natural human language.

This account is OK as far as it goes, but it is incomplete. I will be arguing that it leaves out a crucial dimension of language, namely the element of what in ordinary English we could describe as *commitment* and which I will describe more generally as deontology. Deontology is essential to the nature of human language in ways that I need to explain.

3 SOCIETY AND LANGUAGE

In linguistics and philosophy, there is a more or less orthodox conception of language but there is no such commonality in social science accounts of society. It seems to me that the accounts of society that I am familiar with, ranging all the way from Aristotle to the present, radically misconceive the role of language in that, in an important sense, they take the existence of language for granted and then ask: How does society work, how is it constructed?, and so on. When I say that they take language for granted, I mean that in accounting for the nature of society they do not ask: What is language? Rather, they simply assume the existence of language and go on from there. Perhaps the worst offenders in this regard are the Social Contract theorists, who presuppose beings like us, who have language, and then ask how these beings could form society on the basis of a social contract. The point I will be making is that once a society has a common language, it already has a social contract. The situation with authors such as Bourdieu, Foucault, and Habermas is not really better. They think of themselves as acutely conscious of language and its importance for society, but they do not ask, What is language? in a way that would enable them to ask, How exactly is language constitutive of society?

4 WHAT DOES LANGUAGE ADD TO PRELINGUISTIC COGNITION?

I am not sure how best to argue for the theses that I want to maintain. I think one way to argue for them is, so to speak, genetically. I propose to treat the question as an engineering or designer question. Imagine that there was a species like us, having a full range of prelinguistic conscious experiences, voluntary actions, and prelinguistic thought processes, but no language. What capacities would they have to have in order to create language for themselves and what exactly are they creating when they create a rudimentary language? At one time, animals more or less like us, hominids, walked the earth without language. Now we have language. What happened in between? And when I ask what happened, I do not mean the question historically, but conceptually. What conceptual (logical, cognitive) capacities did they acquire when they acquired language? And what sorts of cognitive capacities did they have beforehand on which language could have evolved? We have a language in a sense that other species do not. What is it that we have and how could we have gotten it? I must emphasize that I am not trying to do speculative evolutionary biology; rather I am trying to do a logical analysis of the relations between prelinguistic cognitive capacities and language, with the aim of figuring out what language is.

In response to earlier drafts of this chapter, some people thought I was trying to enter into current discussions of animal cognition and the actual evolution of language. That is a misunderstanding. I am, to repeat, not engaging in speculative evolutionary biology nor animal cognition. There is currently a sizable amount of research on animal cognition[1] and important work is done on the evolution of language.[2] I am not addressing the empirical issues in these fields. For comparison I will sometimes make reference to other animals, but if it should turn out that everything we currently believe, for example about bee languages and primate thought processes, is false, that would be only marginally relevant to my questions. And even if it should turn out that some animals have full-blown languages in the sense that we do, and that human language did not gradually evolve but was the result of a single evolutionary Big Bang that produced brains with full-blown generative grammars, such facts would be only marginally relevant to the questions I am asking about logical dependencies. I am emphatically not arguing for the superiority of our species. If it should turn out that some other animals have what we have, I welcome them to the club.

When I ask the question, "How could language have evolved?" I mean something quite different from empirical researchers who ask a different question using the same sentence. They are asking: Given what we know about human evolutionary history and animal cognition, how could human languages have developed in our evolutionary history? My question is conceptual. Subtract language from a species like us: What do you have? Now add language: What are you adding?

Notice that the way I am posing the question presupposes that the *nature* of language and the question of the *functions* and *uses* of language by human speakers cannot be separated. We can explore which structural features of language are useful or even essential, by exploring what use humans make of these structures.

There are apparently intermediate cases between humans and species that communicate but do not have language in a human sense. The bees are the best-known example. When a bee returns to the hive she performs a waggle dance that conveys different types of information depending on the variations in the dance. She conveys that there is nectar in the neighborhood, that it is in a certain direction and that it is a certain distance away from the hive. In hot weather, she can communicate the location of water, and even, during swarming, the location of possible hive sites. Different combinations of the elements of the dance convey different elements of information. In one experiment, the experimenters towed a boatful of flowers to the middle of a lake. The returning bee conveyed this information. Her hive mates showed no interest in flying to what apparently they knew to be the middle of a lake.

I will proceed by addressing four specific questions: What features of language are already present in prelinguistic consciousness? What features of language are lacking in prelinguistic consciousness? What special features of consciousness are lacking in language? What functions do humans need language to perform, given prelinguistic consciousness?

5 FEATURES COMMON TO PRELINGUISTIC INTENTIONALITY AND LANGUAGE

I have already said that the hominids have conscious perceptions and intentional actions together with conscious thought processes, all of these in a prelinguistic form. This implies, at the very least, that the animals have beliefs, desires, intentions, and at least some form of memory, enough to enable them to recognize familiar objects and situations.

These prelinguistic forms of intentionality already have some crucial logical properties. Specifically, because perceptions, intentions, beliefs, desires, and so on, are forms of intentionality, they carry within them the determination of conditions of success or failure. An animal that is hungry, for example, has a desire to eat; and pathologies apart, it thus has the capacity to recognize when that desire is satisfied and when it is not satisfied. We can generalize this point as follows: any intentional state determines its conditions of satisfaction, and a normal animal that has intentional states must be able to recognize when the conditions of satisfaction are in fact satisfied. If it is thirsty, it must be able to tell when it has drunk; if it is hungry, it must be able to tell when it has eaten; if it is trying to do something, it must know when it has done it, and so on. We can summarize this point by saying that when we supposed that our animals had intentional states we were already supposing that they had mental representations with propositional contents and conditions of satisfaction. But when I say that, I am speaking logically not ontologically. I am not saying the animals had a set of picture-like or sentence-like entities in their heads called "representations." Rather, to have beliefs and desires, for example, is already to have something that determines conditions of satisfaction, and that implies the capacity to recognize success and failure. Presumably these capacities are realized in neuronal structures but, for our investigation, it does not matter how these capacities are realized, provided only that the realization is rich enough to carry the logical properties. When I say the representations are propositional, I imply nothing linguistic. I mean that there is something that sets the conditions of satisfaction; and because a condition is always a condition *that such and such*, it follows trivially that the conditions are propositional.

We can summarize the formal features of intentionality, prelinguistic as well as linguistic, by explaining the following notions and the relations between them: *propositional content, conditions of satisfaction, psychological mode*, and *direction of fit*. Our evolutionary history has given us different ways in which our mental states relate to reality. The aim of beliefs is to represent how things are; therefore beliefs can be said to be true or false. The aim of desires and intentions is not to represent how things are but how we would like them to be or how we intend to make them be. For this reason, desires and intentions are not true or false, but fulfilled or frustrated. I find it useful to characterize beliefs as having the *mind-to-world direction of fit* (the belief in the mind is supposed to fit the state of affairs in the world) and desires and intentions as having the *world-to-mind direction of fit* (if all goes well with the desires and intentions, the world comes to fit how it is represented in the mind). Not surprisingly these distinctions carry over exactly to speech acts. The assertive class of speech acts: statements, assertions, etc., are expressions of beliefs and are supposed, like beliefs, to represent how the world is and thus they have the *word-to-world* direction of fit. The directive class of speech acts: requests, orders, commands, etc., are expressions of desires and so have the *world-to-word* direction of fit. The commissive class: promises, offers, etc., are expressions of intention and so have the *world-to-word* direction of fit. These different directions of fit are a function not of the propositional content by itself, but of how the propositional content is presented in the speech act. This is why, in standard speech act notation, the total speech act is represented with a distinction between the illocutionary force, or type, of speech act and the propositional content.

Thus

$F(p)$

represents the propositional content p, presented with the illocutionary force F. And this corresponds exactly to the representation of the intentional state as

$S(p)$.

The p represents the propositional content and the S represents the type of intentional state, that is, its psychological mode, whether belief, desire, or whatever.

Our question is: How do we get from the intentional state $S(p)$ to the linguistic resources that would enable us to perform the speech act $F(p)$? Our task is made easier by the fact that the formal apparatus of the content and type, together with conditions of satisfaction and direction of fit, are already present in prelinguistic intentionality.

So far so good. But what about those speech acts where the fit is taken for granted: expressives, such as apologizing and thanking? If you look at the forms of intentionality that correspond to these speech acts, and are expressed in their performance, forms such as regret and gratitude, it seems to me these typically are combinations of beliefs and desires. That is, they are forms of desire based on the presupposition of the truth of the belief.[3] For example, if I regret having done something I must believe I did it and wish I had not. So the existence of speech acts where the fit is presupposed, which have what I have called the null direction of fit, does not pose an insuperable problem for moving from prelinguistic intentionality to speech acts, because the prelinguistic forms also include cases where the fit is presupposed. These cases, such as pride and shame, gratitude and regret, contain beliefs and desires, which do have a mind–world or world–mind direction of fit.

In addition to the problem of expressive speech acts there is a special problem about *declarations*: speech acts that make something the case by declaring it to be the case, such as adjourning a meeting by saying "The meeting is adjourned." Declarations have both directions of fit simultaneously because they make something the case by representing it as being the case. I cannot exaggerate the importance of this phenomenon for answering the question that the title of this chapter poses. These have no echo in prelinguistic thought, and I will discuss them further below.

The categories

Another feature of prelinguistic consciousness – and this will prove crucial for the evolution of language – is that any animal that has the biologically primitive intentional apparatus of conscious prelinguistic hominids already has a hefty number of the traditional philosophical (e.g. Aristotelian and Kantian) categories. It already has *space*, *time*, *causation*, *agency*, and *object*; and with *object* it has to have *identity* and *individuation* together with *property* and *relation*. I do not mean that it has to have concepts corresponding to these categories, but rather, for example, that it has to be able to recognize that one object is over there in front of it and another one on the left (space); it has to recognize that its eating occurred in a temporal sequence (time); that it did something, as opposed to something just happening (agency); that some things it did, made other things happen (causation). Perhaps most importantly, if it can perceive and recognize objects including other hominids, it must have identity and individuation, because it must be able to perceive that this is the same object as before (identity), and that this object is a separate object from that object (individuation). But once it has objects, with their identity and individuation, it already has properties and relations of objects. It can see that this person is next to that person (a spatial relation) and it can see that this object is brown (property). Given all of this apparatus, it also has the category of change; thus it can see that this hominid, who was previously over there, has now moved over here (change from one location to another of the same object). Finally, it can recognize objects of the same type. For example, it can recognize other animals as being or not being of the same species as itself.

6 FEATURES OF LANGUAGE THAT CONSCIOUSNESS LACKS

What does prelinguistic consciousness lack? Perhaps, above all, it lacks *internal* and *controllable* structures in its thought processes. Thus a dog can perceive and hence think that, as we would put it, "Someone is approaching the door." But, unlike us, it cannot distinguish that thought from the thought, "The door is being approached by someone." Furthermore it cannot use its true thought, "Someone is approaching the door" to form the false thought "The door is approaching someone." This is an important point. Prelinguistic forms of intentionality have structure, but they do not have the sorts of *indefinitely manipulatable structures with semantic content* that the syntax of language provides. Thus perception is structured by the sheer physical impact of the objects perceived and by the physiology of the perceptual apparatus. For example, the animal sees a man walk toward the door. The structure of memory is similarly shaped by the sheer physical events and the physiological apparatus. But without syntactical elements the animal does not have a rich structural apparatus the elements of which it can manipulate at will in an indefinite number of ways. Birds can perform new permutations of their songs, and an animal constructing a tool can distinguish removing the leaves from the twig and removing the twig from the leaves. Neither of these cases is, in my sense, a case of freely manipulating syntactic structures with semantic content. The beauty of human languages is not just that they have compositionality and generativity but the user can freely manipulate the *semantically loaded* syntactical elements at will.

I think that what I just said is obviously true but it is controversial. Some philosophers, especially Fodor (1975), think that all thought requires a linguistic syntax, and that humans can acquire a natural language only because they already have an inborn "language of thought" with a syntax as rich as that of any human language. Others, especially Davidson (1975), believe that without language thought is impossible. So, they, incredibly, deny that animals can have intentional states such as beliefs, and desires. I, on the contrary, think that it is obvious that many animals, my dog Gilbert for example, have perceptions, intentions, beliefs and desires, and yet they have nothing like a language with freely manipulatable syntactical structure. And even if I am wrong about Gilbert, there is just too much biological evidence of animal cognition to make Davidson's view credible.[4]

Structure and segmentation

Another difference between the linguistic and the prelinguistic is that the flow of consciousness in prelinguistic thought and perception, though structured in all sorts of ways, does not, or does not necessarily, come in discrete segments in the way that language does. Non-linguistic thought is, or at least can be, a continuous flow, broken only by sleep or other forms of non-consciousness. Language, however, is essentially segmented. The utterance of sentences cannot be a continuous undifferentiated flow, but each sentence, and even each sentence fragment, if uttered as a complete speech act, must be discrete. So the situation we are in when we move from experience to language is analogous to the situation where we move from a movie to a series of still pictures. By thinking in language we break up our thought into words and sentential segments. Though actual discourse takes place in time, the intentionality of the discourse is in discrete segments in a way that the flow of prelinguistic thought and perception in action in conscious life is not in that way in discrete segments. A typical speech act, though performed in time, is, semantically speaking, instantaneous. This is why it does not matter to the identity of the speech act whether, for example, the language spoken requires that the verb phrase comes before or after the subject noun phrase. This difference between unsegmented consciousness and segmented discourse is disguised from us, or at least for a long time was disguised from me, by the fact that beliefs and desires are naturally talked about as if they were discrete units. But when they are, so to speak, in action, when I am actually looking or acting or perceiving, then they become part of the continuous flow. Suppose, for example, I have the following thought in English, "Now I have to go because it is time for dinner." Though that thought occurs in time, because it is expressed in an English sentence it has a kind of discreteness that prelinguistic thoughts do not have. If, for example, I am dancing or skiing, the stream of conscious thought need not contain any words and can be in a continuous flow.

Declarations

A third special feature of language that does not exist in prelinguistic intentionality is that in language we get a type of speech act that I have baptized "declarations." These have a double direction of fit, both word-to-world and world-to-word in the same speech act. These are not two independent fittings but one fitting that goes both ways. Consider the cases where, for example, an authorized person adjourns the meeting, or declares war, by saying "The meeting is adjourned" or "War is declared." Or consider linguistic declarations where somebody makes a promise by saying "I promise" or gives an order by saying "I order." These are performative utterances; and all performatives are declarations (though not all declarations are performatives). In these cases we have the double direction of fit, because we make something the case, and thus achieve the world-to-word direction of fit, by representing it as being the case, that is by representing it with the word-to-world direction of fit. This is one of the most important powers of language: the power to create a reality by declaring it to exist. There is nothing analogous to that in prelinguistic forms of intentionality so we need to be able to show how an extension of the prelinguistic forms to language gives us the capacity to create forms of institutional or social reality that exist only because we collectively and linguistically represent them as existing. We need to show how prelinguistic forms of intentionality could have evolved into human social and institutional reality. What we will require in order to explain this evolution is the notion of meaning and the notion of a convention. I will get to these shortly.

7 SOME SPECIAL FEATURES OF CONSCIOUSNESS. THE UNITY OF THE PROPOSITION AND THE SALIENCE OF OBJECTS WITH THEIR FEATURES

In explaining the transition from prelinguistic intentionality to linguistic intentionality, we have some wonderful resources in consciousness that go beyond the possession of the apparatus of intentionality and the various philosophical categories – space, time, causation, identity, etc. – that I mentioned in section 5. Specifically, in prelinguistic intentionality the problem of the unity of the proposition does not arise. Why? Because the sequence of conscious thought and experience is one where the representation of the conditions of satisfaction is built in at every step of the way. There is no problem about how I can put the elements of my experience together to form a unity in a way that there is a problem about how I can put discrete words together to form a unified sentence. The experience comes with unity built into it. In conscious hunger, thirst, and visual perception, for example, the determination of the conditions of satisfaction is internal to the experience. Another resource that we have is that the actual structure of our conscious, perceptual experiences makes objects with their features salient. We consciously see, and otherwise perceive, distinct objects and their properties. We see, for example, tall trees, ripe apples, and snow-covered mountains.

The combination of the unity of the proposition and the salience of some features of our experience gives us an apparent paradox, but I think it is a paradox we can resolve. Our experiences give us a built-in unity corresponding to the unity of the proposition in language, but at the same time our experiences give us distinct objects and their features as salient, and this corresponds to the noun-phrase verb-phrase structure in language. How do these two apparently inconsistent features relate to each other? We can only succeed in seeing when we see *that something is the case*, see *that such and such*. But all the same we do see objects, we see *that object*. I will attempt to resolve this apparent paradox in section 10.

Another way to put the problem is this. It is easy enough to imagine a language which segments objects differently from the way we do, which treats a tree not as a unified whole, but as a top half and a bottom half. And has separate words for each. That is certainly a logical possibility. It is also possible to imagine a language that does not allow reference to objects, but only to processes as states of affairs. We could imagine a language where instead of saying, "That's a tree," or "That's a stone," we could say "It's treeing here" or "It's stoning here," on analogy with "It's raining here" or "It's snowing here," where the "it" does not refer to any object. We could imagine such a language, but such a language, if it exists, runs counter to our perceptual phenomenology. Our existing perceptual apparatus is constructed so that we naturally treat spatio-temporally discrete entities as single units, and these are represented by typical noun phrases of our language. Furthermore, identity as preserved in memory is crucial to the development of reference over time, because a prelinguistic animal can nonetheless recognize the same object on different occasions, and recognize the same object as having different features on different occasions. The paradox I mentioned earlier is that the unit necessarily represented by an intentional state is a whole state of affairs, not an object. Yet perceptually objects and not states of affairs are phenomenologically salient. In language the problem is to explain the unity of the proposition, given the separate syntactical representation of reference and predication.

8 THE FUNCTIONS OF LANGUAGE: REPRESENTATION VERSUS EXPRESSION

So far, I have attempted to answer three questions concerning (1) features common to language and consciousness, (2) features special to language, and (3) features special to consciousness.

We now go to the last of our four questions. For what primary functions do we need language? By primary functions I mean those functions that are essential to something's being a language at all. We have to specify the primary functions before we can explain the structures which are necessary and sufficient to perform those functions.

The first primary function is this: we need language to provide a mechanism by which our critters can communicate with each other. What does "communicate" mean? And what gets communicated? The standard answer to the second question is that in speaking we communicate information. But "information" is one of the most confused and ill-defined notions in contemporary intellectual life. So I am wary of using it except incidentally. I will just state flatly that what typically gets communicated in speech acts are intentional states, and the point of doing that is that the intentional states already represent the world; so what gets communicated, by way of communicating intentional states, is typically information *about the world*. If I communicate to you my belief that it is raining, the point is typically *not* to tell you about me and my beliefs, but about the weather. But there is no way I can intentionally tell you something about the weather except by way of using my mental representations of the weather, my weather-directed intentional states, such as my beliefs.

Our prelinguistic hominids already have perception, intentional action, and prelinguistic thought processes. All of these are intentional states with full propositional contents. And when one such creature intentionally communicates to another, it tries to reproduce its own intentional content in the head of the other person. When it communicates, for example, "there is danger here" it has the belief that there is danger here and it acts in such a way as to convey this belief to another animal.

The simplest type of communication would be the cases where one animal communicates information about the world by communicating an unstructured proposition to another animal. By unstructured I mean that the propositional content so far has no internal syntax. There is nothing there corresponding to the words of natural languages. This type of communication is already very common among animals. Think of warning cries of birds, mating calls of all sorts of species, and even some dogs' barks. All such examples are cases of what Peter Strawson (1959: 202ff, 214ff) once called "feature placing." We simply communicate the presence of a feature in the environment. In actual languages these feature-placing utterances can often be done with one word. "Danger!" "Rain!" "Fire!" And when we expand one of these into a whole sentence, the other parts of the sentence are sometimes semantically empty, as when we say "It is raining" though there is nothing referred to by "it." Such simple cases of intentional communication do indeed transfer an intentional content from one animal to another, but they are a very small step on the road to real language because they are so limited. The fact that all sorts of animals have this kind of communication should tell us that it is not yet linguistic, or anything like it.

We might say that the first step on the road to language would be to introduce conventional devices for communicating intentional contents from one animal to another. In most of the cases we considered the animals already have natural devices for the communication, but we can easily imagine that our hominids develop conventional devices for intentional states that have no natural external expression. A dog does not need a conventional device to convey aggression. It can just bark aggressively. But humans, for example, do not in that way have a natural way of conveying the fact that it is raining. Such reflections about the distinction between natural ways of conveying intentional states, and evolved conventional ways, will I think force us to distinguish representation from expression. We need to distinguish between those communicative acts that involve intentionally representing a state of affairs in the world and those that simply express (in the original sense of pressing out, of giving vent to) an animal's internal state, where that expression may convey information about the world but it does not do so by representing that something is the case, or by representing other sorts of conditions of satisfaction. Thus if I say "Rain!" I represent the weather even if the representation is unstructured. But if I say "Ouch!" as a spontaneous expression of pain, I convey information but I do not represent anything. Let us now make a generalization that will make our task clearer: simple expressive speech acts, even when performed intentionally, are not "linguistic" in the sense we are trying to make explicit, and the corresponding words of actual languages are not "words" in our sense. "Ouch!" "Damn!" "Yuck!" "Wow!" are all used to express mental states, both intentional and nonintentional, but they are not the kind of linguistic phenomena we are trying to explain. Why not? Because, though they give vent to intentional or other states of the speaker, they do not represent. What we want to understand is, how can our hominids evolve linguistic *representation*?

What is the difference exactly between representing and expressing? If I say "Rain!" my utterance can be literally true or false, because it represents the current state of the weather. I can, for example, lie when I make this utterance. But if I say "Ouch!" though I do convey information about myself, I say nothing that is literally true or false. If I say "Ouch" when I am not in pain I may mislead and misinform, but I do not lie.[5]

So the first thing our hominids have to create are some conventional devices for representing the same states of affairs in the world that their existing intentional states represent. One type of such a device would represent the same state of affairs, the same conditions of satisfaction, as "There is food here," another, "It is dangerous here," another, "It is raining," etc. By producing a token of such a device, in what we might as well call "an utterance," a person can convey to another person the same content as he has in his existing intentional state. For example, he believes it is raining, so he produces the appropriate device to his interlocutor and thus communicates that it is raining.

There is a lot of philosophical weight contained in this simple story, so let us slow down and go over it one step at a time. We are assuming that the prelinguistic people can recognize tokens of the same type. That is a reasonable assumption, because the cognitive apparatus we assumed they came endowed with implies a capacity for recognizing exemplars of the same on different occasions. We assume that the speaker is able to utter a token intentionally. That is implied by his stipulated capacity for intentional behavior. But now what exactly is added when he utters the device for purposes of communication? Well, he already has an intentional state with conditions of satisfaction: for example, the belief that it is raining. So what he does is intentionally impose these conditions of satisfaction on the utterance. The utterance now has the same conditions of satisfaction as his belief, and since we are supposing that he and his hearer both know the convention for using the symbol in question, he can make the utterance with confidence that the hearer will recognize that it has those conditions of satisfaction.

The introduction of conventional devices for representing states of affairs already presupposes the notion of speaker meaning. Any agent who is capable of using those devices must be able to use them meaningfully.

9 SPEAKER MEANING AS THE IMPOSITION OF CONDITIONS OF SATISFACTION ON CONDITIONS OF SATISFACTION

We can now clarify the notion of meaning. We need to distinguish between the conventional meaning of words, sentences, and other symbols, and the speaker meaning which the speaker expresses in making an intentional utterance. In the case we have discussed, the symbol in question has a conventional meaning: it is raining, and when the speaker makes an utterance with this symbol he expresses a speaker meaning, a speech act meaning: it is raining. When the speaker intentionally utters a token of the symbol, the production of the token is the condition of satisfaction of his intention to utter it. And when he utters it *meaningfully* he is imposing a further condition of satisfaction on the token uttered. The condition of satisfaction is: that it is raining. That intentional imposition of conditions of satisfaction on conditions of satisfaction is the essence of speaker meaning.

The capacity to do this is a crucial element of human cognitive capacities. It requires the ability to think on two levels at once, in a way that is essential for the use of language. At one level the speaker intentionally produces a physical utterance, but at another level the utterance represents something. And the same duality infects the symbol itself. At one level it is a physical token like any other; at another level it has a meaning, it represents a type of a state of affairs.

There are two separate aspects to what I have said so far. First, speaker meaning consists in the double level of intentionality I have tried to describe. The speaker intentionally produces an utterance, and he intends that the utterance should itself have conditions of satisfaction, for example truth conditions. But, and this is the next crucial point, if he is to succeed on a regular basis, then there has to be some *socially recognized conventional device*, some repeatable device, the production of which can be regularly and conventionally taken by his interlocutors to convey the message. Now we are getting much closer to language, because the first phenomenon is essential to the performance of speech acts, and the second phenomenon, the repeatable devices, consists typically of words and sentences of a language.

For the sake of explanatory simplicity, I introduced the idea of a convention before that of speaker meaning. But which really comes first, speaker meaning or convention? In the order of logical dependence the speaker intentionality must be logically prior, because these conventions for unstructured propositions encode preexisting speaker meanings. However, without language and its conventions you can only have very simple speaker meanings. You can think, and mean, for example: it is raining here. But you cannot even think, much less say and mean, for example, "It would be nice to visit the zoo next Sunday but I have to stay home and work on my income tax." We will get to this point, the dependence of complex thought and meaning on language, in the next section when we get to symbols that have a compositional structure. For now I will just remark: if the speakers and hearers are to evolve a system where they can communicate effectively, they will have to develop a set of conventional devices for conveying speaker meaning.

When our animals develop a language, they are developing a set of devices for public, social, representation. That means they develop a set of devices, the production of which will be the imposition of conditions of satisfaction on conditions of satisfaction, *by convention*.

This is a first step on the way to language, but only a first step because so far we do not have syntax. The devices we were imagining correspond to unstructured propositions, and have no internal syntactical structure. In English we would have to translate them as one word sentences: "Rain!" "Danger!" "Food!" etc.

10 A FURTHER STEP: SYNTACTICAL COMPOSITIONALITY

A further step on the road to language (and remember, the metaphor of "steps" implies nothing historical – I am speaking of logical components, I have no idea in which order they occurred historically) is the introduction of simple syntactical devices which can be combined with other syntactical devices to produce complex syntactical devices, and each one of the complex devices will be used to communicate an entire intentional state. That is another way of saying that the hominids need to evolve elements that correspond to our words and morphemes and to ways of combining these into sentences in a compositional manner, in a way that enables the participants to figure out the meaning of the sentences from the meanings of the elements and their arrangement in the sentence. For us the minimal unit of communication, the minimal unit of the speech act, is the whole sentence. The principle that guides the selection of the syntactical devices within the sentence is that they must perform a semantic function. There must be repeatable devices each of which can function as a possible communication unit (sentence) and these must be composed of elements (words) which are such that the communicative content of the whole is determined by the elements and by the principles of their combination in the sentence.

How do we introduce these features – words and sentences – where the sentences are systematically built out of the words? We have to build on the resources that the animal already has, and these are in fact quite rich. Because our beasts already have the capacity to identify and re-identify objects, we can introduce names of objects, and because they have the capacity to recognize different tokens of the same type, we can introduce such general names as "dog," "cat," "man," etc., and because the objects have features, we can introduce something corresponding to adjectives and verbs. But notice the crucial constraints on these. We are not assuming that reference and predication, the speech acts corresponding to noun phrases and verb phrases, are in any way simple independent elements, but rather that once we have the total speech act we can abstract these as component elements. Following Frege, we think of the nouns phrases and verb phrases as derived from the total sentence and not the total sentence as arrived at by combining nouns phrases and verb phrases.

What does that mean? Our animals already have unstructured propositional contents. But corresponding to these are structured features of the real world and the animals have the capacity to recognize these structures *and their elements*. So we are not begging any questions when we give the animal a sentential structure that corresponds to the conditions of satisfaction that it already has. The semantic function comes for free because we have already introduced meaning. Here is the basic idea. The animal has perceptual and belief contents that lack syntactic structure: it can see, and therefore believe, something that we can report (but the animal cannot report) as "It is coming toward me." Now if the animal has the capacity to create meaningful events, i.e. speech acts, then it can already represent this state of affairs with the double-level intentionality that I described earlier. From the animal's point of view the representation might be of the form: "Coming-toward-me-thing-now," where we are to think of this so far as if it were one word, without repeatable elements.

The animal has feature placing, but not yet reference and predication. To get reference and predication it needs symbolic devices that break up the propositional content into components. But it already has the material to construct those components from its prelinguistic intentionality. It can see something coming toward it now, and thus believe that something is coming toward it now. But that is enough to give us at least the possibility of introducing devices that can perform the functions of reference and predication, devices that are forms of noun phrases and verb phrases. We will add rules or procedures for arranging those devices (words) into the complex resultant structures (sentences). It does not much matter how we construct these sub-sentential elements or how we combine them as long as they break up the sentence into repeatable components, and as long as the components match the components of the prelinguistic intentional contents. I have been assuming that they are broken up in a style similar to European languages I know, but that is not a necessary assumption. I have been assuming that the presyntactical *coming-toward-me-thing-now* breaks up into a device which refers to a contextually specific object, such as a man, and the predication of coming toward me now, as in the English

The man is coming toward me now.

It is not logically necessary that it be done this way, but doing it this way fits our prelinguistic phenomenology better than some ways we can imagine. As I said earlier, we can imagine a language where what we think of as objects are treated as recurring and repeatable processes, so it would come out as

It is manning now towards me comingly.

on analogy with

It is raining now on me heavily.

But such a language would not reflect the object salience of our perceptual phenomenology.

Furthermore there are built-in structural features of human intentionality which carry the solution to the paradox I mentioned earlier, and any evolutionary account has to face this paradox. The paradox is: how do we achieve the unity of the sentence (and hence the unity of the expressed proposition) when the sentence is entirely composed of discrete entities, the string of words and morphemes that constitute it? A related second question is: how do we explain the pervasiveness of noun phrases and verb phrases in human languages, and how do we explain that typically sentences contain both noun phrases and verb phrases? The solution to the first problem, the unity of the proposition, is provided by the fact that, because of the nature of speaker meaning, it is a requirement on something's being a sentence at all capable of encoding a speaker meaning that it must encode an entire intentional state. All intentionality, conscious or unconscious, perceptual or non-perceptual, comes to us propositionally in the trivial sense that each discriminable intentional state has conditions of satisfaction and a condition is always that such and such is the case. The sentence is designed to encode the entire propositional content of the intentional state. So once we require that sentences encode whole intentional states, the unity of the proposition expressed comes for free. The unity of the proposition is built into the very logical structure of biological intentionality.

Now we turn to the second question. If we now look at the phenomenological structure of our experience, particularly conscious, perceptual experience, we will see that *objects and their features* are salient. Though the conditions of satisfaction of our visual experiences require whole states of affairs, so that we never just see an object, but, for example, we see that an object with such and such features is over there; all the same, phenomenologically, we are aware of seeing objects and seeing that they have such and such features. So the propositional unity expressed by the complete sentence is already provided by pre-linguistic intentionality, and the internal subject-predicate structure is provided by the way our phenomenology presents the propositional content to us.

So far then we have taken three steps on the road to language: first the creation of speaker meaning, that is, the imposition of conditions of satisfaction on conditions of satisfaction. Second, the creation of conventional devices for performing acts of speaker meaning, which gives us something approaching sentence meaning, where sentence meaning is the standing possibility of speaker meaning. Sentence meaning is conventionalized. Speaker meaning is typically the employment or use of those conventions in the performance of the speech act. Third, we have added internal structure to the speech act in the form of discriminable syntactic elements that have meanings, semantic content, but cannot stand on their own in utterances. They are parts of sentences, and thus correspond to words, but they are not yet whole sentences. We also need rules for combining these devices into whole sentences and distinguishing between grammatical and ungrammatical strings. Both of these are crucial to any account of language. The first gives us meaningful units big enough to function in communication; the second gives compositionality. The sentence is composed of meaningful elements and those meaningful elements together with their rules of combination enable us to generate new sentences and to figure out the meanings of sentences and utterances that we have never heard before.

We do not yet have generativity, that is the capacity of speakers to produce and understand a potentially infinite number of new sentences, but it is easy to add generativity to compositionality by simply adding some recursive rules, rules that apply over and over endlessly. Examples of ways of providing generativity are such expressions as "It is possible that," "Sally believes that" or rules for forming relative clauses. What about sentence connectives? They do not seem hard to add either. Indeed we already have an implicit sentence connective when we conjoin two sentences in the speech act. If I say "It is raining. I am hungry" I have already said something equivalent to "It is raining and I am hungry." And we can add explicit connectives to do these jobs, connectives corresponding to the English "and" "or" "if . . . then" and "not."

Notice that with the addition of linguistic syntax to animal intentionality we enable speakers to do something no nonlinguistic animal can do. The speaker can intentionally construct arbitrarily many different representations of actual, possible, and even impossible states of affairs in the world. The speaker can now think and say not only the man is coming toward me now, but the man will come toward me next week, or the mountain will come toward me, and so on endlessly.

With the apparatus so far developed the hominids can extend the vocabulary to enable them to think thoughts and perform speech acts that are literally unthinkable without language. The prelinguistic animal can count on his fingers. Given numerals, initially introduced to match the fingers, he can count indefinitely and have thoughts with numerical components that he cannot have in the prelinguistic form. Without language he might think, "There are three dogs in the field," but with language he can think, "I wish there were a thousand dogs in the field."

11 THE NEXT STEP: DEONTOLOGY

So with meaning conventions plus compositionality and generativity we are well on the road to language.

Why is that not enough? Why are we just on the road and not already there? I think there is a sense in which we are already there if we understand the implications of the account that I have given so far in a certain very specific way. It is essential to see that in the account I have given so far it is implicit that the speaker employing the conventional device in a social setting for the purpose, for example, of conveying some truth about the world to the hearer, is thereby *committed* to that truth. That is, we will not understand an essential feature of language if we do not see that it necessarily involves social commitments, and that the necessity of these social commitments derives from the social character of the communication situation, the conventional character of the devices used, and the intentionality of speaker meaning. It is this feature that enables language to form the foundation of human society in general. If a speaker intentionally conveys information to a hearer using socially accepted conventions for the purpose of producing a belief in the hearer about a state of affairs in the world, then the speaker is committed to the truth of his utterance. I will now try to explain this point.

We saw earlier that the formal structure of the intentional state, $S(p)$, looks a lot like the formal structure of the corresponding speech act, $F(p)$. But $F(p)$ represents an intentional act, and in the cases we are considering it represents an act deliberately performed in accordance with the conventions of a socially accepted language. Recall that the essence of speaker meaning is the intentional imposition of conditions of satisfaction onto utterances, the imposition of the same conditions of satisfaction as the intentional state expressed in the utterance. Thus, if I believe that it is raining and I want to say that it is raining, I express my belief by making an utterance which I intend to have the same conditions of satisfaction as the original belief. And that utterance inherits the direction of fit of the belief and thus, like the belief, the utterance can be true or false. When I say "It is raining," my utterance has the word-to-world direction of fit and will be true or false depending on whether or not the propositional content is satisfied. And so on through the other cases.

But now an interesting problem arises concerning the relation between the speech act and the corresponding intentional state. The speech act involves a commitment that goes far beyond the commitments of the intentional state expressed. This is most obvious in the case of statements and promises, but it is also true of other sorts of speech acts such as orders and apologies. When I make a statement I not only express a belief but I commit myself to its truth. When I make a promise I not only express an intention but I commit myself to carrying it out. Where do these commitments come from? The belief and the intention have nothing like the commitments of the statement or the promise. If we are trying to explain the logical, conceptual evolution of a language that has statements and promises, it is not enough that we explain how a speaker can convey his belief and his intention to the hearer. We need to know how the speaker adds these special deontologies to the speech act. It is tempting, and indeed true, to say that the constitutive rules of the institutions of statement making and promising make every statement into a commitment to truth and every promise into an obligation to do something. The rules typically have the form "X counts as Y in C" (for example, making such and such an utterance X in this context C counts as making a promise, Y). The question is, How do we get the rules?

Notice that one wrong, but very common, answer is to think that the deontic requirements are somehow external to the type of speech act. First we have statement making and then we have a rule that commits us to making only true ones; first we have promise making and then we have a rule that obligates us to keep the promises. This view of the relation of statements to truth is held by philosophers as diverse as Bernard Williams (2002), Paul Grice (1975), and David Lewis (1972). But it is not correct. You cannot explain what a statement or a promise is without explaining that a statement commits the maker of the statement to its truth and the promise commits the maker of the promise to carrying it out. In both cases the commitment is *internal* to the type of speech act being performed, where by "internal" I mean it could not be the type of speech act it is, it could not be that very kind of speech act if it did not have that commitment. But, to repeat the question, how do we evolve the deontic power out of the act of meaning something by an utterance? Does the act of representing the same conditions of satisfaction as those of a belief somehow essentially involve a commitment that goes beyond the commitment of the belief; does the action of representing the same conditions of satisfaction as an intention necessarily involve a commitment that goes beyond the commitment of the intention? Or are these other commitments just add-ons? Are they further accretions that come with the historical development of the linguistic institutions? I think they are internal.

To see why, we have to see that the speech act is more than just the expression of an intention or the expression of a belief. It is above all a public performance. I am telling something to someone else. But I am not just telling him that I have a belief or that I have an intention; I am telling him something about the world represented by those beliefs and intentions. By committing myself to the conditions of satisfaction of the belief I am telling him that this is how the world is; by telling him about the conditions of satisfaction of my intention I am telling him what I am actually going to do. (The self-referentiality of promises comes in here. I do not just promise to do something, but in so doing, I promise to *do* it because I *promised* to do it.) In ordinary parlance, I give my word.

We can summarize this part of our discussion as follows. In evolving a language we found that we needed speaker meaning, conventions, and internal syntactic structure. But if we understand these as relating in a certain way to human intentionality, we can see the different types of illocutionary acts and in so doing, we already get the commitments that typically go with those types of illocutionary acts. Nothing further is necessary to guarantee that speakers will be committed by their utterances. In following the common-sense idea that language could have evolved, and may in fact have evolved, out of prelinguistic forms of intentionality we found that language so evolved provides something not present in prelinguistic intentionality: the public assumption of commitments.

12 THE EXTENSION OF DEONTOLOGY TO SOCIAL REALITY: HOW LANGUAGE ENABLES US TO CREATE SOCIAL INSTITUTIONS

The argument given so far is that intentional acts of meaning, that is the intentional imposition of conditions of satisfaction on conditions of satisfaction, performed according to accepted conventions and with the intention that they should so accord, necessarily involve a deontology. Now, once that deontology is collectively created by these intentional actions, then it is very easy, indeed practically inevitable, that it should be extended to social reality generally. So, once you have the capacity to represent, then you already have the capacity to create a reality that consists in part of representations. Let me give some examples of this. If you have the capacity to say "He is our leader," "He is my man," "She is my woman," "This is my house," then you have the capacity to do something more than represent preexisting states of affairs. You have the capacity to create states of affairs with a new deontology; you have the capacity to create rights, duties, and obligations by performing and getting other people to accept certain sorts of speech acts. Once you and others recognize someone as a leader, and an object as someone's property, and a man or a woman as someone with whom you have a special bond, then you have already created a public deontology. You have already created public reasons for action that are desire-independent. But notice the functioning of the language that we use to describe these phenomena. It creates them. The language constitutes them in an important way. Why? Because the phenomena in question only are what they are in virtue of being represented as what they are. The representations which are partly constitutive of institutional reality – the reality of government, private property, marriage as well as money, universities and cocktail parties – is essentially linguistic. The language does not just describe; it creates, and partly constitutes what it describes.

Compositionality figures essentially in the creation of social and institutional reality. Given compositionality the animal can do much more than just represent existing states of affairs; it can represent states of affairs that do not exist but which can be brought into existence by getting a community to accept a certain class of speech acts. So, for example, the man who says "This is my property" or the woman who says "This is my husband," may be doing more than just reporting an antecedently existing state of affairs; they may be creating a state of affairs by declaration. A person who can get other people to accept this declaration will succeed in creating an institutional reality that did not exist prior to that declaration.

We do not yet have performatives, because they require specific performative verbs or other performative expressions, but we do have declarations with their double direction of fit. If I declare, "This is my property" then I represent myself has having a right to the property (word-to-world direction of fit) and, if I get others to accept my representation then I create that right because the right only exists by collective acceptance (world-to-word direction of fit). And they are not independent: I create a right by representing myself as already having it.

This basic move underlies much of society. It is not easy to see this point but I think it is essential to understanding society. The utterance creates desire-independent reasons for action, and these are then recognized by the collectivity. That same move, that same *X*-counts-as-*Y*-in-context-*C* move, by which you create desire-independent reasons for action in the case of the individual speech act, is now generalizable. So what we think of as private property, for example, is a kind of standing speech act. It is a kind of permanent speech act affixed to an object. It says, the owner of this object has certain rights and duties, and other people, not the owners of this object, do not have those rights and duties. And think of money as a kind of standing permanent speech act. (Sometimes the speech act is written out. On American currency it says: "This note is legal tender for all debts public and private.")[6]

I have throughout this chapter been drawing attention to several remarkable features of human language. None is more remarkable than this: in human languages we have the capacity, not only to represent reality, both how it is and how we want to make it be, but we have the capacity to create a new reality by representing that reality as existing. We create private property: money, property, government, marriage, and a thousand other such phenomena by representing these phenomena as existing.

13 SUMMARY OF THE ARGUMENT SO FAR

There are three essential points I want to get across in this chapter in addition to the analysis of relations of nonlinguistic to linguistic intentionality. First I want to emphasize how the structure of prelinguistic intentionality enables us to solve the problems of the relation of reference and predication and the problem of the unity of the proposition. The second point is about deontology. The basic intellectual motivation that drives this second part of my argument is the following: there is something left out of the standard textbook accounts of language as consisting of syntax, semantics, and phonology with an extralinguistic pragmatics thrown in. Basically what is left out is the essential element of commitment involved in having a set of conventional devices that encode the imposition of conditions of satisfaction on conditions of satisfaction. The third point of the chapter is about the creation of a social and institutional ontology by linguistically representing certain facts as existing, thus creating the facts. When we understand this third point we will get a deeper insight into the constitutive role of language in the construction of society and social institutions. Let me review the steps of the argument so that it is as clear as I can make it.

Step 1.   We imagine a race of beasts capable of consciousness and prelinguistic intentionality. And, of equal importance, they are endowed with a capacity for free action and collective intentionality. They can cooperate and they have free will.

Step 2.   We have to assume that they are capable of evolving proce-dures for representing states of affairs where the representations have speaker meaning, as I have defined it. They can represent states of affairs that they believe exist, states of affairs they desire to exist, states of affairs they intend to bring about, etc.

Step 3.   These procedures, or at least some of them, become conven-tionalized. What does that mean exactly? It means that given collective intentionality, if anyone intentionally engages in one of these proce-dures, then other members of the group have a right to expect that the procedures are being followed correctly. This, I take it, is the essential thing about conventions. Conventions are arbitrary, but once they are settled they give the participants a right to expectations.

Step 4.   We can also imagine that they break up the representations into repeatable and manipulatable components that perform the func-tions of reference and predication.

Step 5.   The central idea in the argument is this: just having a belief or a desire or an intention does not so far commit a person in any public way. Of course, a belief is a commitment to truth and a desire is a commitment to satisfaction and an intention is a commitment to action, but none of these so far are public undertakings. There is no deontology involved, no publicly recognized obligation. But once you freely com-mit yourself to the conditions of satisfaction of these corresponding intentional states and you do this in a public way by imposing condi-tions of satisfaction on conditions of satisfaction, and you do it accord-ing to the conventions of a tribe, then you have a system for creating obligations and other sorts of deontic commitments. Notice that the commitment is to states of affairs in the world and not just to the corresponding intentional states. Thus if I make a statement I commit myself to the existence of a fact, if I make a promise I commit myself to the performance of a future action, and so on.

Step 6. The same basic linguistic move that enables speech acts to carry a deontology of rights, duties, commitments, etc. can be extended to create a social and institutional reality of money, government, marriage, private property, and so on. And each of these is a system of deontologies. Once we introduce the elements of compositionality and generativity into language there is literally no limit to the institutional realities we can create just by agreeing, in language, that we are creating them. We create universities, cocktail parties, and summer vacations, for example. The limits on institutional power are the limits on deontology itself. Deontic powers are powers that exist only because they are recognized and accepted as existing. Sometimes we back them with physical force, in the case of the criminal law for example, but the police and armies are also systems of deontologies.

14 WHY STANDARD SEMANTIC THEORIES FAIL TO ACCOUNT FOR THESE FEATURES

I have now completed the main arguments of this chapter. In this section and the next I will answer some leftover questions.

I said earlier that traditional accounts of language are unable to get at this essential deontic feature. Now, why couldn't, for example, standard truth conditional accounts get at it? The truth conditional accounts that I am familiar with make a connection between truth and meaning. What they do not see is how that connection is necessarily mediated by commitment. It is not enough that there should be a matching or satisfaction relation between the sentence or the utterance on the one hand and its truth conditions on the other; there must also be a representing relation and the representing relation is not explained by a kind of matching or satisfaction. The only way to get the representing relation is to see that an utterance with a meaning does not just match the truth conditions or is satisfied by the truth conditions but rather is a *commitment* to the existence of those truth conditions. You can see this weakness in its most extreme form in the case of the picture theory of meaning. Wittgenstein's *Tractatus* is the classic statement of this view. The problem is that if we are to try to think of the sentence as a picture of a fact, where picturing is defined in terms of the isomorphism of the structure of the picture and the structure of the corresponding fact, then equally the fact is a picture of the sentence. Isomorphism is a

43

symmetrical relation: if *A* is isomorphic to *B*, then *B* is isomorphic to *A*. If this sentence is somehow or other a structural model of the fact, then the fact is equally a structural model of the sentence, and we have lost the representing relation which is essential to language. Now, oddly enough, a similar difficulty affects Tarski-style model-theoretic accounts such as Davidson's, because if we are to say that the key notion is satisfaction, and we can explain satisfaction recursively, then the problem is that if an object satisfies an open sentence, then there must be a relation in which the open sentence stands to the object, the relation of being satisfied by that object. But neither of these, neither satisfier of nor satisfied by, gives us representation or commitment. The particular form of asymmetry that is required between the representation and the thing represented essentially involves a commitment on the part of the speech act to the existence of the state of affairs represented. It is not enough to present language and reality as simply staring at each other blankly. Language is used to represent reality and the notion of representation essentially involves more than the notions of truth or matching, or satisfaction. It involves the notion of a *commitment* to truth or satisfaction.

15 WHY LANGUAGE IS ESSENTIALLY CONVENTIONAL AND WHY THERE ARE SO MANY DIFFERENT LANGUAGES

If language is biologically based, then why is it that we speak so many different languages? If evolutionary biology gave us the capacity for language, why did it not give us a single language which all humans could speak? Humans have, with minor variations, the same way of seeing because they all have the same visual apparatus, but they certainly do not have the same way of speaking. Why not? The answer derives in part from the fact that speaking is a voluntary activity, perhaps the most paradigmatic form of the human freedom of the will, and where free voluntary actions are concerned, people perform these actions in their own free voluntary ways. Biology can give us a basis for talk, but it is up to us how we talk, and it is up to us what we say.

Suppose there had been exactly one primordial language with its own syntax and lexicon. We know from historical linguistics that it would have evolved into different dialects, all of which would be conventional. Even if everyone tries as hard as they can to imitate what they take to be the "correct" way of speaking, variations are bound to emerge. In a sense the Roman Empire gave its subjects a common language, but over two thousand years they evolved into contemporary, mutually incomprehensible, French, Portuguese, Spanish, Romansh, etc. So even assuming one biologically determined language, the free will of language speakers would have evolved the *Ursprache* into any number of conventional dialects, where "conventional" implies both arbitrariness and normativity. There is a right way and a wrong way to speak any language, but the way that the language fixed rightness and wrongness is conventional and therefore arbitrary.

NOTES

This is a revised and expanded version of a talk that I have given at various universities and international conferences. An earlier draft was published in the proceedings of the Twentieth German Philosophy Conference in Berlin (Abel 2006). The tentative title marks the fact that I do not regard this as a finished piece. It is still work in progress. I thank Tecumseh Fitch for his detailed comments on an earlier draft. I am also grateful to Dagmar Searle for her help and advice.

1 For a good survey, see Vauclair (1996).
2 For a good survey, see Fitch (2005).
3 In general this is true of most of what are called the "emotions." The concept of an emotion is not very clear because we are not sure what to count as an emotion and what not. But the paradigm cases of the emotions, strong forms of love, hate, lust, disgust, shame, and pride, I think are all agitated forms of desire, presupposing beliefs.
4 See Vauclair (1996).
5 We can construct examples where what is normally a purely expressive speech can be performed representatively. If my dentist tells me to say "Ouch" if it hurts too much, then in saying "Ouch" I am making a statement to the effect that it hurts too much.
6 These points are developed further in Searle (1995).

PART I

From mind to meaning

Chapter 2

Content, mode, and self-reference

FRANÇOIS RECANATI

1 ILLOCUTIONARY FORCE, PSYCHOLOGICAL MODE, AND THE FALLACY OF MISPLACED INFORMATION

Searle famously characterized speech act types in terms of a number of "conditions" or "rules" they are supposed to obey, including conditions on their propositional content. If I order John to wash the dishes, the content of the order is the proposition that John will wash the dishes – the same proposition that would be the content of an assertion if I *said that* John will wash the dishes, or of a question if I *asked whether* John will wash the dishes. While assertions or questions can have any proposition as their contents, however, orders and directive speech acts more generally are supposed to be more constrained: *their content can only be a proposition bearing upon a future act of the hearer*, as in this particular case. Likewise, promises are such that their contents can only be a future act of the speaker (Searle 1969: 57–8).

In my own book on speech acts I criticized Searle's claim and argued that it rests on what Barwise and Perry later dubbed the "fallacy of misplaced information":[1]

The notion of the hearer's (or speaker's) future behavior does have a role to play in the analysis of commissives and directives, but ... the proper place for this notion is in the analysis of the *illocutionary force* of directives and commissives, not in the analysis of their propositional content. Any proposition whatever can be the content of a directive or a commissive; it suffices that the speaker's utterance express his intention that the hearer (or the speaker), by virtue of this utterance expressing this intention, behave in such a way as to make the proposition true. The "hearer's (or speaker's) future behavior" consists in bringing about the state of affairs that is the content of the speech act. It is not an intrinsic aspect of that state of affairs.

(Recanati 1987: 163; originally in Recanati 1981: 189; see also Sperber 1982: 47)

49

As I pointed out in the same book, Searle's view has unfortunate consequences: it forces the theorist to treat as indirect the illocutionary act of promise performed by means of a sentence such as "You will win" (said by a tennis player to his opponent), while the same act would be performed directly if the speaker had uttered "I will lose" instead. This sounds arbitrary. Again, any future state of affairs can be the content of an order (or a promise) if the utterance manifests the speaker's intention that, because of this utterance, the addressee (or the speaker) will bring about that state of affairs. Even the futurity of the state of affairs is not a genuine constraint on the propositional content of commissives or directives. To be sure, it is a natural constraint that humans can only actualize the future, since the past is beyond their control; but that is not a conventional, linguistic constraint.

In his later work, Searle emphasized the similarity between speech acts and mental states. Both have a propositional content, and both have a dual structure, with the "psychological mode" corresponding, on the side of mental states, to the illocutionary force on the side of speech acts. To assert that p is to perform a speech act whose content is the proposition that p and whose force is that of an assertion. Likewise, to believe that p is to be in an intentional state whose content is the proposition that p and whose psychological mode is that of belief. Now, because of that dual aspect, it is all too easy to "misplace" some of the information carried by a mental state, by ascribing to the content of the state a piece of information that is actually carried by its mode – just as Searle misleadingly ascribed to the propositional content of directive and commissive speech acts what was actually a feature of their illocutionary force.

Indeed, I think Searle himself has been guilty of such misplacement in his insightful analysis of perceptual experiences (a subclass of Intentional states). Besides making the distinction I have just introduced, between the content of the state and its mode, Searle distinguishes two conditions such that the experience counts as satisfied (veridical) if and only if they are both met: the *primary condition* and the *self-referential condition*. (Those are my terms, not Searle's.) For Searle, both the primary condition and the self-referential condition are determined by the propositional content of the experience; he therefore construes that propositional content as self-referential. If I am right, however, the propositional content of the experience only determines the first component of its overall truth conditions – what I called the primary condition. The self-referential condition is not determined by the propositional content of the state, but by its mode. It follows that the propositional content of a perceptual state is not self-referential, even if its overall truth conditions are.

2 THE CONTENT OF PERCEPTUAL EXPERIENCE: SEARLE'S ANALYSIS

Visual experiences have propositional content, Searle claims. The subject does not merely see a flower, he sees a flower there, and this, fully spelled out, means that he sees *that there is* a flower there. I understand Searle's contention as follows: the subject, as part of his visual experience, makes certain perceptual judgments, which determine the (conceptual) content of the experience. So the propositional content of the experience is the content of the judgments that are immediately (i.e. noninferentially) based on it.[2]

Let us ask what the truth conditions of the perceptual judgment are. For the perceptual experience to be veridical, Searle says, there must actually be a flower there, but that is not sufficient. In addition to the primary condition that there be a flower there, an extra condition must be met: it must be the case that the presence of a flower there causes the visual experience (including the judgment that is part and parcel of the experience). Insofar as the propositional content of the state is what determines its truth conditions, the content of the visual experience turns out to be more complex than one might have thought. The content of the visual experience is not the simple proposition *that there is a flower there*, but the conjunctive proposition *that there is a flower there and there being a flower there causes this visual experience* (where "this visual experience" reflexively refers to the experience of which this is the propositional content). Searle therefore provides the following analysis of the perceptual experience of seeing a flower there. As in speech act theory, the capital letters indicate the mode, while the materials within the parentheses specify the content.

VIS EXP (that there is a flower there and that there is a flower there is causing this visual experience)

According to this analysis, the intentional state is a visual experience (mode) and its content is a conjunctive proposition whose second conjunct refers to the very experience of which this is the content, while the first conjunct specifies "the state of affairs perceived" (Searle 1983: 48; I suppose this means something like: the state of affairs which the speaker takes himself to be perceiving). The first conjunct determines a proper part of the judgment's truth conditions, namely the primary condition: that there be a flower there. But there is another truth condition, determined by the second conjunct. That is the self-referential condition: that the perceptual experience be caused by "the rest of its truth conditions," that is, by the state of affairs whose existence is the primary condition. Because of the second condition, the overall truth conditions of the perceptual judgment are self-referential: for the perceptual judgment to be veridical, the state of affairs which the speaker takes himself to be perceiving must actually exist (primary condition), and it must be what causes the speaker's perceptual judgment that that state of affairs exists (self-referential condition).

3 WHAT IS WRONG WITH SEARLE'S ANALYSIS

I agree with Searle that there are these two components in the truth conditions of perceptual judgments. But I deplore Searle's claim that the overall truth conditional content of the judgment, with its two components, is the propositional content of the visual experience (as distinguished from its mode). Insofar as I can tell, this is the fallacy of misplaced information once again.

That the state of affairs represented (there being a flower there) causes the representation of that state of affairs is a condition that has to be met for the representation in question to count as a *perception* (rather than, say, an expectation). It follows that the self-referential condition is determined by the perceptual mode of the state, not by its content.[3] For a representation that p to count as a perception that p, it must be the case that the representation is caused by the fact that p; but what is represented is only the fact that p. In other words: the content of the state (namely, the proposition that p) only determines the primary condition; the perceptual nature of the state is what determines the self-referential condition. Together, the content and the mode determine the overall truth conditions of the state.

Searle might insist that, for him, the propositional content of a state just *is* what determines its truth conditions. Consider the following passage, where he introduces the idea of propositional content:

Every Intentional state consists of an *Intentional content* in a *psychological mode*. Where that content is a whole proposition and where there is a direction of fit, the Intentional content determines the *conditions of satisfaction*. Conditions of satisfaction are those conditions which, as determined by the Intentional content, must obtain if the state is to be satisfied. For this reason the *specification* of the content already is a *specification* of the conditions of satisfaction. Thus, if I have a belief that it is raining, the content of my belief is: that it is raining. And the conditions of satisfaction are: that it is raining.   (Searle 1983: 12–13)

Given this characterization of content, it is legitimate to use the overall truth conditions of perceptual experiences as evidence to determine what their content is. Following this procedure, we end up with Searle's conclusion: the propositional content of a visual experience is self-referential.

But I do not think we can accept this defense. Searle cannot simply "define" the propositional content of a state as that which determines its truth conditions. Or rather, he can, but then the claim that the content so defined is (to some extent) independent of the mode becomes an empirical claim, and it is that claim which I reject.[4] There is a sense of "content" in which the content of perceptual judgments is self-referential; but the "content," in *that* sense, is determined in part by the mode, and in part by . . . the content of the state in a *different* sense, namely, the sense in which "content" and "mode" are two independent dimensions which together constitute the state. My point, therefore, is that Searle cannot simultaneously maintain that the content is what determines the conditions of satisfaction, and that the content is independent from the mode. There are two distinct notions of content: one that is involved in the mode/content distinction inspired from speech act theory, and another one that is involved in the claim that the content of a state is what determines its (overall) truth conditions.

A second line of response is available to Searle. He may insist that *it is part of the subject's perceptual experience* that that experience is caused by its object. The "causation" component is not external to the content of the experience, but an integral part of it. With this I agree – but I do not think Searle's position is thereby justified. The subject is *aware* of the perceptual nature of his experience: he knows he is perceiving rather than, say, expecting or imagining. So there is a sense in which the complete content of his experience is self-referential: but the "complete content" of the experience involves more than the propositional content – it also involves the psychological mode, of which the subject is aware and which determines the additional, self-referential condition.

Once again, the analogy with speech acts can be illuminating. There is a self-referential element in speech acts too, as several authors have pointed out. For example, an order represents a certain state of affairs as a state of affairs such that the addressee complies with the order only if he brings it about. But bringing about the state of affairs in question is not sufficient for compliance: it must be the case that the addressee brings about the state of affairs *as a result of being ordered to do so*. An order, therefore, presents a state of affairs as something which the hearer is to bring about as a result of this order. So there are two components in the obedience conditions of an order: the hearer must do something (primary condition), and the order must be what causes the hearer to do that thing (self-referential condition). But it would be a mistake to consider the second, self-referential condition (that the order be what causes the hearer to do *x*) as determined by the *content* of the order (i.e. what is ordered), as opposed to its force. The speaker orders the hearer to do *x*, period; he does not order her *to do x because of this order*. Yet the fact that the utterance *is* an order (rather than an assertion) means that the hearer's doing *x* will count as satisfying the speech act only if the hearer's doing *x* is caused by the speech act in the proper way. This is a feature of the illocutionary force of ordering. So the correct representation of the speech act of, say, *ordering the hearer to wash the dishes* is not

ORDER (that the addressee washes the dishes and that the addressee washes the dishes is caused by this order)

but simply

ORDER (that the addressee washes the dishes).[5]

I think exactly the same considerations apply in the perception case. The proper representation of the perceptual experience of the subject who sees a flower there is not

VIS EXP (that there is a flower there and that there is a flower there is causing this visual experience)

but simply

VIS EXP (that there is a flower there).

In other words, the content of the perception of a flower is the fact that there is a flower there. That fact can be represented in all sorts of modes; for it to be represented in the perceptual mode, it must be the case that the fact itself causes the representation. But this feature, hence the self-referential component whose importance Searle rightly emphasizes, is a property of the perceptual mode of representation, not a property of the content of perceptual representations. Or rather: it *is* a property of their content, but *not* in the sense in which "content" contrasts with "mode." We should distinguish the strict content of an intentional state (or, for that matter, of a speech act) and its "overall" or "complete" content which includes the aspects of content determined by the mode.

4 REFLEXIVE TRUTH CONDITIONS WITHOUT REFLEXIVE CONTENT

The distinction between the two levels of content is the core of a view I have been trying to develop over the years, within a situation-theoretic framework (Recanati 1996, 1997, 1999, 2000, forthcoming). The basic idea is this: when we think or talk, the content of what we think or say is to be evaluated with respect to some situation (or class of situations), and the truth value of what we say or think depends both upon the content of what we say and think *and* upon the situation with respect to which it is supposed to be evaluated. Not only the truth *value*: as we shall see, the truth *conditions* of the utterance/thought crucially depend upon the situation, and they correspond to the second level of content: the "complete" or "overall" content of the utterance/thought.

In the language case, the situation is often a matter of the speaker's intentions: the situation is tacitly referred to by the speaker. For example, imagine the speaker and his addressee are watching four people playing a poker game, and the speaker says: "Claire has a good hand!" This is true if and only if Claire has a good hand *in the poker game they are watching*. The situation tacitly referred to by the speaker finds its way into the truth conditions of the utterance even though nothing in the sentence stands for that situation. The sentence expresses the proposition that Claire has a good hand, a proposition that would be true if Claire was playing bridge at the other end of town and had a good hand there; but the (complete) content of the utterance is richer than that. It involves that proposition plus the situation the speaker tacitly refers to, and it is true iff the proposition in question is true in the situation in question.

While, in speech, the situation with respect to which the utterance is meant to be evaluated is tacitly referred to, in thought it is often determined by the architecture of the system. Thus a perception is bound to be evaluated in the situation that causally affects the subject's senses and is responsible for the perception. In Searle's flower example, the content of the perception, in the strict sense, is simply the fact that there is a flower; but for the perception to be veridical, that fact must obtain *in the situation that the subject sees, i.e. that which causes his or her visual experience*. On this view the self-referential condition is a crucial aspect of the perception's truth conditions, as Searle claims, but it is captured within the "situational" component of the overall content.

We can extend this analysis to the whole class of Intentional states which involve a self-referential component – the "reflexive states," as Higginbotham (2003) calls them. In what follows I will discuss two examples for which Higginbotham provides detailed self-referential analyses in the spirit of Searle's analysis of perceptual experience.

The first example is episodic memory. For the subject's memory that *p* to be veridical, Searle points out, it must have been the case that *p*, but that is not sufficient: the fact that *p* must have caused a perception that left *the memory* as a trace.[6] In stating the memory's truth conditions we cannot avoid referring to the memory state itself. According to Higginbotham, the subject who remembers having been elected entertains a memory e_1 the content of which is the following proposition:

(1) $(\exists e_2)$ is elected $(\sigma(e_1), e_2)$ and $e_2 < e_1$.

That is the proposition *that there is an event of being elected whose subject is the subject of this memory state and whose time is anterior to the time of this memory state*. The proposition in question is doubly reflexive: it refers to the subject who undergoes the memory state of which it is the content, and it locates the event e_2 as anterior to that memory state ($<$ is the relation of temporal precedence). Searle would presumably add a further component, pertaining to the causal relation between the event e_2 and the memory state e_1.

In contrast to Searle and Higginbotham, I take the content of the subject's memory in Higginbotham's example to be simply the event of being elected. In the Davidsonian framework favored by Higginbotham, this simple content can be represented as (2):

(2) $(\exists e)$ is elected (x, e).

One nice consequence of the view that the overall content of a representation divides into the content proper and a situational component is that the content proper can be made very simple, so simple that in many cases it will be less than fully propositional (in the classical sense of "proposition"). Here (2) is *not* a complete proposition, by Fregean standards; it is only a propositional function. Or, if it is to count as a proposition, it will be in the sense in which Prior's tense logic posits "propositions" that are true with respect to times (Prior 1967, 1968), and Prior's egocentric logic "propositions" that are true with respect to persons (Prior 1977). Indeed (2) is the "proposition" *that one is elected* – a proposition which (given a fixed world) is true with respect to all and only those person-time pairs $<x, t>$ such that x is elected at t. In contrast to classical propositions, which are true or false *tout court*, such a "relativized" proposition is only true (or false) with respect to individual-time pairs.

For a memory with that proposition as content to be true *tout court*, the proposition in question must be true with respect to the subject who remembers and a time anterior to the memory.[7] It follows that if John has, at time t^*, a memory whose content is (2), John's memory is true only if John has been elected prior to t^*. On this view, both the pastness of the remembered event and the subject's involvement in that event derive from the fact that what is represented is represented in the memory mode. Again, we find that the truth conditions are reflexive, but the self-reference bit comes from the mode. The content proper – what the subject remembers – is very simple, and it is not self-referential.

The second example is the state of relief, exemplified by Prior's utterance "Thank goodness that's over!" (Prior 1963). According to Higginbotham (1995), this is a complex state involving an emotion (relief) and, causing the emotion, a doxastic state (the belief that the painful episode is over). The content of the doxastic state refers to the complex state of which it is a part: the painful episode the termination of which brings relief must have been painful to the subject of the complex relief state, and it must be past with respect to that very state. The state is reflexive because its content involves a reference to the state itself.

Again, while I agree that the state is reflexive in some sense, I would offer a much simpler analysis. Following Prior, I would say that in "Thank goodness that's over" the sentence "that's over" expresses a time-relative proposition, true at any time t iff the painful episode is over at t. What brings relief is the subject's belief, at t^*, that this proposition holds. The subject's belief is indeed true iff the time-relative proposition in question is true at the time of the thought episode, that is, at t^*; but this does not make t^* (or the thought episode) a constituent of the proposition that is the (strict) content of the relief-causing belief. t^* only comes into the picture through the act of *asserting* that proposition, linguistically or mentally. To assert the proposition is, in effect, to apply it to the current time.

This type of analysis has several advantages over the Searle–Higginbotham analysis. Among the reflexive states, many are shared with all sorts of animals (e.g. dogs) to which one does not want to ascribe the ability to entertain complex reflexive contents of the sort posited by the self-referential analysis.[8] It is much more plausible to view the self-reference at issue as secured by the architecture of the system. Another advantage of my analysis is that it offers a simple solution to a vexing problem in the analysis of episodic memory. In the last section of this chapter, I briefly present the problem and its solution.

5 TIME AND MEMORY

Episodic memories are mental states which presuppose other mental states, namely perceptual experiences, to which they are related both causally (the memory derives from the perceptual experience, which leaves it as a "trace") and semantically (the memory inherits the content of the perceptual experience). As Evans (1982) puts it, we need to be able to use information gathered through perception at a later time, and for that we need a mechanism for retaining information. Memory is that mechanism. Or, rather, it is a family of mechanisms, corresponding to distinct ways of retaining information. In *semantic memory*, we retain the beliefs once formed on the basis of perception (or on any other basis – what is retained is only the output of the belief-fixation mechanism, so the etiology of the belief is irrelevant). In *episodic memory*, we retain the perceptual experiences themselves. I will be concerned only with the second type of memory, where a memory state is an experience similar to the perceptual experience from which it derives.

The crucial feature of episodic memories, besides their being experiential states, is that they share their content with the perceptual experiences from which they derive: they represent the same event or scene as the perceptual experience which is their ancestor. That is what episodic memory is for – it is supposed to *replicate* the perceptual experience. However, that is not all there is to say about memory. Even though the function of memory is to replicate the perceptual experience and, in particular, to carry the same content as that of the perceptual experience, still there is a fundamental difference in content between memory and the perception on which it is based.

I see that there is a large tree standing in front of me. Later, I remember that there was a large tree standing in front of me. This way of putting things reveals the essential difference: perception and memory relate to the same scene or event, but in memory the scene or event is *presented as past*. I remember that there *was* a large tree standing in front of me.

There is an obvious tension between the two elements I have just mentioned. Does a memory state have the same content as the perceptual state from which it derives, or does it have a different content? The answer seems to be: both! The scene or event the memory is about is clearly the same as the scene or event the initiating perception is about (that is what makes memory memory), but it is not the same since perception represents a present event (and represents it *as present*) while memory represents a past event (and represents it *as past*).

Faced with this tension, the obvious move is to distinguish two components in the content of a memory. One component is common to the memory and the perception from which it derives. Since that component is shared, the memory "has the same content as" the perception. But the content of the memory involves an additional element, which is responsible for the difference between the memory and the perceptual state. Thus William James defines memory as "the knowledge of an event ... of which in the meantime we have not been thinking, *with the additional consciousness that we have thought or experienced it before*" (James 1890: 648, cited in Hoerl 2001: 326; my emphasis). Here the "knowledge of the event" is what is common to the perceptual state and the memory state; the additional component is responsible for the "feeling of pastness" which differentiates memory from perception.

On this view the content of memory is conjunctive. The first conjunct is what is shared with perception; the second conjunct differentiates memory from perception. The first conjunct represents a scene or event in the world; the second conjunct represents the subject's past perceptual experience of that scene or event – hence the second conjunct is metarepresentational. This is very similar to Searle's analysis of the content of perceptual experiences.

Attractive though it is, there is a serious problem with the conjunctive analysis. It takes the content of the memory experience to consist of the content of the perceptual experience together with an additional element. But in what sense does the content of the memory experience contain that of the perceptual experience? In perceiving the flower,

I judge that there is a flower there. In remembering the flower, I do *not* judge that there is a flower there – only that there was one. So it does not seem that one can get to the content of memory by simply adding something to the content of perception.

In response to this objection, we may revise the analysis and interpret differently the idea that the content of memory contains the content of perception as a proper part. We may give up the conjunctive analysis and consider the content of the perceptual experience as occurring in the content of the memory not as an independent conjunct, but as a subordinate, embedded part. Instead of "*p* and I once perceived that *p*" the content would be simply "I once perceived that *p*." (To this, following Searle, we may add the further idea that the present memory state is caused by that earlier perception: "I once perceived that *p* and that perception is causally responsible for this memory experience.") The content of the perception occurs here as *mentioned* in the metarepresentational component, which now exhausts the content of the memory instead of being only a part of it. This view I call the metarepresentational analysis.[9]

This solution to the problem raises another problem, however. The metarepresentational theory presents memory as primarily about our perceptual experience, and only indirectly about the world. I share Evans's protest that

> We no more have, in memory, information that is primarily about our past experiences than we have, in perception, information which is primarily about our present experiences. Just as perception must be regarded as a capacity for gaining information about the world, so memory must be regarded as a capacity for retaining information about the world. (Evans 1982: 240)

In this respect the conjunctive theory fares better than the metarepresentational theory. The conjunctive theory integrates a metarepresentational component (corresponding to the subject's consciousness of being in a state which causally derives from a previous perception), but it also incorporates the direct representation of a state of affairs in the world, and straightforwardly captures the idea that the memory state retains the content of the perceptual state.

The problem we have raised for the conjunctive theory was that memory does not preserve the content of perception but transforms it by putting it, as it were, in the past tense. That is why it does not seem that one can get to the content of memory by simply adding something to the content of perception. Adding is not enough; one needs to

subtract something as well – namely the present tense or, less meta-
phorically, the feeling of presentness which colors the perception of
the scene. In shifting from perception to memory, this feeling is
removed, and it is replaced by the feeling of pastness which colors the
representation of the scene in memory.

In the framework I have sketched, this problem simply does not
arise. As in the conjunctive analysis, there are two components, one of
which represents a state of affairs in the world. But in my framework
that component is temporally neutral – it is a time-relative proposition
which does not, by itself, specify a time – so there is no objection to
saying that it is common to perception and to the resulting memory.

The complete content of a perceptual state is analysed into (i) a
content in the strict sense and (ii) a situation with respect to which
that content is supposed to be evaluated. The complete content is
distributed, and that means that what the situation component supplies
need not be replicated in the content proper. Now the content of a
perceptual experience is relative to the situation of perception (i.e. the
situation which affects the subject's senses and is causally responsible
for the perceptual state). This relativity extends to time: the content of
perception is temporally neutral, but it is evaluated with respect to the
time of the perceptual experience. So the subject has, at t, a perceptual
experience the content of which is the time-relative proposition
that there is a flower there, and that proposition is presented as true
at t, the time of the present perceptual experience.

Since the content of the perception, in the strict sense, is temporally neutral, there is no objection to saying that it is preserved in
memory. In memory, the same time-relative proposition that there is
a flower there is presented as true with respect to the situation (and
the time) of the *earlier* perceptual experience rather than the situation
(and the time) of the *present* memory experience. In the analysis of
memory just as in the analysis of perception, the temporal element is
carried by the situation of evaluation.[10]

NOTES

1 See Barwise and Perry (1983: 38, 164, etc.).
2 I know this is not how Searle himself puts the matter, but the difference in
   formulation is not important in the context of the present discussion.
3 Thus I concur with Kent Bach who writes, in his contribution to this volume
   (p. 74): "It is not the content of a visual experience that determines that its
   cause is its object. Rather, it is the psychological mode. It is the fact that the

experience is perceptual that determines that its object(s) is that which causes, in the appropriate way, that very state."

4 In response, Searle might point out that he never claimed that the content was independent of the other component (mode or force): the very idea of a "propositional content condition" argues against such independence. This point is well taken, but I reply that the distinction between "content" and "mode" (or "force"), by itself, implies that these are relatively independent dimensions. However lightly we construe this "independence" condition, it will not be satisfied (I claim) if we follow Searle and *define* content as that which determines satisfaction conditions. Searle himself concurrently uses a distinct notion of content, namely (for any type of speech act or Intentional state *F*) *what* the subject *F*s: what she believes, what she asserts, what she promises, what she perceives, etc. The content of the act/state, in this sense, satisfies the independence condition, and it is not self-referential (as Searle himself admits).

5 As Savas Tsohatzidis pointed out to me, the analysis of directives I am criticizing here as incorrect (that which construes their content as self-referential) is explicitly endorsed by Searle in *Intentionality* (Searle 1983: 86).

6 "The memory of seeing the flower represents both the visual experience and the flower and is self-referential in the sense that, unless the memory was caused by the visual experience which in turn was caused by the presence of (and features of) the flower, I didn't really remember seeing the flower" (Searle 1983: 95).

7 Again, Searle would (rightly) add a causal condition: the remembered event must be the causal source of the current memory.

8 I am indebted to Ned Block for emphasizing this point. Searle himself has responded to a similar worry expressed by Burge (1991), but I find his response puzzling. Searle says that what he presents as the self-referential content of the visual experience is not something which the subject of the experience (possibly a dog, or a small child) has to entertain or somehow represent. Searle says he only claims that "the visual experience itself functions self-referentially in fixing its truth conditions" (Searle 1991b: 228). But that is precisely my point: the self-reference results from the way perception works, but it is not a feature of the content of the subject's representations, in the strict sense of content. If Searle is right that Burge's objection rests on a misunderstanding, then perhaps this chapter ought to be seen as a clarification of Searle's position rather than a critique.

9 For this analysis to get off the ground, a few adjustments are necessary. First, the paraphrase "I once perceived that *p*" is misleading. It does not capture the experiential component of memory – the fact that in memory, the nonconceptual content of the perceptual experience is retained. A better paraphrase would be: "I had perceptual experience XXX," where "XXX" does not merely specify the conceptual content of the perceptual judgment, but, as it were,

"quotes" the perceptual experience directly. Another adjustment is needed to capture the epistemic value of memory, namely the fact that, if I remember that *p*, I am thereby justified in judging that it was the case that *p*. That would not be the case if the content of memory was simply a representation of a (possibly nonveridical) past perceptual experience. For that reason, Jordi Fernandez has suggested adding the condition that the past perceptual experience which memory represents is *represented as veridical* (Fernandez 2006).

10 At this point the metarepresentational theorist can make the same inadequate response which, in section 3, I said Searle could make. It runs as follows: the feeling of pastness, just like the feeling of presentness that accompanies perception, is an aspect of the *content* of memory. There is a clear *phenomenological* difference between memory and perception, having to do with their respective temporal orientations. This cannot be expelled out of the content, however strictly we construe that notion of content. So, for example, Mike Martin writes: "The mere possibility that recall and experience might coincide in content raise[s] the worry that the phenomenology of recall might *then* have to be identified with that of sensory experience"(Martin 2001: 278; emphasis mine). But there is absolutely no reason to consider that phenomenology supervenes on content in the strict sense. The mode contributes to the phenomenology, since the mode is something the subject is aware of. In the memory mode, the content is presented as true with respect to a past perceptual situation: hence the scene represented is felt as past. In the perception mode, the content is presented as true with respect to the current perceptual situation: hence the scene represented is felt as present. This introduces a difference in the complete content of the respective states, a difference which the phenomenology reflects.

63

Chapter 3

Searle against the world: how can experiences find their objects?

KENT BACH

Here is an old question in the philosophy of perception: here I am, looking at the pen on my desk. Presumably I really am seeing this pen. Even so, I could be having an experience just like the one I am having without anything being there. So how can the experience I am having really involve direct awareness of the pen? It seems as though the presence of the pen is inessential to the way the experience is.

Traditionally, this question was used to raise skeptical worries about perceptual experience and to motivate the sense-data thesis, according to which perceptual experiences, even veridical ones, are directly of mental or private objects and only indirectly of their physical objects. I addressed these epistemological and ontological problems in my dissertation several decades ago, but it is not yet time for me to take them up again. What interests me here is what might be called the semantic problem of perceptual experience. It concerns the fact that experiences are directed at objects. This is what John Searle and many other philosophers call the Intentionality of experience.

Here I am looking at this pen. What makes it the case that it is *this* pen that I am experiencing, that *it* is the one that appears to me of such-and-such shape, size, and color? The problem here is that there is nothing in the character of my visual experience to distinguish this pen from any other pen that would look just like it. If this pen were replaced instantaneously by another, I would not and could not tell the difference. Accordingly, the usual answer to the question of why this pen is the one I am experiencing is that it is the one that causes (in a certain characteristic way) my visual experience. Had another pen been in its place, the other pen would have been the one I am experiencing. Had this pen been replaced instantaneously by another, the other pen would have immediately become the one I am experiencing.

John Searle finds this answer objectionable. It is not so much that the answer is incorrect as that it is given from the "third-person point of view." It is the kind of answer that would be given to the question, what would make a photograph of a pen a photograph of *this* pen? In that case, a straightforward causal answer is clearly the right one. To be the pen "in" the photograph, a pen would have had to reflect light into the camera and on to the exposed film, etc., etc. Had a different pen been the one that did this, it would have been the one in the picture. Appealing to the analogous causal fact in the case of visual experience "fails," according to Searle, "to answer the question as to how this fact gets into the Intentional content" (1983: 63). Searle calls this a "first-person internal" question.

Searle clearly appreciates that in visual (and tactual) perception we are aware of particular things in the world. We are aware of this pen, not just that there exists a thing of a certain sort. In contrast, if we see a shadow or a footprint, we are not aware of the thing that casts the shadow or the person that left the footprint. Seeing a shadow enables us to think of the thing that casts it only under a description like "the thing that is casting this shadow." Seeing a footprint enables us to think of the person that casts it only under such a description as "the person who left this footprint." Similarly, if we saw things only in photographs and films, our cognitive access to them would be equally indirect. We would be in a position even worse than Chauncey Gardiner's, the hero of Jerzy Kozinski's novel *Being There*, whose access to things other than those in his room is only via television. At least he got to see the things in his room.

If actually seeing things were like seeing things in pictures and films, the connection between things in the world and our experience would be merely causal. I have nothing against causal relationships but, as William Alston says, "Causality is no substitute for awareness" (1997: 12). Searle of course would agree. When he sees an object such as his magnificent yellow station wagon, he says that the experience he has "is directly of the object. It doesn't just 'represent' the object, it provides direct access to it. The experience has a kind of directness, immediacy and involuntariness which is not shared by a belief I might have about the object in its absence" (1983: 45). That is why he prefers to call perceptual experiences "presentations" rather than "representations" (1983: 46). The question, though, is whether his official account of the contents of perceptual experience does justice to the fact that experiences are directed at particular things. We will get to that account shortly.

1 THE PUZZLE OF EXPERIENCE AND THE PROBLEM
OF PARTICULARITY

Alston mentions the line of argument which goes from the premise that "hallucinatory experience can be [subjectively or qualitatively] indistinguishable from the real thing" to the conclusion that "we can't regard it as intrinsic to perceptual experiences that there is a direct awareness of objects" (1997: 4). After all, so the argument goes, how can an object be presented to us in experience if a qualitatively indistinguishable experience did not involve the presence of any object? Even when the object is there, it seems inessential to the experience, for the experience could have been just as it is without the object being there.

On the other hand, it does seem that in ordinary perceptual experience we are directly aware of external objects – they appear to us, they are present to us. So we have a dilemma, what J. J. Valberg calls "the puzzle of experience" (this is the title of his 1992 book): how can a perceptual experience be a direct awareness of an object if it is indistinguishable from some possible hallucination? What puzzles Valberg is that the object seems "potentially irrelevant." To make the puzzle vivid, he goes so far as to imagine that during the course of an experience of a certain object, say this pen, God intervenes, eliminating the pen in an instant but preserving our experience. Accordingly, so the argument goes, the experience could be just as it is without the presence of the object. (Arguably, this is merely a doxastic possibility, not a metaphysical one, at least on the plausible supposition that a given event [token], such as an experience, could not have had a different cause from its actual cause, but that does not affect Valberg's point – we can always compare a veridical experience with an hallucination.)

Is it really true, then, that this pen "presents" itself to us? Is appearing really the direct relationship that Alston says it is? The phenomenological support for its directness seems to be offset by simple causal considerations, e.g. that one's experience of the pen could be just as it is even if the brain state underlying it were caused by a drug, an evil demon, or a mad scientist who has immersed one's brain in a bubbling vat. Inveterate internalist that he is, Searle wants to say that he "can have exactly that [experience] even if it is a hallucination, even if the [pen] does not exist" (1991b: 239). In this regard he distinguishes the content of the experience from its object, and maintains that "the content can be exactly the same even if no object exists." He agrees with traditional epistemologists that there is nothing about the character of a perceptual experience that precludes the possibility that it does not have the object – or the cause – it appears to have.

Now in order to make sense out of all this, it is not enough to pay lip service to the phenomenological fact that experiences seem to have objects. We cannot do justice to the fact that ordinary perceptual experiences involve the immediate presence to us of physical objects if we cannot reconcile this with the fact that experiences with the same character could occur in the absence of any physical objects.

Related to the puzzle of experience is the problem of particularity. This problem is posed by Searle's question, "What is it about this experience that requires that it be satisfied by the presence of [this pen] and not just by any [pen] with such and such characteristics type-identical with [this one]?" (1983: 63). Unfortunately, Searle's explicit discussion of the problem of particularity (1983: 62–71) does not address this question. As John McDowell has pointed out, it "is limited to cases where particularity relates to a *prior* identification" (1991: 223). And, as Alston notes, "this is not the problem initially advertised – how the propositional content can be singular in form – but rather the problem of reidentification – how the particular referred to can be picked out as the same one as previously picked out ... It should be obvious that the latter problem presupposes the former" (1997: 18). So let me repeat the question, as Searle himself formulates it, that poses the problem of particularity.

(PoP) What is it about this experience that requires that it be satisfied by the presence of this [pen] and not just by any [pen] with such and such characteristics type identical with this one?

It is easy to see what the problem is: there seems to be nothing about the experience itself, no feature of its character or content, that makes it be an experience of this pen in particular. It seems that the only fact relevant to that is the causal relation between the pen and the experience, but citing this fact, says Searle, does not solve "the first-person internal problem." Then what does?

2 SEARLE'S INHERENTLY DESCRIPTIVIST SOLUTION

It appears that we are faced with a dilemma. We can try to characterize the content of a visual experience either in terms that make reference to the object of the experience or in terms that do not. If we characterize it in a way that does make reference to the object, then we have violated the requirement that "the content can be exactly the same even if no object exists." Call this the "existence-independence" requirement. On the other hand, if we try to characterize the content in a way that meets this requirement, it seems we can do so only in general terms. The dilemma is analogous to a dilemma about proper names in the philosophy of language. There is a strong intuition that proper names "directly refer" to their bearers, that they do not have Fregean senses, and are not equivalent to Russellian definite descriptions. On the other hand, it seems that names without bearers, like "Pegasus" and "Santa Claus," are perfectly meaningful. It is not only meaningful but true to say, for example, that Santa Claus does not exist. In general, it seems that a proper name's having a meaning does not depend on its having a reference. On the other hand, it seems to many philosophers that sentences containing proper names express singular or object-involving propositions. But how can this be in the case where the name does not stand for any actual thing? I cannot go into the problem of proper names here, but I should note that both Searle (1983: ch. 9) and I (Bach 1981, 1994a: chs. 7 and 8) have offered solutions that reject the terms of the dilemma. I mention it just for purposes of analogy. The analogous dilemma is that a visual experience can have its content without having an object and yet it seems to be directly of its object.

Searle rejects the view that the contents of experiences are singular propositions. I totally agree with him on this, because such propositions contain nothing about the way in which the object is (re)presented (Bach 1994a: 14–15). He rejects any view on which the contents of experiences are "object-dependent," such as the Evans (1982)–McDowell (1984a) theory of *de re* senses. Also, he has a long-standing aversion to the notion of *de re* belief. He objects, for example, to Tyler Burge's (1977) view that a *de re* belief or, for that matter, a visual experience is one "whose correct ascription places a [person] in an appropriate nonconceptual contextual relation to the [relevant] object" (1977: 346). Searle maintains that a *de re* belief or a visual experience can be fully characterized in terms of its content. Moreover, he rejects Burge's assumption that to be fully statable the content must be purely conceptual, and completely analyzable in general terms. He thinks "there is a third possibility ... forms of Intentionality which are not general but particular and yet are entirely in the head, entirely internal" (1983: 211). To realize this possibility he invokes the ingenious idea of "causal self-referentiality," a resource that is overlooked on a Fregean or a Russellian approach. That sort of approach, on which the object of the experience is whichever thing satisfies a certain general condition laid down by the experience, would leave us with materials insufficient to determine any one object as the one to which the experience is directed. As John McDowell describes it, Searle's strategy is to exploit "the possibility of anchoring the particular-directedness of the [experiences] in question to the particularity of the relevant experiences themselves" (1991: 216). That is signaled by the phrase "this visual experience" in Searle's specification of the satisfaction conditions of a visual experience (1983: 48; 1991b: 228):

(CVE) Vis Exp (that there is a yellow station wagon there and the fact that there is a yellow station wagon there is causing this visual experience)

The idea here is that any visual experience of the same character determines a condition of satisfaction of this form, but since the condition contains a reference to the particular (token) experience, the requirement that each such experience lays down is distinct – it is that very experience, not just any experience like it, that something must cause to be the object of the experience. CVE is satisfied only if there is an object of the sort the experience represents there to be and if there being such an object causes the experience.

Searle's view is not just a new version of the old causal theory of perception. On his view the causation is "Intentional causation" and the experience is "self-referential": how the experience is caused enters into the conditions of satisfaction that its content determines. (At one point Searle [1983: 49] describes both the content and, three lines later, the experience as self-referential; he has also [1991b: 231] described the condition of satisfaction as self-referential, but I will not quibble about this here.) The question is whether this "causal self-referentiality" is enough to solve the problem of particularity. Does it do justice to the phenomenological fact that in visual experience objects appear to us, are "present" to us? And does it do justice to the psychosemantic fact that visual experience actually puts us in a position to think of and refer directly to particular things in the world, and to do so not merely under a description, e.g. "the thing that causes this visual experience" or "the thing that looks thus-and-so"? In short, has Searle solved the problem of particularity?

In my opinion, he has not. I am not worried by what worries Burge: that the self-referentiality required on Searle's account is "too complex or too sophisticated" (1991: 198). Searle is careful to point out that he does not mean that the experience literally refers to itself, i.e. in the description "the cause of this experience." Obviously small children and animals have visual experiences of particular things, but Searle claims that they can do so without benefit of the concepts of cause or experience. I am inclined to agree that we can experience causal relationships – between objects, between objects and ourselves, and, when we do things, between ourselves and objects – without having the concepts necessary for articulating these experiences. And I am not worried about the skeptical objection that one can seem to see causal relationships that do not actually obtain. This is no more worrisome than the fact that one can seem to see objects that are not really there.

What worries me are two other features of Searle's account. First, the formulation given by CVE does not accommodate the case of misperception. Suppose I am having an experience as of a yellow station wagon but what I am looking at is not a yellow station wagon but a hearse painted orange and seen in yellow light. I am experiencing that hearse, but CVE requires that there be a yellow station wagon causing this visual experience. So CVE, at least as it stands, is too restrictive. Searle needs to find a way, in giving the form of the content of experience, to isolate the representation of the causal role of the object from what the object is represented as. His formulation needs to separate what determines the object of the experience from what features the object is required to have if the experience is to be veridical. I am not sure how such a formulation would go, but I take this first problem to be technical, not fundamental.

There is a deeper problem that worries me about Searle's account, as encapsulated in CVE. As CVE has it, the awareness of the station wagon is only "under a description." I do not mean by this that the experience is in words, but only that the person is aware of the station wagon in a way expressible by a definite description. A definite description, of course, is a phrase that denotes one thing uniquely (if it denotes anything at all). Simple examples include "the discoverer of X-rays" and "the king of France." Notice that a sentence containing a definite description can be meaningful and express a determinate proposition even if nothing satisfies the description. So, for example, the sentence "The king of France is bald" is meaningful and expresses a certain proposition even though France has no king. As Russell demonstrated, even when the description is satisfied, as with the sentence "The discoverer of X-rays was bald," the proposition expressed does not involve the individual who discovered X-rays. That proposition is made true by a fact about that individual, but the proposition itself does not contain that individual as a constituent. This proposition is a general, existential proposition, or what I call a "uniqueness proposition," to the effect that some one individual discovered X-rays and that this individual was bald. It is important to appreciate that phrases containing indexicals or demonstratives, such as "your mother" or "the author of that book," can still qualify as definite descriptions. Sentences containing such descriptions, such as "Your mother is bald" and "The author of that book is bald," although made true by facts about particular individuals (your mother or the author of that book), do not express propositions involving those individuals – they express general, uniqueness propositions.

So you can guess what my worry is about Searle's account. As CVE has it, the condition of satisfaction of a visual experience is a general proposition. Just look at the language: the clause "that there is a yellow station wagon there" obviously expresses a general, existential proposition, and so does the clause "the fact that there is a yellow station wagon there is causing this visual experience." The condition of satisfaction essentially involves the visual experience in question and it does not essentially involve the station wagon. So Searle's account in terms of CVE does not solve the problem of particularity.

Searle rightly claims that visual experience is "not general but particular." The problem is that CVE does not capture this fact. As CVE has it, the content of one's experience of the yellow station wagon is general, albeit in a way that adverts to the particular visual experience. The content is particular with respect to the experience but it is general with respect to the station wagon. CVE represents one's awareness of the station wagon as being only under a description, and has the content of the experience as being to the effect that there exists (a unique) something of a certain sort, namely a yellow station wagon. So, just as Alston says "causation is no substitute for awareness," I say description is no substitute for awareness either.

In saying this, I agree with Burge who, whether or not he is right to complain that Searle's account is too complicated and too sophisticated, rightly comments that "knowledge of the causal relation between visual experiences and physical objects seems posterior to the experience (and knowledge of the experience) of seeing physical objects" (1991: 206). And I agree with McDowell, despite my aversion to his *de re* senses, when he says, "In Searle's picture, 'externally' directed particularity in content is secured indirectly, by way of contents targeted on 'internal' items ... [This] inverts the priority that Searle's discussion suggests of 'this visual experience' ... over 'that [pen]'" (1991: 224); "It is as if Searle has here forgotten, or perhaps never quite took the measure of, the 'direct realism' that he resolutely espouses" (1991: 222–3). Although Searle accepts the naive view that perception is "direct" (1983: 46 and 57) – he is anything but a sense-data theorist – his account of the content of a visual experience in terms of CVE suggests that this relation is indirect: one is aware of the object as just the cause of the experience. I do not mean to suggest that Searle's descriptivism is solipsistic in the way he thinks phenomenalism is solipsistic (1983: 60), but his view does seem to imply that we are aware of physical objects only by proxy. Even though the satisfaction condition of an experience requires that an object of a certain sort stand in a certain relation to the experience, the condition does not specify which object it is. How could it? How could the satisfaction condition, insofar as it is determined by the internal content of the experience, do more than determine what sort of state of affairs must obtain for the experience to be veridical and, in the process, what sort of object(s) must be involved in that state of affairs? The object itself cannot enter into the satisfaction condition because that condition is what it is independently of the existence of that object (or the obtaining of that state of affairs). It seems, then, that Searle's account does not capture the intentionality or direct(ed)ness of visual experience.

3 WHY CONTENT CANNOT DETERMINE CONDITIONS OF SATISFACTION

A central feature of Searle's view of content in general is that the content of an Intentional state determines its conditions of satisfaction (although many philosophers use "narrow content" or "internal content" to mean what Searle means by "content" simpliciter, and use "content" simpliciter to mean conditions of satisfaction, I will follow Searle's usage). I agree with Searle's internalism about content and with the existence-independence requirement: that is, that the content of a state is what it is independently of how the world is (Bach 1982). A brain in a vat could have states with just the contents that ours have. However, I think the problem of particularity cannot be solved unless we give up the supposition that the content of an experience determines its conditions of satisfaction. For the content of the experience cannot determine its object. Even if the condition makes reference to that very experience, as in CVE, it does not require that the object, which in fact

causes that experience, must be the object that causes it. The requirement is only that there be some object or other that causes it.

Solving the problem of particularity requires explaining how the
object gets into an experience's conditions of satisfaction. For Searle
"it is essential . . . that facts [about the presence and features of the object
causing the experience] enter into the Intentional content" (1983: 48). In
his view, the experience represents its object as standing in this causal
relation, and it is not sufficient simply that there in fact be an object in
this relation, represented or not. Searle thinks that those

who rely on perceptual and indexical [states] . . . correctly see that there is a class
of [states] that cannot be accounted for in purely general terms [and] that these
[states] depend on contextual features. [But] they then mistakenly suppose that
these contextual features cannot themselves be entirely represented as part of
the Intentional content.   (1983: 214)

Searle *claims* that the element of causal self-referentiality does the trick:

Once you understand that the visual experience [of a man wearing a red cap]
has a causally self-referential propositional content you don't need to worry
about "describing" or "conceptualizing" anything in words in order to individ-
uate the man: the Intentional content of the visual experience has already
done it.   (1983: 212)

But it cannot do this, not if it is as Searle formulates it:

(There is a man there causing this visual experience and that man is wearing
a red cap.)

This is a blatantly general, existential proposition, the condition on
whose truth requires merely the existence of a man of a certain sort.
Once again Searle's actual formulation of the content does not do justice
to the fact that the experience is of a particular individual, one who
figures essentially in the experience's condition of satisfaction. The
contents of experiences are not general propositions.

It seems to me that Searle is constrained to specify experiential
contents as general propositions because, first, he recognizes that they
cannot be singular propositions but, second, because he cannot shake
the assumption that contents determine conditions of satisfaction. The
contents of experiences cannot be general propositions, but they cannot
be singular propositions either, because such propositions contain
nothing about the way in which the object is (re)presented. But if the
contents of experiences are not singular propositions and they are not

general propositions either, what are they? In my view, they are not propositions at all, at least not complete propositions – they are indexical. We can make sense of this idea once we give up the supposition that the content of a perceptual experience determines its condition of satisfaction.

Before trying to make sense of it, let me raise one other problem for this supposition. What is to prevent a state other than a perceptual experience, say a vivid fantasy (not an hallucination), from having the same condition of satisfaction as a perceptual experience? If the content of the experience determines its condition of satisfaction, then why would a fantasy with the same content not have the same condition of satisfaction? Searle might object that a fantasy could not have the same content, because it does not contain any self-referential causal element. But one could turn the point around and say that it is not a difference in *content* that makes the difference in conditions of satisfaction between the perceptual experience and the fantasy but rather, as I wish to suggest, their difference in psychological mode.

4 THE INDEXICALITY OF EXPERIENCE: WHY THE RELATION BETWEEN OBJECT AND EXPERIENCE IS NOT PART OF CONTENT

Whereas for Searle an experience must represent its object as standing in a certain causal relation, in my view it is sufficient simply that there in fact be an object in this relation, represented or not. One is visually aware of the object not because one *represents* the relation between oneself and the object but because one is *in* that relation – the condition is imposed simply because the state in question is a visual experience. It is not the content of a visual experience that determines that its cause is its object. Rather, it is the psychological mode. It is the fact that the experience is perceptual that determines that its object(s) is that which causes, in the appropriate way, that very state. (Analogously, as argued in Bach [1978], it is the psychological mode of what Searle calls an "intention in action" that determines that the change that fulfills its condition of satisfaction is the one that it causes in the appropriate way.)

On the indexical view, the causal self-referentiality of an experience, or what I prefer to call its token-reflexivity, resides not in its content but in its condition of satisfaction. In this respect, its content does not fully determine its condition of satisfaction. The content determines only a schema for the condition of satisfaction of any particular experience with that content. Specified schematically, the content includes a slot, represented by a free variable, for the object that is the cause of the experience. In the case of seeing a yellow station wagon, it takes the form

(IVE) Vis Exp (yellow station wagon there [x])

The object that fills that slot is whichever object (if any) is in the relevant causal relation to that experience. A different experience with the same content can have a different object or even no object at all – not because the content is a general, existential proposition but because the content is schematic. It is filled in by the object of the experience. Notice that IVE does not include any information about how the object of the experience is determined. The fact that the psychological state in question is a visual experience makes it the case that its object is whatever is in the appropriate causal relation to that experience.

I wonder if the above is not what Searle really believes. In a very revealing passage he writes, "the sense in which the visual experience is self-referential is simply that it figures in its own conditions of satisfaction. The visual experience itself does not *say* this but *shows* it" (1983: 49). He seems here to be holding on to the claim that the content of the experience determines its condition of satisfaction while at the same time recognizing that there is nothing in the content of experience that is equipped to do the job. Indeed, he has since conceded that it may have been inadequate to describe the self-referentiality which determines an experience's conditions of satisfaction as "*shown* but not *stated* by the visual experience," and suggests that it might "have been better to put the point without using the notion of reference, but e.g. that of token-reflexivity" (1991b: 238).

In my view, an experience is token-reflexive not because it refers to itself but because, being perceptual, its content is context-sensitive. The condition of satisfaction is experience-relative. To experience a certain event or state of affairs is to experience it from a certain point of view. That is, you experience it in a spatio-temporal relation to your point of view. But though you experience it in an experience-relative way, you do not experience it under an experience-relative description. It is by having the experience at a certain time and place, with a certain orientation, that the time and place of the event or state of affairs experienced can be represented as being when and where it is. But you do not have to represent the time and place of the experience in relation to which you represent the time and place of the event or state of affairs. Your experience is essentially perspectival.

On the indexical view, the experience (*qua* type) *is* the indexical. Even if you are aware of this pen as the cause of your experience (token), or even if, in what amounts to the same thing, you are aware of it as the thing that looks thus-and-so to you now, it is not the fact that you experience it as such that makes it the object of your experience. It is not the object of your experience because it satisfies a condition determined by the content of your experience. It does satisfy the description, "the object of this visual experience," but it does so independently of there being anything in the experience that imposes this condition. The object of the experience is, as I like to say, determined not "satisfactionally" but "relationally". (Bach 1994a: 12).

By treating experiences as themselves indexicals, we avoid the difficulty that McDowell raises for Searle's account, namely, of locating the particularity in the wrong place. Why, McDowell asks, does Searle allow an element of content of the form "this experience" but not one of the form "this pen" (1991: 218)? If an experience can refer to itself, why can it not reach out to the world? After all, Searle has always been a direct realist. He rightly thinks that we see pens and pigs, not sense-data of pens and pigs (and that we see pens and pigs not by way of seeing sense-data of pens and pigs). So he should not insist that an experience can "refer" to itself but not to this pen. Saying that the experience refers to the pen, i.e. that it is directed at the pen, does not imply the pen is part of the content of the experience – it is the object of the experience.

Nor is it implied that the content of the experience is a singular proposition. After all, as Searle says, experience (and thought, for that matter) is always under an aspect. Visual experience, for example, is always from a point of view, from which certain portions of an object are visible and not others, and selective, insofar as only certain of the object's properties figure in how it appears. But it is the experience itself that provides this perspective on the object.

On the indexical view you can be aware of this pen and be in a position to refer to it as "this pen" just because it is in the right relationship to you. What makes your experience an experience of this pen is not that it meets a condition laid down by the content of your experience but that it enters into a certain causal relationship to your experience (such that its features affect what you experience and changes in its features or in which features are accessible to you differentially affect what you experience). Searle's descriptivist view gets the "direction of fit" backwards (if I may borrow one of his favorite phrases) between the object and the content of the experience. The object does not have to satisfy any element of the content in order to be the object – it is the object because of its causal relation to the experience.

5 AFTERTHOUGHTS

I want to finish with a brief comment on Alston's dispute with Searle, followed by a speculative hypothesis about the dependence of thought on experience.

In Searle's view, "the content of [a] visual experience, like the content of [a] belief, is always equivalent to a whole proposition. Visual experience is never simply *of* an object but rather it must always be *that* such and such" (1983: 40). I have argued that the content of a visual experience is equivalent only to an incomplete proposition, which is completed when its objectival slot is filled by the object causing the experience. Alston disagrees with Searle for quite a different reason. He maintains that visual experience is a matter of "direct, unmediated awareness of . . . objects," that objects are simply "displayed" or "presented to awareness." It seems to me that Searle agrees with this. After all, he grants that visual experiences have objects and that these are physical objects, not private objects like sense-data. And yet he holds that "the whole content [of an experience] must be propositional (even though phenomenologically it seems a matter of just perceiving an object)" (1991b: 235). I think Searle's view can be reconciled with Alston's if, first, instead of saying that "visual experience is never simply *of* an object but rather it must always be *that* such and such," Searle were to say that it must always be of an object experienced *as* such and such. In other words, seeing is always seeing-as, not seeing-that. Secondly, except when explicitly stating his theory, Searle could avoid the cumbersome language of causal self-referentiality and just say that the content of an experience is, for example, "this yellow station wagon looks old." He could do this by arguing that the causal self-referentiality is built into the word "looks." After all, to say that this station wagon looks old is just another way of saying that one sees a certain thing as an old station wagon.

I would like to end on a friendly note by offering a hypothesis that indirectly supports Searle's (1992) controversial "Connection Principle," which says that every mental state either is conscious or is at least potentially or in principle conscious. I will not try to defend the CP directly, though it would be helpful to try to pin down the force of the expressions "potentially" and "in principle" so that the CP does not turn out to be trivially true. Presumably Searle does not want to count as mental a state involved in visual edge detection or a state involved in the phonological parsing of a heard sentence. The problem is to explain in precisely what sense such states are not potentially or in principle conscious.

Anyway, let me tentatively offer a different though related principle. I call it "Experience First." It says that only beings that enjoy phenomenal states are capable of being in Intentional states at all, as opposed to mere informational states. In other words, only beings with perception and sensation are capable of thought. If this is so, there can be no such thing as a pure thinking machine. Nothing qualifies as a thinking thing unless it qualifies as a sentient one. A robot, no matter how sophisticated its sensors and its processing of the information received from them, does not qualify as a thinking thing, a conscious being, unless it has experiences.

The rationale for Experience First is this: you can't have general thoughts unless you have singular thoughts, and having singular thoughts depends on being in perceptual relations with particular things. Moreover, thoughts about things involve concepts of physical properties and having such concepts requires having experiential or recognitional concepts. Having such first-person concepts requires having, or having had, perceptual experiences. In short, no concepts without percepts. Sound familiar?

To conclude, I have argued that Searle's account of the content of visual experience is, despite its element of causal self-referentiality, essentially a descriptivist theory. As such, it does not solve the problem of particularity. To solve that problem I have suggested an indexicalist alternative to the various *de re* accounts that Searle criticizes. No doubt he will criticize this account too, but, as he says in reply to his other critics,

I do not know of a demonstrative argument to show that visual perception includes a causal component in such a way that the analysis of the content must contain the causal self-referentiality that I allude to ... In the end, perhaps, it is one of those points in philosophy where you either see it the way I do or you don't.   (1991b: 236)

NOTE

This is the text of a talk given at a mini-conference on the philosophy of John Searle held at the University of Notre Dame in April 1997. If I were writing it today, I might use "character" in place of "content," and "content" interchangeably with "condition of satisfaction."

Chapter 4

Seeing what is there

ROBIN JESHION

In *Intentionality* (1983), John Searle poses one of the most fundamental of questions within philosophy of language: how does language express facts about the world? In particular, how can utterances have meaning, have *aboutness*, when the expression of such utterances are only sounds and marks that are simply physical phenomena in the world? Searle offers us a long, rich, extensively argued answer. The short crude version of his answer is that utterances have meaning by being derived from the intrinsic and basic intentionality of the mind. Mentality has various forms of intentionality – among them, most importantly, perception and intentional action – and the aboutness of language is rooted on them.

In his theory of intentionality, Searle famously commits himself to internalism, Fregeanism, and realism. *Internalism* is the thesis that all intentional content is completely "in the head." The intentional content of all perceptual experiences, beliefs, desires, utterances is constituted exclusively by what is internal to the thinker that has them. A thinker's intentional contents are constituted by both linguistic and nonlinguistic representations. Intentional contents, however, never include the real-world objects, events, locations, or moments "outside" the thinker that the thinker's thoughts are about. Such objects, events, locations, and moments may figure in the truth conditions of the intentional contents, but not in the contents themselves.

Searle's theory of intentionality is also Fregean in spirit. By this I mean that he adopts the central Fregean tenet that all *aboutness* is secured by virtue of objects "satisfying" or "fitting" intentional contents. Our perceptual experiences, thoughts, and utterances are *about* the particular objects they are about because those objects "fit" certain satisfaction conditions. This Fregeanism is most easily exemplified in linguistic reference. Sometimes we speak in fully general terms about individuals. So, for example, "The smallest prime number greater than 15 is odd" contains a singular term "the smallest prime greater than 15" that refers to 17 by virtue of the fact that 17 satisfies the condition *being the smallest prime greater than 15*. The number 17 figures in the truth conditions on the sentence. What makes the sentence true is the fact that 17 is the smallest prime number greater than 15 and it is odd. Likewise, "The oldest yellow station wagon in Berkeley is still running" is about whatever individual happens to be the oldest yellow station wagon in Berkeley, and its truth depends upon whether that station wagon is still running. The contents of the sentences are purely general, constituted exclusively of concepts, and the objects that are the truthmakers are *only* truthmakers; they do not figure into the content of the sentences themselves. In these examples, the satisfactional mode of aboutness-determination imports language – words themselves – as the vehicles for expressing contents that the relevant objects must "satisfy." But it need not. It can use other representations as well. So, for example, a satisfactional account of perceptual experience could understand, say, vision as computing nonlinguistic, but still conceptual representations of what is seen. The object that the visual experience is about would be that object that "fits" the conceptual representation.

Searle's theory of intentionality is committed as well to naive realism. The objects our perceptual experiences (and the thoughts and beliefs rooted on them) are about are real-world objects. In perceptual experience, perceivers directly perceive the intentional objects that satisfy the intentional contents of their perceptual experience. Naive realism here contrasts with sense-datum theories on which one does not ever directly perceive real-world objects themselves. All that one directly perceives is one's sense-data of the real-world object.

Internalism is a thesis about *what* is included in intentional content and Fregeanism is a thesis about *how* aboutness is secured. Still, it is easy to see the close connection between the two theses. If all intentional content is constituted entirely of the thinker's representations of the world, then the particular objects that the thinker's perceptual experiences, thoughts, beliefs, desires, utterances are about must be, in some fashion, determined or selected. Yet any means of direct, nonsatisfactional means of selection would appear to conflict with internalism, because a direct means of object determination would automatically import an external object into the intentional content. A satisfactional means of object determination appears to be the only way to preserve internalism. In the other direction, a purely satisfactional means of object determination, one in which there is no direct reference at all, quite clearly allows – indeed it requires – that all intentional content resides in the thinker.

THE PARTICULARITY OBJECTION

Many have rejected internalist and Fregean analyses of intentionality because it seems that while some intentionality is satisfactional, not all is. Perceptually based beliefs mark off a class of problem cases. Such beliefs are intentionally directed toward *particular* individuals. I see that particular object there and, given naive realism, my perceptual beliefs based upon that experience are true or false depending upon how things are with that very object. How things are with distinct qualitatively type-identical objects is irrelevant to the truth conditions of my particular-directed perceptual experience. Yet, it seems that a satisfactional analysis of aboutness determination cannot properly capture which individual object my perceptual experience is about. No matter how detailed my intentional perceptual qualitative "description" of the object gets, we can always imagine a situation in which there exists a duplicate having all those qualities; yet it seems that a satisfactional account of aboutness determination has no way to determine that my perceptual experience is about this object, and not the qualitatively identical duplicate. Let us call this the *particularity objection*.

Intentionality can be seen as Searle's attempt to defend an internalist, Fregean analysis of intentionality against the particularity objection without giving up on naive realism. Searle's main claim is that critics have seriously underestimated the resources of Fregean analyses of intentionality. There is a way to secure the particularity of intentional contents within the confines of a satisfactional account of aboutness determination. His central strategy is to anchor the particular object-directedness of perceptual experience in the subject's particular perceptual experience itself.

Suppose that I see the yellow station wagon that is in front of me. Then I have a certain particular visual experience of it. For Searle, the intentional content of my visual experience is given entirely by its satisfaction conditions, conditions specifying what has to obtain in the world for my experience to be veridical. The veridicality of visual experiences depends upon the world being "as it visually seems to me that it is, and furthermore its being that way must be what causes me to have the visual experience which constitutes its seeming to be that way" (1983: 49). In this case, what must obtain is that there is a yellow station wagon there before me and that that yellow station wagon is the cause of my having this very visual experience of it. Here is how Searle articulates the intentional content of visual experience: "I have a visual experience (that there is a yellow station wagon there and that there is a yellow station wagon there is causing this visual experience)." This analysis of the intentional content of visual experience makes clear that it is, in a certain sense, "self-referential."[1] The content of any particular visual experience "specifies" the object of visual experience as the cause of the visual experience itself.

Searle regards this analysis as a satisfactory way to answer the particularity objection. Suppose that you and your twin are experiencing type-identical visual experiences of different yet type-identical yellow station wagons. If the external environment is equally type-identical, then you and your twin have phenomenologically identical visual experiences. Yet, most of us agree, your visual experience is about the particular yellow station wagon you see while your twin's is about the particular yellow station wagon she sees. Some externalists have thought this alone shows that externalism must be right – that the different station wagons are a part of the intentional contents of you and your twin's visual experiences or perceptual beliefs. Searle's causal self-referential account of visual intentional content shows, however, that, by itself, this argument does not establish that our visual experiences or beliefs based upon them include the objects they are about, something outside or external to the perceiver. For Searle found a different way to secure particularity. On his account the intentional content of my visual experience directly involves my visual experience, and the intentional content of my twin's visual experience directly involves her visual experience. Since the intentional contents themselves differ, the objects that they determine satisfactionally – the different yellow station wagons that are *there* and that are the causes of the two distinct visual experiences – differ as well. The aboutness of intentional content can be of the particular individuals that are seen without the intentional content including those objects themselves. Particularity is preserved within the confines of internalism, Fregeanism and naive realism.

Searle's causal self-referential account of perceptual intentional content provides a rather brilliant solution to the problem of particularity. However, it is not without its own problems. It has come under fire for various reasons, but by far the most serious and widespread objections stem from a common concern that Searle's intentional perceptual content is too rich. It is too complicated, involves overly sophisticated conceptual abilities, incorporates excessively robust intentional ontological commitments. I think that, on the contrary, Searle has the resources to sidestep these complaints, and indeed has largely met most of the objections. But I am not convinced that his account of visual intentional content can stand. In contrast with the orientation of others' objections, I think that Searle's account is not too rich, but rather too impoverished to solve the particularity objection while remaining committed to internalism, Fregeanism, and naive realism.

I am going to present a problem for Searle's account of the intentionality of perception. The problem is that his analysis of the intentional content of visual experience incorporates the locations of intentional objects, to what Searle specifies as "there." And he is correct to include the spatial aspects of visual experience. I think that they are essential features of the intentional contents of visual experience. But, since locations of objects are external to the perceiver, Searle will need a way of specifying satisfaction conditions for locations. Yet, I shall argue, he has no way of doing this that will preserve his ability to solve the particularity objection while retaining his internalism, Fregeanism, and naive realism.

It is worth highlighting at the outset that the problem I am shaping for Searle's theory does not appeal to the social, interpersonal features of language as a basis for rejecting internalism and Fregeanism. I am, by and large, with Searle in thinking that the intentionality of perception and action is more primitive than the intentionality of language, and that the latter is, to a large extent, rooted on the former.[2]

I begin by briefly discussing key features of Searle's account of the intentionality of visual experience. I then turn to evaluating the objections to Searle's theory based on its excessive richness. The detour through these well-known objections will both help situate my own criticism within the literature and help sharpen the problem I shape for Searle. The bulk of the chapter will be devoted to developing the idea that Searle cannot successfully account for the spatial aspects of the intentional content of visual experience, and consequently cannot provide a fully general solution to the particularity objection. I end the chapter with an all too brief account of certain empirical facts about vision that may compound problems for Searle's theory and may provide independent reasons for thinking that the intentionality of visual perception is non-Fregean and externalist.

THE INTENTIONAL CONTENT OF VISUAL EXPERIENCE

For Searle, the intentional aspects of perceptual experience characterize the way that the world seems to be to the subject of the perceptual experience. Searle tends toward an analysis that separates experiences according to the sense modalities that give rise to them. So, for example, there is an intentional content of visual perception that aims to capture the way that the world seems visually to the subject. In discussing the intentional content of perception, I have thus far been speaking almost exclusively about the content of visual experience, to the neglect of the intentional content of other sense modalities. In this, I follow Searle in confining discussion mainly to visual perception. It is worth keeping in mind the other sense modalities since, ultimately, Searle wants his theory to smoothly generalize to them.[3]

For Searle, visual experiences are akin to beliefs and other attitudes insofar as the intentional contents of such experiences are "whole propositions." So the intentional content of visual experiences is never merely *of* a certain seen object, but is rather *that* something is the case. I never have a visual experience that is simply of the yellow station wagon, full stop. The content of my visual experience rather "requires the existence of a whole state of affairs if it is to be satisfied. It does not just make reference to an object" (1983: 40). It is for this reason that, according to Searle, my visual experience of the yellow station wagon will include an intentional propositional content *that there is a yellow station wagon there.*

Searle maintains that this thesis is an immediate and trivial consequence of the fact that visual experiences have satisfaction conditions, and satisfaction conditions are always given propositionally. I worry that this apparently trivial consequence is false – and, indeed, that there is a way to give satisfaction conditions for visual experiences that allows that their intentional contents are not propositional.[4] Furthermore, my main criticism of Searle's account of the intentionality of visual perception will at least pave the way toward challenging this claim that we never have intentional visual experiences of objects that are not "fully propositional." Still, in evaluating Searle's own position, I will try as far as possible to go with the assumption that all intentional visual experiences involve predications, and that their intentional contents are propositional.

According to Searle the intentionality of vision is realized in visual experiences that are conscious mental events. All unconscious aspects of visual experience are excluded from intentional contents. In criticizing Searle's theory, I shall simply assume this famous and controversial thesis about the intentionality of vision.

THE RICHNESS OBJECTIONS: REFERENCE TO VISUAL EXPERIENCE AND PERCEPTION OF CAUSES

Two main, related criticisms stand out within the literature. While distinct, they join forces in charging that Searle's account of the intentional content of visual experience is overly rich. Both maintain that Searle's account includes elements that are not in fact features of the content of visual experience. Both of them are, in effect, embodied in Armstrong (1991), Burge (1991), and Soteriou's (2000) complaint that causal self-referential intentional contents are "too sophisticated" or "too complicated" to be the contents of all visual experiences. After all, young children and animals lack the conceptual resources to have intentional contents containing the concepts *cause* and *visual experience*. As David Armstrong (1991: 154) put it:

Could it be the case, I wondered, that the intentional object of a dog's perception should include, besides an external scene including the dog's bodily relation to that scene, the self-referential component that the perception itself, something in the dog's mind, should be caused by the external scene? It seems a bit much. What concern has the average dog with its own perceptions? Is it even aware of having them?

The first complaint that is packed within this objection is that, on Searle's account, perceivers must make some kind of explicit reference to their own visual experiences. In having the visual experience, one has or forms a second-order thought or belief about the visual experience itself. And this is plainly too sophisticated or too complex a thought for dogs and young children who lack the concept *visual experience* and so could not make reference to their own visual experiences. The second complaint is that, according to Searle, the intentional content of visual experience involves our perceiving the intentional objects as causing our visual experiences. When I see the yellow station wagon, I must see it as the cause of my experience of it. And this is too sophisticated or complex a requirement, and does not inhere in the intentional content of visual experience. While we *can* conceive of intentional objects as the causes of our experiences, we need not do so, and very young children and dogs, and other nonhuman animals, typically do not do so.[5]

Searle replied to the first objection by maintaining that it is rooted on a misunderstanding. In holding that visual experience is causally self-referential, he does not commit himself to the idea that for every visual experience the perceiver explicitly makes reference in language or in thought to her visual experience. "It is emphatically not part of my claim that dogs or people have to have some verbal equivalent to 'this visual experience' or references to their visual experiences or thoughts about causation in order to have visual experiences" (Searle 1991b: 228).[6] There need be no ascent, semantic or otherwise, in the subject's visual experience or beliefs based on the visual experience. For Searle's self-referential satisfaction conditions to obtain, no one, the perceiver included, needs to make second-order reference to the visual experience at all. Searle holds, rather, that "the visual experience itself functions self-referentially in fixing its conditions of satisfaction" (1991b: 228). In other words, the intentional content of my visual experience is self-referential only to the extent that the visual experience figures in its own satisfaction conditions and is that which determines those satisfaction conditions.

To underscore the point, Searle makes analogies with other instances in which satisfaction conditions are determined by an intentional aspect of an experience or speech act, yet there is no requirement that the experiencer herself needs to make reference to them in order for the conditions to obtain. So, for example, a very young child, say, may use a word referentially, and her use will determine satisfaction conditions the intellectual account of which will describe the subject as having made reference to an object. But she need not herself comprehend or have within her cognitive repertoire a concept of *reference*. Searle also gives the example of issuing an order as an instance in which satisfaction conditions are self-referential. Fulfilling the order requires that it be carried through because of (or as a response to) the order itself. Yet the order-giver need have no intellectual grasp of the way that the order itself determines its self-referential satisfaction conditions (Searle 1991b: 231–2).

On this charge, Searle's defense of his theory seems to me correct. We must be able to admit that perceivers can have intentional contents that determine self-referential satisfaction conditions, yet the perceivers need not themselves conceptualize their intentional content in a way that makes *explicit* its self-referentiality. However, one thing needs to be completely clear – and it will be important in connection to my own criticism of Searle. Because Searle's account of the intentional content of visual experience must determine its objects satisfactionally, as opposed to directly, there needs to be a way to represent the propositional content of the subject's visual intentional experience, and it must be a proposition expressive of how things seem to the subject. *There must be a propositional content graspable by reflective subjects that express the intentional content of the visual experience, and this must obtain for every visual experience.*

The second component of the "too sophisticated" charge is that in every visual experience we experience the intentional object as causing the experience of it. The charge, pressed especially by Burge (1991), is that it is implausible that we experience visual objects as causing our experience of them. On this matter, Searle claims that he holds that we do experience visual intentional objects as causes of our experience, though we may not have the resources to describe them as such, and may not consciously think of them as causes of our experience of them. Nevertheless, we do experience them in this way. Searle gives an interesting analogy with tactile experience. I experience a sharp object pressed into my back as causing that very tactile sensation of pain or pressure. It is part of my tactile experience that I experience the intentional object as the experience's cause. He suggests that visual experience is analogous.

Here again, I am inclined to think that Searle has, if not a decisive reply, at least a deep point to make about our tactile experience, and about how the point transfers to visual experience. I think, however, that the points about both tactile experience and visual experience stand in need of extensive, at least partially empirical, defense. Connections between visual perception and action, and in particular how our capacity to act on the objects of visual perception affects our visual perception, would need to be explored.[7]

THE POVERTY OBJECTION: THE REPRESENTATION OF SPATIAL LOCATION

The problem that I see in Searle's account differs starkly from the foregoing criticisms. I maintain that Searle's analysis of intentional content is too poor. It is not rich enough to account for the representation of the particular spatial locations of objects while retaining its internalism, Fregean satisfactionalism, and naive realism, and consequently it is unable to solve the particularity objection.

The problem I see is Kantian in its inspiration. I start with the idea that visually experiencing particular objects in the world involves seeing them as spatially located. When I see the yellow station wagon, I see the yellow station wagon *there*. I see it, experience it, as located in a precise place. My experience of it as spatially located involves my seeing it as *there*, identified egocentrically, as Evans would say, from my own visual perspective. Yet the spatial locations of visually perceived objects are "external" to the perceiver. So, on Searle's internalist account, they may not be directly represented, directly referred to, and so may not occur as constituents within the content of visual experience. Yet, because visual experience represents objects as spatially located, Searle needs some way to represent an object's spatial location that is sufficient for satisfying the particularity objection and yet is consistent with Searle's Fregeanism. And this, I think, Searle's account cannot do.

My claim is that Searle's analysis of the content of visual experience is unable to capture the representation of objects as spatially located. The argument is fairly straightforward: the locations of objects are represented in visual experience. Because Searle's avowed aim is to capture the intentional aspects of visual experience, the way the world is visually experienced by us, he needs for his account of the intentional content of visual experience to represent objects' locations.[8] Yet Searle has no way to uniquely represent objects' locations that is sufficient for capturing their particularity yet is compatible with the other central tenets in his theory of intentionality.

The first premise is, I believe, relatively uncontroversial. Our visual experience of objects involves our experiencing them as having particular locations. My perception of spatial locations within my visual field is an essential feature of the way that the world seems, visually, to me. Furthermore, seeing objects as spatially located is an essential feature of the way that the world is visually presented to us. Consequently, spatial features, including the locations of the intentional objects of visual perception, are an essential part of the intentional content of my visual experiences.

I think it is clear that Searle agrees. In his many examples, he aims to provide a way to mark the location of objects within the content of visual experience. He explicates the content of his favored visual experience as an experience not merely of a yellow station wagon but rather that there is a yellow station wagon *there* (1983: 41). In addition, he separates the satisfaction conditions into two components: one, that there is a yellow station wagon there; the other, that the yellow station wagon that is there is the cause of this visual experience. That they are two distinct conditions highlights the importance of the experience of the wagon as spatially located. This of course coheres with his central aim of being able to capture the particularity of the content of intentional visual experience. For such particularity is specified in part by the representation of the locations of seen objects within the content of visual experience.

The upshot of this point might not be entirely transparent, and is significantly more potent than it initially seems. It entails that Searle will not be able to fully capture the content of a visual experience of an object exclusively by reference to a characterization of it as "the cause of this visual experience" or "the cause of this aspect of visual experience" or even "the yellow station wagon that is the cause of this visual experience." For such characterizations only represent the object that is the cause of the experience or the aspect of the experience. They do not represent its location (or represent the object as located). And my point was that the object's location (or locatedness) is represented in – is a feature of – visual experience.[9] So Searle may not omit it from the content of visual experience, *even if he has an alternative way of getting the right intentional object into the satisfaction conditions.*

There is one place in *Intentionality* in which Searle appears to excise the independent locational satisfaction condition, relying solely on the causal condition. He seems to regard the description "the cause of this visual experience" as sufficient for representing an object in terms of its location. It occurs somewhat obliquely in the course of critically evaluating Donnellan's argument against a descriptivist analysis of the content of proper names, the details of which are unnecessary to go into here (1983: 254). Suppose a person sees two colored patches on a screen, A on top, B on the bottom. Apart from their different locations, A and B are type-identical – identical in size, color, shape. Our subject does not know it but he is wearing inverting lenses, so that the one he thinks is on the top is on the bottom and vice versa. How, at the level of intentional content, does he distinguish them? The trouble is, of course, that, from the stance of our subject, "the one on the top" describes A, but "the one that is causing this visual experience" describes B. And it seems that, from Searle's own analysis, they should both contribute to the content of the subject's perceptual experience. But the answer that Searle offers is this:

A is the one he actually sees right *there*. It is the one causing *this* visual experience. You couldn't ask for a better identifying description than that. Expressions like "the one on top" are strictly for public consumption, and though one can imagine cases in which they would take precedence over the Intentional presentation, in most cases the presentational content is primary.

(1983: 254)

Searle seems to be suggesting here that the description "the one causing this visual experience" serves as the sole description determining the satisfaction conditions.[10] By opting for this description alone, Searle has a way of ensuring that the patch that appears to the subject to be on top is in fact the patch that is the object of his visual experience. But taking this way out comes at a cost. By replacing "there" with "the cause of this visual experience" (or "the cause of this aspect of visual experience", since, presumably, the two patches are seen in one visual experience), Searle excises the object's locational features from the content of the visual experience. Notice that I am *not* maintaining that Searle should here resort to characterizing the patch's location as "the one on top." I only maintain that he needs to give *some* description of the object's location – give some descriptive content to "there" – that does not excise the object's location, as it appears to the subject, from the content of the visual experience.

For roughly the same reason, Searle cannot capture the representation of an object's location in visual experience by describing it as, say, "the location of the yellow station wagon" (or, somewhat more precisely, "the location of the yellow station wagon that is the cause of this visual experience"). This too conflicts with our first premise. For this description fails to reflect the *subject's* experience of the object as located. The location of the yellow station wagon will of course satisfy the description "the location of the yellow station wagon," but it will fail to represent the way that that location is presented to the subject in visual experience. To the perceiver, the location of the yellow station wagon is represented egocentrically, from the perspective, the visual vantage point, of the perceiver. The description fails to capture this entirely. Likewise, in the subject's visual experience, the object's location is specifically identified as distinct from other locations in the perceiver's visual field. Yet the description offers no such specific identification, no such particularity. The significance of the point is easily seen by imagining that there are two yellow station wagons in front of me. "The location of the yellow station wagon" will not suffice to identify one rather than the other.

The first premise pinpoints the fact that spatial locations of objects are properties of the objects they are spatial locations of, but they differ from other qualitative properties of objects insofar as they inextricably involve a demonstrative element. The yellowness of the station wagon, and the station wagon shape of the station wagon may, perhaps, both be represented conceptually, nondemonstratively. But the station wagon being precisely there, as seen from here, cannot be. We visually perceive objects as spatially located and need a way to capture our situated representation of objects' spatial locations within the contents of our visual experiences.[11]

This brings us to the central controversial premise of my argument. I maintain that Searle cannot capture our representation of objects' locations with sufficient precision to satisfy the particularity constraint without compromising his internalism, Fregeanism, or naive realism. I will develop this point in stages. The first few remarks give constraints on Searle's specification of the locations of objects.

First and most obviously, Searle cannot represent the locations of objects directly, with a demonstrative. "There" cannot be a device for directly referring to the location of an object or a location in space. Searle's internalism and his Fregeanism rule this out.

Notice also that Searle may not rely upon prior individuation of perceptually given objects as a way to specify locations. Such a strategy would presuppose what needs to be accounted for. Searle is aiming to specify the location of objects as a way to uniquely describe the particular objects that our visual experiences are about, and so cannot help himself to those objects as a means of specifying their locations.

Searle's commitment to naive realism demands that when the intentional content of a visual experience of a real concrete object has "veridical" satisfaction conditions – when things are in the world as they seem to the perceiver to be – "there" designates a real-world location. "There" does not designate the visual experience itself; neither does it designate a part or aspect of the visual experience, nor a spatial location "within" the visual experience. If it did, then the subject, in locating the yellow station wagon as *there*, would be locating the yellow station wagon as within her visual experience, or at some part or aspect or spatial location of her visual experience. But that is not where yellow station wagons reside.[12]

The natural way to go here would be to take "there" as equivalent in intentional content to the content of a description that captures the perceiver's situatedness by using the perceiver herself as an anchor to the perspective. This is in fact the tactic that Searle seems to be partial to. In numerous places in *Intentionality*, he casually substitutes "in front of me" for "there"(1983: 41, 42, 61). He also includes "there" in his catalogue of indexicals (1983: 224). So it appears that he is implicitly using a description to refer by way of a satisfaction relation to the location of the seen object. Such a route would be consistent with his general approach toward supplying descriptive content to indexicals. Consequently, to understand how Searle handles "there," we need to examine his analysis of indexicals, which advances a very clever response to the general challenge that indexicals are essentially indexical, that there is no descriptive content that is sufficient to determine the relevant referents.

Kaplan and Perry famously argued that there is no completing descriptive content that suffices for generating the right truth conditions for sentences containing indexicals (Kaplan 1989; Perry 1977, 1979). So, to use the well-worn examples, if Hume and Heimson both say "I am David Hume," only Hume's utterance is true. Is it possible to secure the right truth conditions with a completing Fregean sense? Kaplan and Perry claim it is not possible. They argue that "I" cannot be interchanged with any simple content-supplying description, such as "the author of the *Treatise*," because Hume's belief that he is David Hume is a different belief from the belief that the author of the *Treatise* is David Hume. "I" cannot have the same content as a proper name, say "David Hume," because Hume's belief that he is David Hume is a different belief altogether than the belief that David Hume is David Hume. To reinforce the point, we can see that if Hume and Heimson both utter "The author of the *Treatise* is David Hume" or "David Hume is David Hume," the content of their utterances, and their truth conditions, are the same. But then those descriptions cannot be candidates for supplying the relevant descriptive content of "I" because, as just noted, their respective utterances of "I am David Hume" must have different truth conditions. Hume's is true, Heimson's is false. From these considerations, Kaplan and Perry go further. They hold that there is no descriptive content available that is sufficient for securing the correct truth conditions.

It is here where Searle objects. He reinstates his self-referential apparatus to provide an alternative way to secure the right truth conditions, and to do so in a way that respects his Fregeanism. He notes that his ambition is to secure the right truth conditions for utterances with the indexicals "I," "you," "she," and "he" designating agents, "now," "then," "today," and "tomorrow" designating times, and "here" and "there" designating places.[13] His key device is to characterize the referent of these indexicals in terms of their relations to the utterance. Searle is clear about his technique: "What is the essence of indexicality? The defining trait of indexical expressions is simply this: In uttering indexical referring expressions, speakers refer by means of indicating relations in which the object referred to stands to the utterance of the expression itself" (1983: 221). So, for example, "I" has the lexical meaning of "the speaker of this utterance" and so refers to the speaker of the utterance; "now" has the lexical meaning "moment of this utterance" and therefore refers to the moment of the utterance; "here" has the lexical meaning "place of the utterance" and so refers to the place of the utterance. Searle maintains that none of this implies that the indexicals are *synonymous* with the descriptions that specify the relevant truth conditions. Indeed, he denies that they are synonymous. All he is committed to is that the utterance containing indexicals has an intentional content whose truth conditions are satisfactionally determined by reference to the relation that the objects have to the utterance itself. In this sense, the utterance figures in the truth conditions and its intentional content is self-referential.

Now, our question is, with this analysis of indexical reference, does Searle have a way to account for how locations figure in the intentional content of visual perceptual experience? Does he have a way to capture the intentional content of "there"? I think that the answer must be negative. The problem with resorting to Searle's analysis of indexicals is that while certain indexicals like "I," "here," "today," "yesterday," and "now" can plausibly be regarded as having lexical meanings that "complete" the content, "there" cannot be so regarded. The lexical meaning of "there" is quite plainly *not* "place in front of the speaker of the utterance." "There," in language and in thought, marks off all varieties of locations – those to the right of the speaker, those above her – not just those in front and center of the speaker/perceiver.[14]

It might seem that Searle has an easy fix here. After all, he astutely recognizes that utterances of some demonstratives do not by themselves carry a lexical meaning sufficient for determining truth conditions.

Utterances of sentences containing "this" and "that" typically require, in addition to the content of the utterance, also "the intentional content of the awareness by the speaker and hearer of the context of the utterance" (1983: 225). So if, for example, I say "That man is happy," the intentional content of the utterance involves the intentional content of my perceptual experience that accompanies the utterance, the very perceptual experience that I intend "that" to be anaphoric on. I am making reference to someone that I am seeing, and my utterances' truth conditions depend upon and incorporate the intentional content of my visual experience. Consequently, the full analysis of utterances with such demonstratives expresses both the intentional content of the demonstrative expression and the intentional content of the perceptual experience they are tied to.

Is "there" akin to "this" and "that" insofar as it just needs supplementation with the intentional content of visual experience in order to fully complete its descriptive content? Again, the answer must be "no." Such an analysis would make use of the very content that we are trying to account for. While utterances involving "this" and "that" can be filled out by showing how their contents are dependent upon the contents of certain visual experiences, the intentional content we are searching for is an aspect or feature of the content of visual experience itself. "There" linguistically marks the locational aspect of the content of visual experience, so it will do no good to regard its content as somehow being supplemented by the content of visual experience.[15]

Let us try a different route, one that Searle may be implicitly employing when he substitutes "in front of me" for "there." On this analysis, perceivers always represent objects' spatial properties by conceptually marking off their location, egocentrically characterized. When I see the yellow station wagon that is right in front of me, I think of it as the yellow station wagon *that is right smack in front of me*. When I see the yellow station wagon that is to my right, I think of it as the yellow station wagon *that is in front of me and to my right*. And so on. This account allows Searle to sidestep the problem discussed above with taking "there" as having the *lexical meaning* "place in front of the speaker of the utterance." "There," in thought and talk, can be used to pick out locations other than those right in front of the speaker. On this alternative analysis, the perceiver does not rely on any lexical meaning, but instead conceptualizes each visually perceived object's location, and such conceptual representations are what mark the spatial aspect of the intentional content of visual experience.

This looks to be the best solution yet. It specifies a propositional content as the content of intentional visual experience; that content explicitly represents a location, one that captures the perceiver's visual perspective; and it is Fregean and internalist, at least to the extent that intentional contents of other indexicals "centered" on the utterance are internalist. And it looks as though we have a way to solve the particularity objection. Supposing there is a single yellow station wagon parked in the yard that is just to the right of center of my visual field, "The yellow station wagon in front and to the right of me" is satisfied by just the right object.

I want to suggest that while, *for this example*, the conceptualization of the object's location is a satisfactory way of getting the right intentional object into the content of visual experience, this method cannot succeed in solving the particularity objection for all cases. It cannot be a correct general method for capturing objects' locations as they occur within the intentional content of visual experience.

Certain visual situations underscore the inadequacy of this method. Consider a scenario in which you see twenty type-identical circles, all of them randomly dispersed on a screen that exhausts the center of your visual field. The only way to visually distinguish the circles is in terms of their locations. You attend to a particular circle within the bunch. Which description will serve to solve the particularity objection? Resources are limited. The ordinary description from our example above will not work. "Circle in front of me" does not distinguish the circle you are attending to from the other nineteen circles in front of you. Let us choose a description that does uniquely characterize the relevant circle – take, for example, "Circle that is a half inch to the left of the uppermost circle." But this (and other relational descriptions of its kin) will not do because it characterizes the location by reference to other objects or other objects' locations, which themselves stand in need of a uniquely characterizing description. "Circle I am attending to" does not work for two reasons. First, like the description "the cause of this visual experience," it conflicts with our first premise, for it fails to specify the seen, perspectivally characterized locational property of the object of visual perception. Second, this description will not always provide a means of uniquely selecting the relevant particular object. In this example, we are assuming that you are attending to only one circle. But in an alternative situation, you could be simultaneously attending to more than one, so this fails as a general method. It is hard to see what other descriptions could serve that will provide a general means of uniquely describing the relevant object. I do not claim that I have surveyed all possibilities here. But I have detailed problems for several natural ways of going, and the problems appear to me to be insurmountable. Searle needs to come up with an alternative.[16]

EMPIRICAL CONSIDERATIONS

I have given nonempirical reasons for thinking that Searle's account is too weak to be a general solution to the particularity objection. There are, in addition, empirical reasons for thinking that his account of visual intentional content is inadequate. I wish to close our discussion by presenting some empirical evidence for thinking that visual reference to seen objects is direct, nonconceptual, and hence nonsatisfactional. The empirical research is largely due to Pylyshyn, his collaborators, and those inspired by his research. I will inevitably present (rather, squeeze in) only the smallest dash of this rich body of empirical work on vision and visual perception, and its theoretical underpinnings. In discussing Pylyshyn's work, I shall be bracketing the *a priori* reasons adduced above for thinking that there is no completely purely conceptualist way of encoding locations sufficient for dealing with the static case involving numerous identical objects in a single visual field. That is, I shall here confine all problems with the satisfactionalist approach to those arising from empirical considerations. It should be noted at the outset that this research was not even in its infancy when Searle published *Intentionality*, so he could not have confronted it.

Pylyshyn has extensively investigated our ability to execute what he calls multiple-object tracking (MOT), the tracking of objects as they change locations in the visual field. In a paradigmatic multiple-object-tracking situation, a subject initially views a randomly scattered array of static visually identical objects, like our circles, numbering anywhere from eight to twenty-four objects. A subset of the objects, the "targets," are designated to the subject, typically by flashing them on the screen. Then all of the objects move in unpredictable ways about the screen. The subject's task is to track the targets and, once the objects are again static, say after ten seconds, to identify which objects are the targets. The results of the massive research on MOT are numerous and complex, but, for present purposes, we can focus on one finding that has been repeatedly established experimentally: subjects can successfully track between four and five targets in a field of ten moving objects.[17]

We need an explanation of how we can execute this task. Since the visual tracking of objects is conscious, Searle should count it as part of the content of intentional visual experience. Now, for Searle, or anyone that adopts a conceptualist account of intentional visual content, the only way to account for this phenomenon is by holding that subjects track the target objects by encoding their locations, because, at any given time, their locations are the only things that distinguish them from the other objects on the screen. Since the objects' locations are constantly changing, the conceptualist needs to continually update target objects' locations. Pylyshyn supplied a hypothetical algorithm for such updating. It required that subjects first scan each target in turn, encoding its location; then, once the targets are in motion, subjects must return to an initial encoded location of one target and search in the vicinity of that location for the closest object, and update the location of the found closest object with the new location of the place in which it is found. The subject would have to do this for all the target objects, and must do so serially, so the subject would then have to move on to the next encoded location of a different target, and update it in the fashion of the first target. After the first "round" of updating, the subject would have to, in effect, go around again with the updating, and continue doing so until the objects come to rest and the subject reports on the final locations of the target objects.

Using some rather conservative assumptions about the speed of focal scanning, Pylyshyn simulated this strategy and found that this serial scanning and encoding procedure would result in a far higher incidence of errors than in their actual experiments. (On average, subjects track with 85 percent accuracy.) He concluded that the targets could not be tracked by a unitary beam of attention that scans and stores a unique description of each of the target objects. Although there are logically possible alternative processes for taking up the slack of the speed of focal scanning, all are riddled with problems on straight empirical grounds.[18]

Pylyshyn hypothesized that the best explanation of this experimental result is that we have the primitive ability to visually track objects directly, i.e. deictically and nonconceptually. We do so without representing the objects by Frege's method – descriptively, by, for example, encoding their locational properties. On Pylyshyn's view, we visually track objects with what he calls "fingers of instantiation" or FINSTS, mechanisms built into visual perception that track objects, even identical objects, directly, without individuating them.

Searle's main objective in *Intentionality* was to demonstrate not that his internalist-Fregean theory was superior to externalist-direct reference theories, but rather to show that his theory has the philosophical resources to answer the particularity objection. Searle never set out to demonstrate that his account of visual intentional content is empirically superior, or even empirically adequate. I have argued above on purely philosophical grounds that his theory lacks the resources to solve the problem of particularity. Pylyshyn's research suggests that even if there is a way to skirt those difficulties and conceptually encode and identify objects, we just do not do it that way. As we close in on a quarter-century since the publication of Searle's brilliant work, it would be enlightening and satisfying to learn how Searle himself sees how his theory of visual intentional content fares in the wake of newer developments.

NOTES

I wrote much of this chapter while I was a fellow at the Center for Advanced Study in the Behavioral Sciences. Thanks to CASBS and the ACLS for supporting me as a Burkhardt Fellow; and to the University of California, Riverside, for freeing me from other obligations. Thanks to Michael Nelson and Manuel Garcia-Carpintero for helpful, engaging discussion of these issues, and to Savas Tsohatzidis for inviting me to contribute to this volume and for his excellent editorial assistance.

1 "Token-reflexive" is a better characterization of what Searle is requiring, given that he does not maintain that the visual experience involves explicit reference to itself. Searle acknowledges this point in Searle (1991b). For simplicity, in the text I will stick with the term "self-referential" that Searle uses in *Intentionality*, making clear that it does not require explicit linguistic self-reference.

2 I almost surely accord more social impact on *semantics* than Searle does. But these differences will not play any role in this chapter.

3 I have serious doubts about whether it can, but this is a separate concern from the one I focus on here. I am inclined to think that visual experience presents the most natural platform for Searle's analysis of the intentional content of perceptual experience.

4 If I am having a visual experience in which I am visually attending to a particular object, then that visual experience will be "satisfied" just in case the very object I am visually attending to is causing the visual experience I am having. The satisfaction condition includes the object itself and the relation it has to my visual experience of it. It employs a "direct" way of selecting the object, by way of my visual attention. Here, satisfaction conditions are not

given in terms of truth values, but rather in terms of the success of the fulfillment of the function of the visual experience. Details, and complex situations with mirrors, holograms, illusions, misidentification of properties, etc. would have to be filled out. I do not maintain that I have here shown or even tried to make a case for the claim that the content of visual experience can be just of an object, rather than a state of affairs. But I do maintain that, from what Searle has said, he has not ruled out this alternative.

5 These two components to the "overly sophisticated" objection are neatly separated in both Burge (1991) and Searle (1991b).

6 Searle made the point in passing within *Intentionality*. He claimed that while his philosophical discussion of the intentional content of visual experience makes explicit linguistic reference to the subject's visual experience, this is just an artifact of the fact that he was linguistically explicating those conditions. In having my visual experience, I do not make explicit reference to it. And I do not have to explicitly think of it. And it is not part of what I see. Searle puts this well in noting "what is seen are objects and states of affairs, and part of the conditions of satisfaction of the visual experience of seeing them is that the experience itself must be caused by what is seen" (1983: 49).

7 The recent work by Melvyn Goodale and David Milner (1995, 2004) distinguishing two functions of the visual system – one for representation, one for action on objects – bears on this complex philosophical and empirical issue.

8 Alternatively, we might say that Searle needs a way to represent objects *as spatially located*. I will sometimes switch back and forth between both ways of speaking. Nothing hinges on whether we think of visually perceiving locations or perceiving objects as located.

9 In saying that visual experience represents visually perceived objects as spatially located, I am not maintaining that our visual experience of the objects' location is more basic than our visual experience of the object itself. In fact, I think that our experience of objects is basic in the sense that visual experience represents objects directly. It need not and sometimes does not identify them by reference to location. Still, visual experience does often record objects' locations as properties of objects as it tracks and represents them. What I am saying is just that on Searle's account of the content of visual experience, neither the objects of visual experience nor the locations of the objects of visual experience can be represented directly. Both must be represented satisfactionally. Notice that, on any view that allows for direct reference, it is fine to maintain either that objects are directly represented in visual experience and locations are represented descriptively by reference to objects, or vice versa. And the view that both are represented directly in visual experience is, of course, also adequate. Indeed, this is the view I prefer and that I think best captures visual intentional content. The overall problem I am specifying is just that one cannot adequately capture the content of visual experience unless either objects or locations are directly represented.

10 Alternatively, he might be taking "there" as directly referring to a perceived location. Obviously, this route is unavailable to him, for it goes against his Fregeanism. And if "there" is supposed to refer only to a perceived location, rather than a real-world location, it goes against his naive realism.

11 You might disagree with this point if you are inclined to hold that many qualitative properties of objects are also nonconceptually represented. I am, in fact, one who thinks just this. (I was making a concession above.) As I see it, the only way to represent the precise yellowness of that station wagon is nonconceptually. But some conceptualists, notably McDowell (1994, 1995), have attempted to "conceptualize" qualitative properties like color by describing them with a so-called demonstrative concept like *that color*. If one takes this line, my point then is not that spatial locations differ from other qualitative properties insofar as we are unable to represent them with a nondemonstrative "concept," but that spatial locations are among the most fundamental aspects of visual experience in the sense that most other qualitative properties of physical objects may be selected by reference to their location.

12 In "Intentionality *de re*," McDowell wonders whether the particularity problem is solved in cases in which several type-identical objects – in his example, men – are before the subject. He maintains that Searle has solved the problem, claiming "there is no risk that the specificatory material made explicit here might be satisfied by the wrong man" (McDowell 1991: 216). He claims that Searle can solve this instance of the particularity problem by using "there" to "function to select the right aspect of the visual experience and so secure that the specification selects the right man." But this cannot work. Requiring that "there" selects aspects of visual experience puts the location of the objects that are *there* within visual experience: not a happy result.

13 Searle remarks that in English and other actual languages there are but four kinds of indexicals: the three mentioned above indicating time, place, and utterance directionality, plus devices of discourse reference, like anaphoric pronouns. I have confined my discussion to the first three for simplicity, as Searle largely does.

14 One might be inclined toward a semantics on which "I," "here," and "now" may also, in certain contexts, refer to objects other than the speaker, place, and time of the utterance. But, typically, such semantical views will admit that these indexicals do have, if not the lexical meaning that Searle assigns them, at least a default character (in Kaplan's sense) such that uses of these indexicals normally deliver as referents the speaker, place, and time of the utterance. Not so for "there."

15 It is easy to see this point by examining the way that Searle analyzes, say, my utterance of "That man is drunk" in a context in which I am using "that" as anaphoric on the individual I perceive in visual experience. For Searle the

truth conditions of this utterance specify both the intentional content of my utterance and the intentional content of my visual experience, and "show how the latter is nestled in the former": ([There is a man, x, there, and the fact that x is there is causing this vis exp] and x is the man visually experienced at the time of this utterance and x is drunk). See Searle (1983: 226–7). "There" is still a part of the full content of the visual experience.

16 In his contribution to this volume, Bach also argues that Searle cannot solve the problem of particularity, which he characterizes thus: what is it about this visual experience that requires that it be satisfied by the presence of this particular object and not by another object type-identical with this one? His primary reason why Searle cannot solve the problem of particularity is that Searle's analysis of the intentional content of visual perception structures that content like a general proposition, and so does not capture the fundamental particularity – the direct object-directedness – of visual perception. While I agree with Bach that this essential feature of intentional visual experience is missing from Searle's account, I worry that Searle could rightly regard Bach's complaint as question-begging, for it simply lays claim to the idea that the object of awareness cannot be selected satisfactionally. To appreciate this point, notice that Bach's complaint is not really that Searle has not found a way to solve the problem of particularity: that is, that he has not found a way to, in effect, get the right object in the satisfaction conditions. His claim is rather that Searle has not captured "the phenomenological fact that in visual experience objects appear to us, are "present to us" (p. 69). That is a related, but distinct issue. My argument here is strictly about whether Searle can get the right object in the satisfaction conditions, and as such begs no questions against Searle's satisfactionism.

17 The experimental paradigm was initially discussed in Pylyshyn and Storm (1988). Cf. also Pylyshyn (2002, 2003). You can see demonstrations of MOT experiments on Pylyshyn's website http://ruccs.rutgers.edu/faculty/pylyshyn/DemoPage.html.

18 So, for example, instead of a unitary beam of attention, it is at least *logically* possible that there is a beam of attention corresponding to each tracked object, and that each one scans, stores, and updates the locations of the targets independently. Pylyshyn regards this analysis as highly implausible on empirical grounds.

Chapter 5

Intentionalism, descriptivism, and proper names

WAYNE A. DAVIS

John Searle is famous for his description theory of names. Most regard this theory as having been refuted by Kripke. Yet Searle's theory has definite advantages over the Millian and causal alternatives. I show that the advantages are due to his explaining meaning in terms of the contents of mental states. The arguments against descriptivism refute only the claim that the relevant contents are descriptive. We get a better theory of names by keeping Searle's Intentionalism and dropping descriptivism.

1 SENSE, REFERENCE, AND INTENTIONAL CONTENT

Searle addressed fundamental questions about proper names: *Do names have senses? In virtue of what do names refer to objects? How in the utterance of names do speakers succeed in referring to objects?* In answering these questions, Searle develops a broadly Fregean account in which the notion of "Intentional content" plays the fundamental role. Searle's basic principle is that the meaning and referential properties of all linguistic units are derived from the intrinsic Intentionality of mental states (1983: vii, 27).

Since linguistic reference is always dependent on or is a form of mental reference and since mental reference is always in virtue of Intentional content ... proper names must in some way depend on Intentional content.

(Searle 1983: 231ff)

In order that a name should ever come to be used to refer to an object in the first place there must be some independent representation of the object. This may be by way of perception, memory, definite description, etc., but there must be enough Intentional content to identify which object the name is attached to.

(Searle 1983: 259)

Because names refer in virtue of Intentional contents, Searle affirms that names have a sense as well as a reference. He takes the Millian theory that names have a reference but no sense to be "simply a refusal to answer the question," namely, "In virtue of what does a name (or a speaker in using a name) refer to an object?" (Searle 1983: 242). Everyone should grant that names – certain letter or sound sequences – do not refer in virtue of their intrinsic properties. Names refer only because of certain facts about the people who use them. Specifically:

[T]he speaker refers to the object because and only because the object satisfies the Intentional content associated with the name. (Searle 1983: 234; see also 197)

The name itself refers to the object for the same reason. The questions now are: *What are Intentional contents?* And: *Which Intentional content is "associated" with any given name, or any given use of a name by a speaker?*

Searle follows Brentano (1874) in using *"Intentionality"* to refer to the "aboutness" of mental states.

Intentionality is that property of many mental states and events by which they are directed at or about or of objects and states of affairs in the world. If, for example, I have a belief, it must be a belief that such and such is the case; if I have a fear, it must be a fear of something or that something will occur. (1983: 1)[1]

Searle (1983: 4) acknowledges that Intentional "aboutness" is not an "ordinary relation" because we can be in a mental state that is of or about an object even though that object does not exist, as when a child is afraid of ghosts or believes something about Santa Claus.

Searle (1983: 5–6) next distinguishes between the *"Intentional content"* of an Intentional state and its *"psychological mode."* Believing that the war will end soon and hoping that the war will end soon have the same Intentional content, namely, the proposition that the war will end soon. The states differ because the mode is believing in one case and hoping in the other. Such Intentional states *represent* the "conditions of satisfaction" determined by their Intentional contents. "Thus, if I have a belief that it is raining, the content of my belief is: that it is raining. And the conditions of satisfaction are: that it is raining" (1983: 13).

Whereas the Intentional contents of beliefs and desires are whole propositions, the Intentional contents of other mental states are not (1983: 6–7). In the case of *loving Sally*, the Intentional content is Sally, not a proposition. With the introduction of nonpropositional Intentional contents, our first problem arises. Searle later introduces the notion of an *"Intentional object."* "To call something an Intentional object is just to say that it is what some Intentional state is about. Thus, for example, if Bill admires President Carter, then the Intentional object of his admiration is President Carter" (Searle 1983: 16). In this case, the Intentional content appears to be identical with the Intentional object. But Searle defines "Intentional object" using the relational rather than the Intentional sense of "about."[2] So Intentional objects must exist. They are external to the mental state for Searle, whereas Intentional contents are internal (1983: 22). Consider now the Intentional state of *looking for the king of France*. Searle would say that this state does not have an Intentional object because there is no king of France. What then is the Intentional content of the state? It has to have an Intentional content, since that is how looking for the king of France differs from looking for the king of Prussia. Moreover, Searle's account of reference presupposes that Intentional contents are distinct from Intentional objects even when the objects exist. For otherwise there is nothing mental associated with the name for the object of reference to satisfy.

A natural solution to the first problem is to take Intentional contents in general to be *concepts* (or *ideas*), defined as *propositions (thoughts) or parts thereof* (Davis 2003: part III; 2005: chs. 2 and 3). Then the Intentional content of looking for the king of France is the concept of the king of France, which is a part of the proposition that the king of France is bald and countless other propositions. A speaker refers to an object when he uses a term provided the object satisfies the individual concept associated with the term. Thus I can use "the third planet" to refer to Earth because Earth satisfies the concept of the third planet.[3] Searle says that reference is "unsuccessful" if the speaker expresses an Intentional content which nothing in reality satisfies.[4]

Suppose that Steve believes that Kennedy was the fortieth US president, and as a result said "The fortieth president was assassinated by Lee Harvey Oswald." In using "the fortieth president," Steve was trying to refer to Kennedy. On Searle's theory of reference, Steve succeeded provided *Kennedy satisfies the Intentional content associated with "the fortieth president."* The second problem is that this phrase is associated with many different Intentional contents. It is associated with the concept of the fortieth president by the rules of English; with the concept of Kennedy because the speaker was using the term to express the idea of Kennedy; and even more indirectly with the concept of Oswald as well as the concept of the thirty-ninth president. Every noun "N," moreover, is associated with the metalinguistic concept of being called "N." So a key term in Searle's theory of names suffers a serious failure of its uniqueness presupposition: "the Intentional content associated with the name."

Without going into numerous complexities, we can make progress by replacing "associated" with *"expressed"* (Davis 2003: part II; 2005: chs. 7–8). We must first underscore the distinction between *speaker expression* and *word expression* that parallels Grice's (1957) distinction between speaker meaning and word meaning and Kripke's (1977) distinction between speaker reference and word reference. Thus the *phrase* "the fortieth president" itself expresses the idea of the fortieth president: that is the concept the conventions of English assign to the phrase. The phrase does not express the idea of Kennedy or other associated ideas. Nonetheless, *Steve* used "the fortieth president" to express the idea of Kennedy. We can now say: *A speaker S refers to an object x in using "N" iff x satisfies the concept S used "N" to express*; and *a name "N" refers to x iff x satisfies the concept "N" expresses*. Speaker expression can be defined in terms of speaker intention, word expression in terms of conventional speaker expression.

2 ADVANTAGES OF INTENTIONALIST THEORIES

Intentionalist theories have critical advantages over Millian and causal theories.[5] Searle (1958: 166) began with Frege's argument that names must have senses distinct from their referents, otherwise all true identity statements involving names would be as trivial as "N is N." If the meaning of a name were its referent, then "Shakespeare was Bacon" would be synonymous with "Shakespeare was Shakespeare" if it were true. Yet they are clearly not synonymous even though serious scholars have made the case that the former is true. The Intentionalist can say that whether or not Shakespeare and Bacon were the same person, the idea of Shakespeare and the idea of Bacon are different. They have to be since most people who think of Shakespeare are not thinking of Bacon, and vice versa.[6] Thus Searle can say that even if these names have the same referent they have different senses because they express different Intentional contents.

Similarly, Searle observed that Millian theories are unable to account for the truth of negative existential statements like "Santa Claus does not exist." Since "Santa Claus" does not have a referent, Millianism rules that it does not have a sense. But that implies that the negative existential is meaningless rather than true. The Intentionalist observes that even though Santa Claus does not exist, the idea of Santa Claus does exist and is expressed by the name. "Santa Claus" has a sense because it expresses this Intentional content, allowing the negative existential to be meaningful and true.

According to the causal theory, a name "N" acquires a referent when a person, place, or thing is "baptized." It retains this referent as the use of the name spreads from one person to another. When I use "Aristotle" today, I am referring to Aristotle because a causal chain connects my use of the name to the initial baptism of the person. Evans (1973) observed that if the causal theory were true, then "Madagascar" would refer to a portion of the east coast of Africa rather than the big island to its east. For when the term was originally introduced, it referred to a part of the mainland. But when Marco Polo heard the name, he thought it referred to the island, and used it accordingly. The causal theory has even more difficulty with "Santa Claus" than Millian theories. For not only is it not connected to Santa Claus by any causal chain, it may be connected by a Kripkean causal chain to the historical St. Nicholas, bishop of Myra (d. AD 343). On Searle's (1983: 237) view, what determines the referent of "Madagascar" today is the Intentional content we use it to express today (the island). Similarly, since children do not use "Santa Claus" to express the Intentional content "St. Nicholas," they are not referring to the historical saint.

Devitt and Sterelny's (1987: §4.4, §5.3) unsolved "*qua*" problem is also unproblematic for Searle. If "Mt. Everest" is causally connected to Mt. Everest by its initial baptism, then it is also causally connected to the Earth by its initial baptism. So why on the causal theory does "Mt. Everest" not refer to the Earth? Searle can answer that the name does not express the Intentional content "the Earth."[7]

3 NAMES AND DESCRIPTIVE CONTENT

To deepen his account, Searle (1958: 170) asks how names differ from other terms used to refer to things, namely demonstratives and definite descriptions. All three categories have a referential function, but they perform this function differently. The referent of a proper name is not determined by special features of the context the way the referent of "this" or "that" is. In this respect, proper names resemble common nouns like "cat," "tree," and "star," as well as definite descriptions like "the smallest prime" or "the fortieth president." But like demonstratives and unlike definite descriptions, *names are not used to describe the objects they refer to* (1958: 167). "Unlike definite descriptions, they do not in general *specify* any characteristics at all of the objects to which they refer" (1958: 170). If we point to a star and say "That is Betelgeuse," we have identified the star, but have not yet described it. Searle parts company with Frege here, denying that the name "Aristotle" is synonymous with any identifying description like "the author of *De Anima*," or "The man called 'Aristotle'" (1983: 244). One argument would be that "Aristotle is the author of *De Anima*" is not a trivial logical truth like "Aristotle is Aristotle." A fortiori, Searle denies that "names must be exhaustively analyzed in completely general terms" (1983: 232ff).

Despite these observations, Searle brought a storm of objections upon his head by adopting the now notorious *description theory of names*. This is remarkable not only because Searle explicitly denies that names are used to describe, but also because I explained his theory above and illustrated its many advantages over competitors without once mentioning that the Intentional contents expressed by names are in any way descriptive.

Searle often seems to assume without argument that all Intentional content is descriptive. Consider:

> Thus, if a proper name occurs in an existential statement, it seems that it must have some conceptual or descriptive content. But if it has a descriptive content, then it seems Frege's theory must be correct, for what could that descriptive content be except the sense of the proper name? Thus, the occurrence of proper names in existential statements poses another grave difficulty for the non-sense theorists. (Searle 1967: 488)

We have seen why names must have *conceptual* content: in order for "Santa Claus does not exist" to be meaningful and true, the name "Santa Claus" must be expressing the concept of Santa Claus rather than that of the bishop of Myra or nothing at all. That is, the name must express the subject concept in the thought that Santa Claus does not exist. But what reason is there to assume that names must have *descriptive* content? How could they have descriptive content if they are not used to describe things? Similarly:

> The only chain that matters is a transfer of Intentional content from one use of an expression to the next; in every case reference is secured in virtue of descriptivist Intentional content in the mind of the speaker who uses the expression. (Searle 1983: 245)

The name "Madagascar" refers to the island because it expresses a particular Intentional content, namely, the idea of Madagascar – the subject concept of the proposition that Madagascar is in the Indian Ocean. If "Madagascar" expressed the idea of Mozambique instead, it would refer to part of the mainland. The reference is "secured" by virtue of an Intentional content. Why must it be descriptivist?

> Both definite descriptions and indexicals serve to express at least a certain chunk of Intentional content ... But what about proper names? They obviously lack an explicit Intentional content, but ... Since linguistic reference is always dependent on or is a form of mental reference and since mental reference is always in virtue of Intentional content including Background and Network, proper names must in some way depend on Intentional content.
>
> (Searle 1983: 231ff)

It is at least as obvious that names express a certain chunk of Intentional content as it is that definite descriptions and indexicals do. "Aristotle" expresses the subject concept of the proposition that Aristotle was a philosopher just as obviously as "the author of *De Anima*" expresses the subject concept of the proposition that the author of *De Anima* was a philosopher. Given that the name "Aristotle" expresses the concept of Aristotle, why is its Intentional content any less "explicit" than that of descriptions or indexicals? *If* all Intentional content were descriptive, then it would make sense to say that the name has implicit content. For the concept it expresses would then have components that are not separately expressed by components of the name. Why assume that?[8]

> "[I]dentifying description" does not imply "in words", it simply means: Intentional content, including Network and Background, sufficient to identify the object. (Searle 1983: 243ff)

If we know that the name "N" expresses the concept of Madagascar, that is sufficient to identify the object that "N" refers to: it refers to Madagascar. Only Madagascar fits or satisfies the concept of Madagascar. In the same way, if we know that "D" expresses the concept of the fortieth president, that is sufficient to identify the object that "D" refers to: the fortieth president. Of course, if a man does not know what Madagascar is, the given information will not enable him to identify the referent of "N." But in the same way, if a woman does not know who the fortieth president is, the given information will not enable her to determine the referent of "D." The concept of Madagascar satisfies the definition of an identifying description. But what is descriptive about it?

When he rejects Frege's view that names are analyzable as definite descriptions, Searle repeatedly stresses that: "[I]n some cases the only 'identifying description' a speaker might have that he associates with the name is simply the ability to recognize the object" (Searle 1983: 232ff; see also 1967: 491; 1969: 90; 1983: 241). Searle had to put "identifying description" in scare quotes because abilities are obviously not descriptions or descriptive concepts. Indeed, the ability to recognize an object is not an Intentional content. Searle (1983: 143) describes recognitional abilities as "non-representational capacities that constitute the Background" that makes Intentional content possible. So Searle cannot be satisfied with the fact that some names are "associated" with nothing but an ability to recognize an object. For that would undermine his thesis that names refer only because they are associated with Intentional contents. Fortunately, having the ability to recognize George Bush does entail having the concept of George Bush, just as having the ability to recognize red entails having the concept of red. Recognition is one of the ways in which concepts manifest themselves. So "George Bush" does express an Intentional content even for those people who can recognize Bush but are unable to give an identifying description of Bush. In the same way, "red" expresses an Intentional content even for people who are able to recognize red but are unable to define red. There is so far, then, no reason to think that a name expresses a *descriptive* Intentional content.

Searle candidly describes an obvious problem for descriptivism.

Following Strawson [1950] we may say that referring uses of both proper names and definite descriptions presuppose the existence of one and only one object referred to. But as a proper name does not in general specify any characteristics of the object referred to, how then does it bring the reference off?

(Searle 1958: 170)

Searle's basic principle provides the answer: the name refers to the object because the name is used to express a concept that represents that object. Thus "Madagascar" refers to Madagascar rather than Mozambique because it expresses the concept of Madagascar rather than Mozambique. In the same way, "red" refers to red rather than green because it expresses the concept of red rather than green.

Despite having an answer in his own basic Intentionalism to what appears to be an insoluble problem for the descriptivist, Searle appears to believe that only descriptivism provides a solution.

How is a connection between name and object ever set up? . . . I want to answer by saying that though proper names do not normally assert or specify any characteristics, their referring uses nonetheless presuppose that the object to which they purport to refer has certain characteristics. But which ones? Suppose we ask the users of the name "Aristotle" to state what they regard as certain essential and established facts about him. Their answers would be a set of uniquely referring descriptive statements. Now what I am arguing is that the descriptive force of "This is Aristotle" is to assert that a sufficient but so far unspecified number of these statements are true of this object.

(Searle 1958: 171)

I presume that users of the name "Aristotle" generally regard many things to be established facts about Aristotle: Aristotle was a man, a philosopher, and a Greek, among other things. This fact, however, does not establish any semantic connection between the name "Aristotle" and any or all of those properties. In order to get any connection, we have to be given that "Aristotle" expresses the subject concept in the proposition that Aristotle was a man, a philosopher, and a Greek. The fact that users of "Aristotle" believe that Plato was a man obviously tells us nothing about the meaning or reference of "Aristotle" because it does not express the subject of the proposition that Plato was a man. But given that "Aristotle" represents the concept of Aristotle, that suffices to identify the name's referent: Aristotle. Even if what people believe about Aristotle was in fact uniquely true of Plato, that would not make the name "Aristotle" refer to Plato. For "Aristotle" expresses the concept of Aristotle, which Plato does not satisfy.

One of Searle's main arguments for descriptivism relies on *"the principle of identification,"* according to which "an utterance of a proper name must convey a description just as the utterance of a definite description must if the reference is to be consummated" (1969: 165). When he says that a reference is "consummated," Searle (1969: 85) means that the speaker uttered an expression that enabled the hearer to identify who or what the speaker is referring to.

By "identify" here I mean that there should no longer be any doubt or ambiguity about what exactly is being talked about. At the lowest level, questions like "who?", "what?", or "which one?" are answered. Of course at another level these questions are still open: after something has been identified one may still ask "what?" in the sense of "tell me more about it", but one cannot ask "what?" in the sense of "I don't know what you are talking about". Identifying, as I am using the term, just means answering that question. For example, in an utterance of the sentence "the man who robbed me was over six feet tall" I can be said to refer to the man who robbed me, even though in one sense of "identify" I may not be able to identify the man who robbed me. I may not be able, e.g., to pick him out of a police line-up or say anything more about him. Still, assuming one and only one man robbed me, I do succeed in making an identifying reference in an utterance of the above sentence. (Searle 1969: 85)

The conventions of English enable hearers to determine that a speaker is referring to Aristotle if he uses the name "Aristotle," and to Madagascar if he uses "Madagascar." Speakers may not be able to pick Aristotle out of a line-up, or say anything more about him, but that does not prevent hearers from knowing who speakers are talking about when they use "Aristotle."[9]

Searle infers descriptivism from his principle of identification because he assumes that the *only* way to answer the question "Who or what is the speaker referring to?" is by using a demonstrative or definite description (1969: 86). This assumption is false. We standardly answer such questions by using proper names. If a speaker says "The big island off Africa has unusual primates," and the hearer says "Which island are you referring to?" the speaker can perfectly well answer "Madagascar." If Searle's assumption were true, names could not be used to make consummated references in the first place. Of course, some hearers do not understand the word "Aristotle." They either do not have the concept of Aristotle, or do not know that the word "Aristotle" expresses it. If I say "Aristotle was a realist," such a hearer will not be able to identify who I am referring to. The same goes for descriptions. A hearer who does not understand "the cube root of eight" will not know what I referred to when I said "The cube root of eight is smaller than three." Whether I can provide some other term that identifies for this hearer who or what I am referring to depends on facts about me and this particular hearer that have little to do with the questions about names we are addressing.

Searle used another principle of identification to argue for descriptivism earlier:

It is characteristic of a proper name that it is used to refer to the same object on different occasions. The use of the same name at different times presupposes that the object is the same; a necessary condition of identity of reference is identity of the object referred to. But to presuppose that the object is the same in turn presupposes a criterion of identity, that is, it presupposes an ability on the part of the speaker to answer the question "In virtue of what is the object at time t_1, referred to by name N, identical with the object at time t_2, referred to by the same name?" (Searle 1967: 489)

If the name "Aristotle" is used on two different occasions, a necessary and sufficient condition of the objects referred to being identical is that they both be Aristotle.[10] Speakers can provide such an identity criterion if they are clever enough. They can answer Searle's question by saying "In virtue of the fact that both are Aristotle." This follows from a principle Searle laid down earlier:

> So suppose we ask what are the necessary and sufficient conditions for applying a particular name to a particular object. Suppose for the sake of argument that we have independent means for locating an object; then what are the conditions for applying a name to it; what are the conditions for saying, e.g. "This is Aristotle"? ... Briefly and trivially, it is ... its identity with Aristotle that constitutes the necessary and sufficient conditions for the truth of "This is Aristotle."
> (Searle 1958: 169–70)

Of course, Searle was assuming that an "identity criterion" would be a definite description that Aristotle and only Aristotle satisfies at any time. There is no reason to think such an identity criterion needs to be provided, and no one to my knowledge has succeeded in providing one for any concrete object. The most widely accepted criterion for the identity of material objects over time is spatiotemporal continuity. But that fails in some possible worlds if not the actual world, and takes the form of a two-place relational predicate rather than a definite description. Aristotle is a person, moreover, for which spatiotemporal continuity is generally not thought to be an appropriate condition of identity over time. The use of proper names by competent speakers of English does not require them to have a solution to the problem of personal identity.[11]

Another argument Searle offers for descriptivism is that it is necessary to explain how we learn and teach the use of proper names:

> But now let us ask how it comes about that we are able to refer to a particular object by using its name. How, for example, do we learn and teach the use of proper names? This seems quite simple – we identify the object, and, assuming that our student understands the general conventions governing proper names, we explain that this word is the name of that object. But unless our student already knows another proper name of the object, we can only *identify* the object (the necessary preliminary to teaching the name) by ostension or description; and, in both cases, we identify the object in virtue of certain of its characteristics. So now it seems as if the rules for a proper name must somehow be logically tied to particular characteristics of the object in such a way that the name has a sense as well as a reference.
> (Searle 1958: 167ff)

One way I could teach a native Spanish speaker to use the name "Mars" is to explain (in Spanish or English) that it is the English name for the fourth planet. I would then be using a description to teach the use of the name. But no *logical* connection is established between "Mars" and "the fourth planet." These singular terms do not have the same meaning, and could have different referents. I could also teach the name "Mars" by pointing to Mars in a picture of the solar system. In this case, it is not even clear that I identified Mars in virtue of its characteristics. What is required in both cases is that what I said made the learner think of Mars, and learn that "Mars" expresses the concept of Mars.

4 THE EXPLANATION ARGUMENT

I have argued that Searle could explain how a name is connected to its referent in terms of the fact that the name expresses an individual concept that represents that object. Thus "Aristotle" expresses the concept of Aristotle, which represents Aristotle. Only Aristotle satisfies that concept, so Aristotle is the referent of "Aristotle." Some would now raise a further question: *What makes it the case that the concept of Aristotle represents Aristotle?*[12] Searle should give the same answer he gives for any other concept: the Intentional content of a mental state is an intrinsic property. For a concept to represent Aristotle is for it to *be* the concept of Aristotle. We can no more explain why the concept of Aristotle represents Aristotle than we can explain why the concept of red represents red.

We could explain why a concept is of what it is of if the concept could be analyzed into descriptive components. The concept of the author of *De Anima* is of the author of *De Anima* because it contains the concept of an author and the concept of *De Anima* in a certain relationship. But if we have to explain why the concept of Aristotle represents Aristotle we are also going to have to explain why the descriptive concepts we use to define it represent what they represent (Devitt 1990: 83). What makes the concept of an author represent authors? Not all meaningful terms can be defined. Indeed, much of our basic vocabulary is undefinable; the descriptive term "red" is a good example.[13] Even if we insist *per impossibile* on defining everything, there is no more reason to insist that names be defined in terms of descriptions than there is to demand that descriptions be defined in terms of names ("nominalism").

Inspired by Putnam (1981: 2–4), Devitt (1990: 90) dismisses Searle's thesis that Intentional content is an intrinsic property as "magic." He does so because he believes that Searle is committed to "a mental state having intrinsic properties that reach out and grasp things that are outside the head."

How could something inside the head determine reference, which is a relation to particular things outside the head? Nothing internal and intrinsic could ever determine such a relation. (Devitt 1990: 83; see also 94)

It is tautological that intrinsic properties are not relations to external objects, and do not suffice to determine any relations to external objects. If Searle is claiming that Intentional content is an intrinsic relation to external objects, he is not engaging in magic, he is contradicting himself. But Searle is not committed to any such foolishness. The mistake lies in Devitt's thinking of Intentional aboutness as "grasping." Recall Searle's observation that Intentional "aboutness" is not an "ordinary relation." It is not that it is an extraordinary relation: *Intentional aboutness is not a relation at all*. A fortiori, it is not a connection, and is not like being a photograph of something. Tautologically, the concept of Santa Claus is of Santa Claus. Being of Santa Claus is an essential property of the concept, part of its identity. Being of Santa Claus cannot be a relation between the concept of Santa Claus and Santa Claus because there is no Santa Claus for the concept to be related to. Similarly, the property of being of the author of *De Anima* that the concept of the author of *De Anima* possesses is not a relation to the author of *De Anima*; for if it were, then the concept of the husband of Pythias should equally well be of the author of *De Anima*. But it could not be of the author of *De Anima* without being the concept of the author of *De Anima*.[14]

Of course, there is a relation between the concept of Aristotle and Aristotle. The concept of the author of *De Anima* stands in the same relation to the author of *De Anima* and the husband of Pythias. The concept of Santa Claus does not stand in this relation to anything. This relation is the inverse of *satisfaction*, and may be called *reference* (in a relational sense of that term). Aristotle satisfies the concept of Aristotle, so the latter refers to the former. This relationship is not expressed by "of" in its Intentional sense, but the relation exists nonetheless. The mere fact that the concept of Aristotle is of Aristotle does not suffice to determine that it refers to Aristotle. It is also required that Aristotle exist and that he *be* what the concept is *of*. In general, *x* satisfies *c* and *c* refers to *x* iff *x* is what *c* is of. There is nothing magical here.[15]

Devitt (1990: 99) also thinks Searle's belief that Intentional content is intrinsic commits him to dualism: "How *could* Intentional content be biologically realized?" he asks incredulously. This question is no more unanswerable than the question "How could pains be neural events?" or "How could water be H_2O?" The evidence for physicalism is evidence that concepts are physical. Suppose we learned that a certain neural event is the concept of Santa Claus, based in part on the evidence that people think of Santa Claus when and only when that neural event was occurring to them, that this neural event is part of the more complex neural event that occurs when and only when people think the thought that Santa Claus is jolly, and so on. Then we would know that the neural event was of Santa Claus.

5 THE DISJUNCTIVE AND SECOND-ORDER DEFINITE DESCRIPTION THEORIES

Searle rejected Frege's view that the sense of a name "N" can be given by a definite description. The problem is not merely that our language does not have the words to express the descriptive content expressed by a name, but that a name does not have the sort of content a definite description has. How, then, can Searle be a descriptivist? Since the sense of a term is its meaning, how can a name "N" have its sense in virtue of being associated with a descriptive intentional content "D" unless "N" means "D"?

Frege's *implicit* or *shorthand definite description theory* is a strong form of descriptivism. The question is whether any other description theory is viable. Searle first advocated the *disjunctive definite description theory*:

Suppose we ask the users of a proper name, say "Aristotle," to state what they regard as essential and established facts about him. Their answers would constitute a set of descriptions, many elements of which would be identifying descriptions, and the totality of which would be an identifying description. For example, Aristotle was a Greek; a philosopher; the tutor of Alexander the Great; the author of the *Nichomachean Ethics*, the *Metaphysics*, and the *De Interpretation*; and the founder of the Lyceum at Athens. Although no particular single one of these descriptions is analytically tied to the name Aristotle, some indefinite subset of these descriptions is . . . It is a necessary condition for an object's being Aristotle that it satisfy at least some of these descriptions. This is another way of saying that the disjunction of these descriptions is analytically tied to the name "Aristotle." (Searle 1967: 490)[16]

Kripke (1972: 278–98) observed that there is a possible world in which Aristotle satisfied none of these descriptions. Aristotle might have been a Macedonian, who pretended to be a philosopher, putting his name on the books of others, and so on. Kripke also observed that "Aristotle" is a rigid designator, referring to the same individual in every possible world. It follows that "Aristotle was a Greek, or a philosopher, or the tutor of . . ." cannot be analytic.

The following argument may nonetheless seem persuasive:

> A classical scholar might discover that Aristotle never tutored Alexander or that he did not write the *Metaphysics*; but if a classical scholar claimed to discover that Aristotle wrote none of the works attributed to him, never had anything to do with Plato or Alexander, never went near Athens, and was not even a philosopher but was in fact an obscure Venetian fishmonger of the late Renaissance, then the "discovery" would become a bad joke. (Searle 1967: 490)

We would dismiss such a claim out of hand. But this can be explained by the fact that we (or others) have so much evidence that Aristotle was a Greek, and so much evidence that he had something to do with Plato, and so much evidence that he lived in Athens, and so on, that the imagined scholar's claim would be literally incredible. He would need a staggering amount of evidence to prove that all of these things are false. A much more likely hypothesis is that the scholar was using the name "Aristotle" to refer to someone other than Aristotle; another is that he was playing some kind of hoax. This explanation of our reaction to the claim is more plausible, surely, than that a disjunction of seemingly logically independent propositions is analytic even though no one of them is.

In his criticism of the causal theory, Searle (1983: 249) objected that Aristotle could not possibly be an odd number. It is plausible that different classes of proper names fall under different "sortals" or "categories."[17] In one sense, "America" is a place name; in another, it is a country name. If the speaker is not thinking of a country, he is not using "America" in the country sense. The sortals Searle proposed were much too specific, though: "man" for "Aristotle," for example. It is logically possible that Aristotle was not a man but a god, a Martian, or an exceptionally sophisticated machine planted on earth by gods or Martians. "Concrete object" is more defensible. Either way, the sortals that might be part of the meanings of names are far too general to be identifying.

Technical problems include the fact that the disjunction of the descriptions Searle lists for "Aristotle" is not an identifying description, and cannot be what enables the typical person to learn "Aristotle," or explain who he is referring to. With "Santa Claus," it is unclear what if any descriptions would go into the disjunction. For adult users do not believe there are any established facts about Santa Claus other than that he does not exist. And if "Santa Claus" is analytically tied to a disjunction that includes anything like "the man who wears the familiar red costume with white trim," then the theory will rule that "Santa does not exist" is false. So this theory is not supported by the considerations that led Searle to adopt descriptivism.

Other passages in Searle's earlier work propose the "cluster theory" Kripke attacked. On this view, names are analytically tied to a *second-order* description: *"The individual satisfying a sufficient number of the descriptive contents users of 'Aristotle' believe to be established facts about Aristotle"* (1967: 490; 1958: 171, 173). This description is so vague, however, we do not even know whether it is true of Aristotle. There seems to be no hope of answering "Sufficient for what?" in a noncircular fashion. Moreover, it is not an Intentional content the typical user of "Aristotle" would ever express. So it is hard to see how it could have anything to do with the meaning of "Aristotle." In fact, no description referring to a name can be analytically tied to that name. The meaning of "Aristotle" does not guarantee that its referent is named "Aristotle" or bears any relation at all to that name. And if someone asks a user of "Aristotle" who he is referring to, it would beg the question for him to answer using the second-order description italicized above.

As we observed in section 3, the criterion Searle uses to determine that a description "D" is tied analytically to the name "Aristotle" is that speakers believe the proposition that *Aristotle is D*. Searle correctly presupposes that speakers have the concept of Aristotle, and that this concept is a part of many propositions they believe. Without this presupposition, Searle would not be able to pick out the set of descriptions he did. Yet, given this presupposition, there is no need for him to insist implausibly that the descriptions are analytically tied to the name. He can maintain that the name has a sense because it expresses that Intentional content.

6 THE VARIABLE DEFINITE DESCRIPTION THEORY

Searle later espoused the *variable definite description theory*. On this view, a name does not express a particular Intentional content. It is used to express different descriptive contents on different occasions, all of which refer to the same object.

In this respect, proper names differ from general terms. Since the point of having proper names is just to refer to objects, not to describe them, it often doesn't really matter to us much what descriptive content is used to identify the object as long as it identifies the right object, where the "right object" is just the one that other people use the name to refer to. (Searle 1983: 246)

Thus, in Kripke's terms I am providing a theory of reference but not a theory of meaning. However, the distinction is not as sharp as he suggests, for the following reason: the Intentional content associated with a proper name can figure as part of the *propositional content* of a statement made by a speaker using that name, even though the speaker's associated Intentional content is not part of the *definition* of the name. (Searle 1983: 256)[18]

On this theory, the relation of names and descriptions is the reverse of what we find with the referential use of definite descriptions. Mary can use "The president is a Republican" to express the proposition that George Bush is a Republican, and Jane on another occasion can use the same sentence to express the proposition that Bill Clinton is a Republican. On the variable description theory, Steve can use "Aristotle was a philosopher" to express the proposition that the author of *De Anima* was a philosopher, while Mark uses it to express the proposition that the husband of Pythias was a philosopher. The big difference is that while "the president" expresses an Intentional content, "Aristotle" does not on this theory. In consequence, the variable description theory does not solve the problems that motivated Searle's theory in the first place. On this theory, names do *not* have a sense. None of the Intentional contents associated with the name are what it means. The theory inherits the problems of Millianism as a result. It does not account for the marked difference in meaning between "Cary Grant is Cary Grant" and "Cary Grant is Archibald Leach." And in addition to ruling that "Santa Claus does not exist" has no meaning, it provides no criterion for what descriptive truths it can nonetheless be used to express. The allowed descriptions cannot be described as the ones that pick out the "right object," because there is no such object.

The variable description theory could be formalized using Kaplan's (1989: 505–7) notion of a "character." A character is a function from contexts to "contents." On the variable description theory, proper names, like indexicals, are associated with different contents in different contexts. For Searle, however, contents are descriptive Intentional contents rather than intensions (functions from possible worlds to objects). And, unlike indexicals, the character function associated with a proper name on Searle's view has the restriction that its values all refer to the same object in the actual world. This makes it even clearer that the variable description theory does not account for the meaning of "Santa Claus" or the difference in meaning between "Cary Grant" and "Archibald Leach."

The variable description theory also fails to account for the *rigidity* of names (Kripke 1972: 269–70, 306). Whereas names designate the same object in every possible world, definite descriptions typically do not. If the variable description theory were correct, there would be no reason to expect names to be rigid. On this theory, (1) is used to express a statement like (2).

(1) "Aristotle" refers to x in w iff x is Aristotle in w.

(2) "Aristotle" refers to x in w iff x is the author of *De Anima* in w.

But whereas (1) is true for every world w, (2) is false for any world w in which Aristotle is not the author of *De Anima*.[19]

Furthermore, modal sentences of form (3) have a well-known structural ambiguity: the first "NP" can be understood as inside or outside of the modal operator.

(3) NP is NP in every possible world.

Both interpretations are possible whether "NP" is a name or a definite description. With descriptions, (3) typically expresses a truth when the first "NP" is inside, and a falsehood when it is outside. But because names are rigid designators, the structural ambiguity does not affect the truth value of the resulting statement: on both interpretations, the sentence expresses a truth. Thus (4) expresses a truth whether this is saying that the person who is Aristotle in any possible world is Aristotle in that world, or is saying that Aristotle is such that he is Aristotle in every possible world.

(4) Aristotle is Aristotle in every possible world.

If the variable description theory were correct, however, (4) should have the semantic properties of a sentence like "The author of *De Anima* is the author of *De Anima* in every possible world"; this is true on one interpretation, false on the other. The description theorist could try to avoid this problem by claiming that speakers always use names to express rigid descriptions, like "the author of *De Anima* in *this* world (the actual world)," or descriptions giving identity conditions for the object named.[20] But this claim is psycholinguistically implausible. The variable description theory makes the additional false prediction that (4) could be false on both interpretations. For the speaker could be using the different occurrences of the name to express different descriptions. Thus, on some occasions, (4) could have the content "The author of *De Anima* is the husband of Pythias in every possible world," which is false whether the first description is inside or outside (assuming that the second description is inside the modal operator).[21]

The variable description theory is inadequate even as an account of speaker meaning and reference. As we observed at the outset, Searle (1958: 170) observed that names differ from definite descriptions in that names are not used to describe the objects they refer to. Names do not themselves convey any particular descriptive contents, on this view. But if names are always used to express descriptive contents like definite descriptions, then they are always used to describe their referents.

Furthermore, there is much the variable description theory cannot explain about speaker meaning and reference. Assuming that Steve and Mark are typical, they *mean the same thing by "Aristotle"*; they *express the same proposition*, namely, that Aristotle was a philosopher; they *directly contradict* someone who says "Aristotle was not a philosopher"; and they are thinking of Aristotle *as Aristotle*.

(i) The variable description theory does not entail that Steve and Mark mean the same thing by "Aristotle," because there is no Intentional content both use it to express. To see how far they might be from meaning the same thing, suppose that Tony mistakenly thinks "Aristotle" is the name of Plato, and mistakenly believes that Plato was the author of *De Anima*. Then like Steve and Mark, Tony could use "Aristotle was a philosopher" to express the proposition that the author of *De Anima* was a philosopher, and would be using "Aristotle" to express a descriptive content that identifies Aristotle.[22] But it is obvious that Tony did not mean by "Aristotle" what we mean by it.

(ii) Steve and Mark both express the thought that Aristotle was a philosopher. This is distinct from the thought that the author of *De Anima* was a philosopher as well as the thought that the husband of Pythias was. These three thoughts are logically independent, and can occur to people independently. On the variable description theory, however, there is no thought both speakers expressed.

(iii) If Mary said "The fortieth president was a Republican," referring to Reagan, and Jane uttered its negation referring to Clinton, then what they *said* was contradictory even though what they *meant* was not. But on the variable description theory, if Mary says "Aristotle was a philosopher" and Jane utters its negation, then there is no reason to maintain that what they said was contradictory. For neither sentence expresses a proposition. What they meant would not be contradictory either unless by chance they happened to have expressed the same descriptive content.

(iv) Thinking of Aristotle *as Aristotle* is different from thinking of Aristotle *as the author of De Anima*.[23] The latter would occur if someone were thinking that the author of *De Anima* was a philosopher, but did not realize that Aristotle was the author. Someone entertaining the proposition that the author of *De Anima* is a philosopher need not have Aristotle in mind at all. In this case, he could not mean "Aristotle" by "Aristotle," and is not intentionally referring to Aristotle. On the variable description theory, however, there is no important difference between that case and typical cases. There is no way to express the difference between thinking of Aristotle as Aristotle, and thinking of him as the author of *De Anima*. For on this theory there is no distinctive Intentional content for the second occurrence of "Aristotle" in "S is thinking of Aristotle as Aristotle" to express.

The variable description theory also faces problems with *belief error* and *ambiguity*.

(v) Many people believe Columbus discovered America. Hence they use "Columbus" to express the idea "the discoverer of America." In fact, others got to America first. So, are these people using "Columbus" to refer to Columbus improperly (because they are using a descriptive content that does not pick out the right object)? Or are they using "Columbus" improperly to refer to Leif Ericson (or the first human to arrive). Neither answer is appealing. Most people have a mistaken belief about Columbus, but use the name "Columbus" properly.[24]

(vi) Finally, suppose that Carol says "Aristotle was a philosopher," and that the only descriptive content that goes through her mind as she does so is "the author of *De Anima*." The variable description theory would seem to rule that Carol is referring to Aristotle. But

Carol may have meant "Aristotle Onassis" by "Aristotle" on this occasion; "the author of *De Anima*" occurred to her because she mistakenly believes that Onassis wrote *De Anima*. The variable description theory cannot account for the fact that Carol meant "Aristotle Onassis" by "Aristotle."

Let us ask *why* a speaker might have used "Aristotle" to express the idea "the author of *De Anima*." Why did the speaker not use "Aristotle" to express the idea "the author of *The Republic*" or "the second husband of Jackie Kennedy"? The answer cannot simply be that "the author of *De Anima*" identifies the object other people use "Aristotle" to refer to. For the same thing is true of "the second husband of Jackie Kennedy." The answer, surely, is that the speaker wanted to refer to Aristotle (the philosopher), and believed that Aristotle is the author of *De Anima*, not the author of *The Republic* or the second husband of Jackie Kennedy. When the speaker does use the same name to express the idea "the second husband of Jackie Kennedy," that is because he wants to refer to Aristotle Onassis on that occasion, and believes that he was the second husband of Jackie Kennedy. That is, certain definite descriptions are associated with a name because speakers use it to express the subject concept of certain descriptive beliefs. It is that subject concept, not the associated descriptive concepts, that provides the sense of the name. Searle could have avoided all the criticisms his descriptivism engendered by recognizing that not all Intentional contents are descriptive.

NOTES

1 See also Searle (1994, 2004: ch. 6).

2 Searle (1983: 17) notes that "of" and "about" have an extensional or relational sense in which their grammatical object must denote something that exists, and an Intentional sense in which it does not. When Searle defined "Intentional content," he was using "about" in the Intentional sense.

3 On my view, though, contents are not concepts or propositions (Davis 2003: §15.4, §15.6). Concepts and propositions themselves have Intentional contents, which determine the Intentional contents of mental states that consist in relations to those concepts or propositions.

4 Searle uses "S refers to N" relationally, so that the existence of N is required. It is also used Intentionally, in which sense children can and do refer to Santa Claus (Davis 2003: §6.2; 2005: §2.8).

5 Mill (1879: §1.2.5); Russell (1918); Wittgenstein (1922); Putnam (1962, 1973); Donnellan (1972: 373); Kripke (1972: 298–303, 330–1); Devitt (1974, 1981; 2, 25, 33, 64); Devitt and Sterelny (1987: ch. 4).

6 If "of" is used relationally, we can still observe that few people who think of Shakespeare think of him *as* Bacon.

7 For a more complete and thorough survey of advantages of Intentionalist theories of names over competing theories, see Davis (2005: part III).

8 Cf. Devitt (1990: 102, fn. 9).

9 In other contexts, of course, the use of "Aristotle" enables hearers to know that the speaker is referring to Aristotle Onassis.

10 This presupposes that the speaker is using "Aristotle" the way we are. If the speaker is instead using "Aristotle" to mean "Aristotle Onassis," then the identity condition is that both objects are Aristotle Onassis.

11 I rebut other arguments from identification in Davis (2005: §13.7, §14.7).

12 See e.g. Devitt (1990); Margolis and Laurence (1999: 55). Cf. Wittgenstein (1953: 177).

13 See e.g. Fodor (1975: 124–56; 1981: ch.10; 1994: chs. 2–3); and Davis (2005: §13.1).

14 As noted in note 2, there is a relational sense of "about" and "of" in which the concept of Santa Claus is not of anything, and the concept of the author of *De Anima* is of the husband of Pythias. But we are concerned with Intentional aboutness.

15 See Davis (2005: §8.5) for a fuller argument.

16 See also Searle (1958: 172).

17 Cf. Searle (1967: 489); Geach (1980: 83–4); Wiggins (1980: 48); Cocchiarella (1984: 335–7); Soames (2002: 122); Davis (2005: §13.4).

18 See also Searle (1967: 491; 1969: 172; 1983: 255, 260).

19 Searle himself seems to have made essentially this point using a different description years before Kripke advanced his modal argument. See the passage quoted above (1958: 169–70) in which he says that the necessary and sufficient conditions of the truth of "This is Aristotle" is the identity of the referent with Aristotle.

20 Searle (1983: 257–9). See also Kaplan (1978); Plantinga (1978). A common mistake is to assume that "actual" rigidifies a description. "The actual author of *De Anima*" is itself nonrigid. For in a world in which Plato wrote *De Anima*, Plato was the actual author of *De Anima*. What we can say is that such descriptions tend to take wide scope in modal contexts.

21 Cf. what Searle says about "Hesperus is Phosphorus" (1983: 256).

22 This is true in the referential sense of "refer to N" that Searle is using. In the Intentional sense in which people can refer to Santa Claus and other non-existent objects, Tony was not referring to the same person as Steve and Mark. The variable description theory does not account for speaker reference in the Intentional sense.

23 In Frege's terms, these are two different "modes of presentation" or "ways of thinking" of the object. In Searle's, they are different "aspects" under which the object is represented (e.g. 2004: 133).

24 What if they also use "Columbus" to express the idea of the person called "Columbus"? Are they then using the name both properly and improperly, or are they referring to both Columbus and Leif Ericson? Searle (1983: 248, 251–2) assumes that the speaker would have to "give precedence to" or "fall back on" one description rather than the other. But he does not say what either expression means, or why this must be true.

Chapter 6

On the alleged priority of thought over language

CHRISTOPHER GAUKER

Language, I contend, is the medium of conceptual thought. By "language" I mean spoken and written languages, such as English, Arabic, and Chinese. I deny that there is any such thing as a universal "language of thought"; so that is certainly not included in what I am calling "language." By "conceptual thought" I mean the process of thought that consists in making *judgments*. For instance, the judgment that *that* (a certain object) *is a reptile* is a conceptual thought, and the judgment that *some reptiles can swim* is a conceptual thought. So my claim is that every judgment is an act of saying something, either out loud or *in foro interno*, in some language. But what I am calling conceptual thought is definitely not the only kind of mental process that deserves to be called "thought." For example, there might be a kind of imagistic thought that does not necessarily involve the application of concepts. Perhaps very little of our mental problem solving is actually conceptual thought.

Exponents of the doctrine of language-independent conceptual thought like to portray themselves as heretics defying orthodoxy.[1] However things might have been at one time, the language-independence of conceptual thought is now certainly the orthodox position, not the heresy. Anyone who dares to deny it can expect to be met with mockery and derision rather than serious arguments. Not long ago, a well-known linguist said to me, in all seriousness, in front of a large audience, that on my view it should be possible to get a chicken to think by teaching it language. So I expect that there will be some who have already stopped reading, persuaded by the first paragraph that all that follows is incorrigible nonsense.

In this short chapter I do not have space for a thorough exposition of a positive account of the nature of conceptual thought, but I can confront some of the main reasons for thinking that language just *cannot* be the medium of conceptual thought. (The chicken argument is not one of them.) Some of these are reasons that we find in the writings of John Searle, especially in his 1983 book *Intentionality*; it is these on which I will focus. But not all of the main arguments are arguments that Searle would endorse; so I will survey some additional arguments as well.

INTRINSIC INTENTIONALITY

Searle's own version of the now orthodox position takes the form of the claim that the intentionality of mental states is *intrinsic*, whereas the intentionality of speech acts is *derived*. In saying this he means not only to assert that the intentionality of mental states has primacy over that of speech but also that various attempts to explicate the intentionality of mental states all fail (1983: viii–ix).

Searle's explicit argument for this position is unique. I have not encountered it anywhere else. Here is what he says:

> The actual performance in which the speech act is made will involve the production (or use or presentation) of some physical entity, such as noises made through the mouth or marks on paper. Beliefs, fears, hopes, and desires on the other hand are intrinsically Intentional. To characterize them as beliefs, fears, hopes, and desires is already to ascribe Intentionality to them. But speech acts have a physical realization, *qua* speech acts, that is not intrinsically Intentional. There is nothing intrinsically Intentional about the products of the utterance act, that is, the noises that come out of my mouth or the marks that I make on paper. (Searle 1983: 27; see also 1983: viii, 22, 26, 28–9)

In other words, there is an asymmetry between our characterizations of mental states such as beliefs and our characterizations of speech acts that justifies us in calling the intentionality of mental states intrinsic and the intentionality of speech acts derived. We cannot, for instance, characterize a belief *as such* without characterizing it as contentful. To characterize something as a belief is to imply that, for some proposition *p*, the belief is a belief that *p* – a belief that the house is on fire, or a belief that bats are birds, or some such. In contrast, we can very well characterize a speech act as an *utterance* without implying that it has any content. We can characterize it as a sequence of sounds or vibrations in the air.

The answer to this argument is that the purported asymmetry does not exist. As Searle himself says, intentional states "are *realized* in the neurophysiology of the brain" (1983: 15). So a belief can be characterized either *qua* content-bearing state or *qua* neurophysiological entity. We are not presently able to give the neurophysiological description, but since each particular belief *is* a particular neurophysiological entity, the description is there to be had. So there is a perfect symmetry between the case of speech acts and the case of mental states. A speech act can be described as an assertion that *p* or as a commanding that it be the case that *p*, or as some other speech act, and it can also be described as an utterance consisting of a sequence of sounds or of marks on paper. Likewise, a mental state can be described as a belief that *p* or as a desire that it be the case that *p*, or as some other kind of conceptual thought, or as a neurophysiological entity.

Here I have assumed that both in the case of such things as beliefs and desires and in the case of such things as statings and commandings, a thing can be *identified* with its realizer. Thus, because a belief that the house is on fire is *realized* by a certain neurophysiological entity we can say that the belief *is* the neurophysiological entity, and because a certain act of *asserting* is realized by a given utterance, we can say that the assertion *is* the utterance. Perhaps this is objectionable in the case of belief and we should not identify a belief with the entity that realizes it. Fine. But whatever objections might lead us to deny the identity of a belief with its realizer should lead us to deny as well the identity of a speech act with the utterance that realizes it. So there is still a perfect symmetry between the case of things like beliefs and desires on the one hand and things like assertions and commands on the other.[2]

The claim that a particular belief *is* or is *realized* by a particular neurophysiological entity does not entail that the belief can be correctly characterized as a belief that *p just because* it is or is realized by that neurophysiological entity. Rather, we should expect that the neurophysiological entity will qualify as being a belief (or as realizing a belief) only because of the way it is embedded in a larger system of neurophysiological entities, and perhaps only because of the way that larger system is embedded in a larger world. Searle himself acknowledges this when he observes that something in Jimmy Carter qualifies as being (or as realizing) the desire to run for President only because the neural configuration that realizes his desire is embedded in a network of other neural states that realize other intentional states and only because this whole network functions against a background of non-representational mental capacities (1983: 19–20).

So given a neurophysiological description *B* of some state that *is*, or *realizes*, some intentional state characterized in intentional terms as *M*, the following is a perfectly serious question: what is it about *B*, its intrinsic properties, its relations to other neurophysiological states and to objects and events in the rest of the world that makes it the case that it is intentional state *M*? Elsewhere, Searle claims that, in asking such a question, one is presupposing that if intentionality is not something mysterious, then "it is really something else, that it is eliminable by an eliminative reduction" (1998: 97). But no, what I am asking for is not an identification of intentionality with something *else*. What I am asking is what intentionality *is*. It is not an answer just to explain in neurophysiological terms how state *B arises* (see the discussion of thirst, 1998: 95–6). To answer in that way would be to confuse a question of genesis with a question of constitution. It is also not an answer just to say that "It is internal to the state that it has this intentionality" (1998: 97).

Still, one might contend that there is a different asymmetry between things like beliefs, on the one hand, and things like assertions, on the other, namely, this: the intentionality of speech acts is imposed on them by the mind inasmuch as the mind intentionally confers on these utterances the conditions of satisfaction that are intrinsic to the mental states that the utterances express (1983: 27), whereas mental states do not have their conditions of satisfaction imposed on them. But if this is right, then we need some reason to believe that it is apart from the first asymmetry claim, which has fallen through. Thus I turn to Searle's 1983 theory of speech acts.

SPEECH ACTS

That the intentionality of thought is intrinsic is a basic tenet of Searle's theory of speech acts. More precisely, the tenet is that the intentionality of thought is at least *relatively* intrinsic in that the intentionality of speech acts is *derived* from that of the intentions with which they are performed. According to Searle, acts of speech are meaningful only insofar as their conditions of satisfaction are "imposed" on them by the intentions with which they are made (1983: 167–9). So there has to be something having conditions of satisfaction that are not likewise imposed, and those are things such as beliefs and intentions. Moreover, we can define the distinctions between the several kinds of speech act (such as assertions and commands) in terms of the differences in content between the intentions that motivate them (1983: 166). It is here, I suspect, that we have the argument that really moves Searle, for it is here that the assumption that the intentionality of thought is (at least relatively) intrinsic appears to do some explanatory work.

According to Searle, whenever someone performs an act of speech he or she acts with a "meaning intention," the essential component of which is an "intention to represent" (1983: 165–6). (The other, optional part of a meaning intention is an "intention to communicate.") When an agent performs an act with an intention to represent that *p*, the agent performs a gesture or sound (an utterance) of kind *K* with the intention that *this very intention* will cause the agent to perform an act of kind *K* that has as its conditions of satisfaction that *p*. Searle gives a military example in which he raises his arm as a prearranged signal that the enemy has retreated. In this case, the intention to represent is the agent's intention that his arm go up as a result of his having that very intention and that his arm's going up should have as its condition of satisfaction that the enemy has retreated (1983: 167–8). The conditions of satisfaction that a speaker thus intends an utterance to have are said to be "imposed."

One of the peculiarities of Searle's theory is the idea that the content of the intention includes a reference to that very intention, but I will not make an issue of that peculiarity here. What I do want to make an issue of is that it is completely unclear what it means to say that an utterance *has* conditions of satisfaction *as a consequence* of their being imposed. I can understand why one would want to say that an utterance has conditions of satisfaction. One could say that an utterance has conditions of satisfaction as a consequence of its conventional meaning and the context in which it is uttered and that it is knowing that the utterance has these conditions of satisfaction that enables an audience to recognize the belief or other intrinsically intentional state that underlies and motivates the act of speech. But that is not what Searle says. He does not think that the conditions of satisfaction that one imposes are the conditions of satisfaction that an utterance has by virtue of the conventional meaning of the sentence uttered. In fact, there cannot be any substantive conditions that an utterance must meet in order to have these conditions of satisfaction, other than the speaker's intending it to have them, because then the conditions of satisfaction could not be simply *imposed*. The speaker could not guarantee that the utterance will actually have them just by intending that it have them. Consequently, if we ask about the content of this intention – *what it is* that a speaker intends in intending that his or her act have certain conditions of satisfaction – there is none but a circular answer.

So set aside for a moment Searle's insistence that conditions of satisfaction are simply *imposed*. At one point (1998: 140; see also 2002: 152), Searle does acknowledge that the conventional meaning of a form of words constrains what a speaker can mean by that form of words. So the content of the speaker's intention might be, for instance, to speak words to which convention assigns certain conditions of satisfaction. In that case, a speaker might fail to achieve what he or she intends if convention does not in fact assign those conditions of satisfaction to the words he or she speaks. One question is whether in that case there will be anything left to the claim that the intentionality of words is *derived*. Nowhere, as far as I can see, has Searle attempted to explain how the *conventional* meanings of words derive from the intentionality of speakers' thoughts (as, for instance, Grice [1968] did).

Assuming that conditions of satisfaction have some kind of independence from speakers' intentions, a further objection to Searle's account of the intention to represent will be that ordinary people cannot speak with such intentions because they do not even have the concept of such conditions of satisfaction. The problem is not that they do not know what the phrase "conditions of satisfaction" means. The problem is not even that when we try to teach them what it means, they have a hard time and make all kinds of mistakes about it; perhaps they just have a hard time bringing the concept to consciousness. The problem is that even philosophers of language do not share a concept of conditions of satisfaction.

When we theorists contemplate conditions of satisfaction we encounter all sorts of difficult cases that elicit arguments over whether some condition belongs to a thing's conditions of satisfaction or not. (Think about the debates concerning conventional implicature. Think about the debates concerning context-relativity.) And we encounter fundamental questions such as whether we should be able to analyze the reference relation in naturalistic terms. We are not at the stage where we can say that we know in general what kind of thing conditions of satisfaction are and that the only question is *which* conditions of satisfaction particular thoughts and utterances have in particular cases. So even we who work on such things do not all share a concept of conditions of satisfaction. So it seems to be out of the question that ordinary people apply this concept every time they perform a meaningful act of speech.

According to Searle, a speech act having a certain condition of satisfaction also *expresses* a mental state having that condition of satisfaction, and, moreover, the speaker's being in that mental state is a condition on the sincerity of the speech act. Thus, to assert that p is to express the belief that p, and having that belief is a condition on the sincerity of the assertion. One of the virtues Searle claims for his theory is that it explains *why* a speech act and the mental state required by the sincerity condition for that type of speech act have the same condition of satisfaction. (The task is set on p. 165 [point 2] of Searle [1983], and Searle's claim to have achieved it is on pp. 174–5.) But as far I can see, Searle does not in fact explain that. Any explanation of that would have to explain what it means to say that a speech act with a certain condition of satisfaction *expresses* a mental state with that same condition of satisfaction, and, as far as I can see, Searle has no special explanation of that at all. Searle also claims that his theory explains why people who hear an assertion have a reason to believe that which is asserted (1983: 179). But I do not see that his theory does that either.

So if Searle's account of the content of the intention that characterizes a meaningful act of speech is not correct, what is the correct account? Here is an unenlightening answer that might, despite its unenlighteningness, be all that we can expect: The characteristic intention is an intention to *say something*. More precisely, there is always some type of speech act such that it is an intention to perform a speech act of just that type. What is the difference between the case in which *I* say, "The program is not responding," and the case in which a like-sounding sequence of sounds is generated by a laptop speech processor? Well, the first, but not the second, is the product of an intention to *say* something, specifically, to *assert* something. What is the difference between an utterance of "The bartender did it" in a court of law and an utterance of those same words by an actor on the stage? In the first case, the accuser intended to *assert* that the bartender did it, whereas, in the second, the actor intended only to *pretend* to assert something. For any type of speech act, the intention that characteristically accompanies the making of that type of speech act is precisely the intention to make a speech act of that type.

If this is right, then there must be some way to characterize the *content* of such an intention other than as the intention to make a speech act of such and such type. For example, if we are to say that the characteristic intention of an assertion is the intention to make an assertion, then we must be able to say something about what an assertion is other than that it is a speech act that results from the intention to make an assertion. The alternative that I would like to propose for the case of assertion begins with an account of an explicitly normative concept that *appropriately applies* to those utterances that qualify as assertions, namely, the concept of *assertibility*. Many philosophers associate the term "assertible" with some kind of epistemic standard, but I want to propose a different way of defining it, in terms of the goals of the conversation to which an assertion belongs.

Paradigmatically, a *conversation* is a linguistic exchange between two or more people aimed at the achieving of some goal. The goal might be practical, such as obtaining food to eat, or it might itself be linguistic, such as answering a theoretical question. In less-than-paradigmatic cases, a conversation may involve just one person who, as it were, talks to himself, and in less-than-paradigmatic cases the goal that drives a conversation may be merely pretense. The distinctive function of sentences in declarative mood is to shape the means by which inter-locutors seek to achieve the goals of a conversation. They do this insofar as interlocutors *accept* and act in *accordance* with declarative sentences. A declarative sentence is *assertible* in a conversation if and only if, as a consequence of the conventions of the language, the goals of the con-versation and the way the world really is on the occasion of utterance, the interlocutors *ought* to accept it and act in accordance with it. An *utterance* is assertible in a derivative sense if the *sentence uttered* is assertible relative to the conversation in which it is uttered.

Next, an *assertion* may be defined as an act of speech that may be appropriately *appraised* for assertibility. Typically, an assertion will elicit appraisals from the other interlocutors. They will accept it as assertible or reject it as unassertible (because it is deniable or because it is just irrelevant). The assertions are the utterances of declarative sentences appropriately subjected to this kind of appraisal. So a rock is not an assertion because it is not an utterance of a declarative utter-ance in any language. A song might not be an assertion, even if it contains some declarative utterances, because it might not be appro-priate to appraise those utterances for assertibility. But a lie will be an assertion because we appropriately appraise the lie as unassertible and on that basis blame the liar for asserting something unassertible.

In this way, a type of speech act may be defined in terms of the normative concept that appropriately applies to it. Similarly, acts of speech such as commands and promises may be defined in terms of the normative concepts that appropriately apply to them. For exam-ple, a command is an utterance of an imperatival sentence that may be appropriately evaluated for imperatival legitimacy. Granted, this kind of definition does not make it any easier for us to *recognize* the type of a speech act; recognizing a speech act as such remains as difficult as deciding which normative concepts appropriately apply to it.[3]

One consideration that might seem to favor the attempt to define speech acts in terms of intentions over my own approach is that each of us knows better than anyone else whether he or she has made an assertion or issued a command or performed any other type of speech act. This authority that each of us has over his or her own speech acts might be accounted for as follows: each of us is authoritative on the question of what he or she intends; so since it is an intention that determines the type of the speech act, each of us is authoritative on the question of the type of his or her speech act. Whereas, if speech acts are not *defined* in terms of intention, then the authority we have over our own intentions will not immediately carry over to authority over the type of our speech acts. I do not find Searle arguing in quite this way; however, he does seem to assume that we are completely authoritative over what our words mean, for instance, when he writes that "Entities which are not intrinsically Intentional can be made Intentional by, so to speak, intentionally decreeing them to be so" (1983: 175).

The answer to this is that in fact we are not perfectly authoritative over the type of our speech acts. Though the intention characteristic of a type of speech act is precisely the intention to make a speech act of that type, that characteristic intention is not a necessary condition on the performance of that type of speech act. A person can make a promise without intending to do so, for we consider people to have made a promise if they give every appearance of having made one. Similarly, a person can make an assertion without intending to do so. Suppose I say something insulting about a colleague but misjudge the situation, thinking that everyone will recognize that I was only pretending to be the sort of person who would say such a thing about Professor Cheesewitz, when in fact my interlocutors all take my act as confirmation that I am precisely the sort of person who would say something like that. If I am supposed to be authoritative over the type of my speech acts, then we will say that I did not make an assertion; I merely acted misleadingly in such a way that people believed I had made an assertion. But I do not think that is what we would say. We tend to think that the type of a speech act cannot be very different from what it seems to be, so that we have to pay attention to make sure that what we do is what we intend to do. So what we would say is that, whether I had intended to or not, I did indeed assert that Prof. Cheesewitz lacks a philosophical temperament.

ANIMALS AND BABIES

Searle has another argument for the priority of the intentionality of beliefs and desires over the intentionality of utterances. He says that it "seems obvious" to him that "infants and animals that do not in any ordinary sense have a language or perform speech acts nonetheless have Intentional states" (1983: 5), and he says that before there was language humans might have had beliefs and desires (1983: 177). The fact that infants, nonhuman animals, and prelinguistic hominids have intentional states, if it were a fact, would not show that the intentionality of mental states is "intrinsic" in any sense, but it would show that the capacity for thoughts with semantic properties does not depend on the possession of a language, contrary to my hypothesis.

We can say that a baby "wants milk" or that a dog "thinks that its master is at the door" (Searle's examples), but it is a serious question whether we should take these attributions literally. If we think that the baby literally desires that it be the case that it drink milk, then we have to suppose that the baby literally has the concept *milk*. But I think it is plainly doubtful that an inarticulate infant literally conceives of milk *as such*. To this it might be said that our use of the word "milk" in ascribing a desire to a baby is just a kind of loose talk that we resort to because we do not know exactly what concept it is under which the infant thinks of that white liquid (cf. Searle 2002: 66). Maybe so, but then what is the argument? The force of the argument from infants and animals lay in its appeal to common sense and our ordinary ways of talking. If now we have to deny that our ordinary ways of speaking are to be taken at face value, we can no longer maintain that the sheer ordinariness of these ways of talking ought to persuade us that infants and animals really do have conceptually contentful thoughts.

In his paper, "Animal minds," Searle describes a dog barking up a tree and claims that the dog's behavior would be "unintelligible" without the assumption that the dog believes there is a cat in the tree (2002: 68). But is the dog's behavior any more intelligible if we are told that the dog believes that there is a cat in the tree? What does a dog expect to achieve by barking at a cat in a tree? If you tell me that the dog thinks there is a cat in the tree, then that does in a way explain what I see. It is a shorthand description of what has happened. Perhaps a cat ran into the brush toward a tree; the dog chased after it; but the cat slipped under the brush and did not go up the tree after all. But all of this is explanatory only because I know something about dog tendencies. I recognize the dog's behavior as an instance of a pattern. The description works just because the behavior in question is in some ways similar to the behavior of someone who literally believes there is a cat in a tree and has some reason to pursue that cat. But the description leaves me completely in the dark about motives and mechanisms.

There is, of course, an extensive literature on the cognitive capacities of animals and young children, which I cannot review here. What a review would show, I contend, is that there is no simple demonstration that nonhuman animals or prelinguistic children are capable of conceptual thought. We can conceive of a great variety of thought processes that might do a lot of cognitive work but which do not deserve to be called "conceptual thought." For example, there is the ability to track the movements of individual objects through space (cf. Pylyshyn 2003). The power of forming visual and other sorts of images may extend to the ability to imagine long sequences of events – including the consequences of one's own actions. There is also the ability to locate objects and situations in a multidimensional space of perceptible qualities, such as color, shape, texture, and manner of motion (Gärdenfors 2000). By locating objects or situations in such a space and comparing distances between them in this space, creatures may be able to recognize that an object or situation x is more like an object or situation y than it is like z and consequently to expect that x will subsequently behave more like y than like z. Before we concluded that we must attribute conceptual thought to nonhuman animals and prelinguistic infants, we would need to make sure that their cognitive achievements could not be just as well explained in terms of such nonconceptual mental processes. I am not confident that psychologists and philosophers have seriously tried to do that.[4]

COMPUTATIONALISM

Many philosophers of mind have been inspired by an analogy between the mind and a digital computer – the computational model of the mind. John Searle is definitely not one of them. He makes that perfectly clear in his most famous single essay, "Minds, brains and programs" (1980a). For those who are inspired by the computational model it is difficult to conceive of spoken language as the medium for conceptual thought for at least two reasons. First, the analogy is supposed to account as well for the processes by which spoken languages are learned. So the language of computation cannot itself be spoken language. Second, the meaning of spoken words is not always very clearly reflected in the grammatical structure of, and choice of words in, the sentence spoken. So computations cannot very well be defined over spoken sentences; they must be defined over sentences in the *language of thought*.

According to the computational model, language learning must itself be the product of computational thinking. If we allowed that something that is as characteristic of our kind of intelligence as spoken language did not rest on computational thinking, then we would have little reason left to think of thought as computation at all. Moreover, once we have supposed that language learning is computation, it seems inevitable that we will conceive of word learning as a matter of mapping spoken words into mental representations (Fodor 1975; Bloom 2002; Murphy 2002). Nouns, verbs and adjectives will be learned by discovering their extensions – by *defining* those extensions in the language of thought (which might give us their intensions as well).

The problem with the resulting theory of word learning is that it essentially begs the question by assuming that the mind already possesses a vocabulary adequate to the task of defining the extension of each of the words that can be learned. If we suppose that the language of thought is *acquired*, then we can ask why spoken languages cannot be acquired in the same way, without the language of thought. If it is supposed that the language of thought is *innate*, then the assumption is that concepts such as *parliament*, *Wednesday*, and *lepton* can all be defined in terms of concepts that were possessed as well by the earliest members of our species, which is not only absurd but also question-begging. It is question-begging because until we are told how the language of thought might have *evolved* in the first place, we may speculate that the process by which spoken languages are learned by individuals has much in common with the process by which the language of thought first evolved in the species.

It has sometimes been said that while this is a puzzle – how the concepts that the mind maps words into could arise in the mind or in the species independently of language learning – it is a puzzle that we *must* solve because languages clearly *are learned* and they are learned by means of *thinking*. On the contrary, while it is certain that language learning is the product of some kind of thinking, it is not at all obvious that the thinking that makes language learning possible is *conceptual* thought. There is some kind of mental processing that makes language learning possible, but we do not have to assume that that mental processing is a matter of applying concepts of a sort that words might be said to express. One can maintain that spoken languages are the very medium of *conceptual* thought while maintaining also that relatively little of the thinking that enables us to negotiate our way through life is conceptual thought. At the end of the previous section, I listed some other kinds.

The other reason I mentioned to deny that spoken language is the language of computation was that too much of the meaning that a sentence has in any given context is not explicitly expressed in the surface structure of a sentence. In all sorts of now familiar ways, which Searle was one of the first to emphasize through his conception of the "background" (1983: ch. 5), the words we explicitly speak may fall short of the meaning our utterances actually express. Since this meaning nonetheless *exists*, it is tempting to suppose that it must be somewhere explicitly *written out*, and for this reason one might posit a language of thought distinct from the languages we speak. For example, if someone says, "That one looks delicious," then what is written in his language of thought might be (i.e. translate as) "The peach pie that I am now looking at looks delicious." Or if someone says, "Samuel is late," what is written in her language of thought might be (translate as), "Samuel is late *for his dissertation defense*." The reason to think that the full meaning must be explicit in what is written in the language of thought is that only in that case will the computational processes of thought be sensitive to every part of what is meant (Pinker 1994; Levinson 1997).

This argument presupposes that the only way in which we can be sensitive to the meanings we express with our spoken words is by in some way *writing those meanings out*. In other words, it is presupposed, and not shown, that thought has to be treated as a process of computation. The presumption can be denied by allowing that another way in which the mind might be sensitive to the meanings expressed is by being sensitive to *mental imagery* that the speaker associates with the words he or she speaks. Or it may be that sometimes it is features of the situation in which the speaker spoke that determine aspects of meaning beyond those explicit in the sentence uttered and that the very availability of those features to perception obviates the need for the speaker to explicitly represent them at the time at which he or she spoke.

Christopher Gauker

MEANING AND COMMUNICATION

Above I complained that while Searle ascribes Intentionality to mental states, he declines to tell us what Intentionality is, excusing himself on the grounds that it is intrinsic. My assumption was that one cannot both maintain that *there is* intentionality and deny any need to explain what it is. I did not mean to commit myself categorically to explaining what meaning *is*. I acknowledge that if one sought any kind of reductive theory of meaning or reference, one would look first for an account that would apply to language-independent conceptual representations. The reason is just that if we posit language-independent conceptual representations, then it will be easy to suppose that there are many more of them than there are utterances in spoken languages, and so such representations will constitute a richer field of relations than the field of overt utterances in which to formulate our theories of meaning.

There are indeed many theoretical concerns that lead philosophers to posit something called *meaning*, or intentionality, and then to try to explain what meaning *is*. If we are to avoid positing language-independent conceptual thoughts, we will have to face up to these and show that they do not, after all, commit us to conceiving of conceptual thought as prior to and independent of spoken language. Here are some of the reasons why philosophers have thought it necessary to suppose that the world contains something called *meanings*:

1. *Translation*: What does the French word "maison" have in common with the English word "house"? An answer would be: a meaning (or, more precisely, a *character* in the sense of Kaplan [1989]).
2. *The semantics of "S believes that p"*: In the sentence, "Vladimir believes that Mark Twain was a Mexican aristocrat," what does the phrase "that Mark Twain was a Mexican aristocrat" refer to? An answer would be: a meaning (or, more precisely, a proposition).
3. *Logical relations*: What is the relation of logical implication? An answer would be: it is a relation of containment between two meanings. So one sentence logically implies another if and only if the first sentence expresses a meaning (a proposition) that contains the meaning (proposition) that the second sentence expresses.
4. *Communication*: What happens when one person says something and another person understands what has been said? An answer would be: the hearer grasps the meaning of the sentence that the speaker uttered (the proposition that it expresses in context) and on that basis

138

identifies the meaning (proposition) that the speaker had in mind in speaking.

I do not have space here to discuss all of these motives for introducing meanings.[5] But I want to say a little more about the last item on the list, communication, which in my opinion is the root of the others, both historically and conceptually. The basic idea is that the typical result of the speaker's speaking some words or making some other kind of sign is that the speaker and hearer come to share a *thought* – that the hearer comes to have a thought with the same propositional content as the thought that the speaker expressed with his or her words. On some versions, the hearer may be supposed to form a *belief* having this content; on others, the hearer's thought is only a belief that the *speaker* has a belief with that content. Further, there will typically be something about the speaker's words or other signs that the speaker and hearer understand in common, which could be called a conventional meaning. Different versions of the basic idea may offer different accounts of this conventional meaning and the role that it plays in bringing about the requisite sharing of thoughts. Call all of these theories collectively the *philosophical theory of communication*.

It is sometimes claimed that this philosophical theory of communication is supported by common sense. We do sometimes ask what people mean by what they say, and we sometimes complain that their meaning is not clear. But saying these things is still a long way from claiming that in general communication is a matter of grasping meanings. Our everyday talk of meaning normally occurs in the context of *conversational repair*. Someone has said something that we have not understood; so we ask "What did you mean?" and in that way elicit a reformulation that we might understand better. Or someone misunderstands what someone else has said and we clear up the misunderstanding by distinguishing between "meanings." It is not at all obvious that these devices of conversational repair reveal a commonsensical foundation for the philosophical theory of communication.

It is also sometimes thought that the philosophical theory of communication provides the framework for a psychological theory of language learning and language use. Some psychologists may indeed have taken the philosophical theory as a starting point, but it is not obvious that they ought to. Again, we may countenance varieties of thought – of mental processing – other than conceptual thought. Cognitive scientists have not worked very hard at conceiving of these other varieties because they have been fixated on a model of thought according to which thinking is essentially the application of concepts. Neuroscientists freely posit "representations," but the representations they have discovered (such as edge-detectors) do not much resemble the building blocks of judgment; so we should not be surprised to find that the most basic kinds of mental process are not well conceived as applications of the sorts of concepts that, according to the philosophical theory of communication, words are supposed to express.

Another place at which we might put to use the philosophical theory of communication is in formulating the *norms of discourse*. Talking is something that we think of as governed by various kinds of rules. There are not only rules pertaining to the *how* of speech – rules of logic, grammar, usage, and style. There are also rules pertaining to the *what* of speech – what we may say under the given circumstances. For example, we are expected to say only what we believe and, moreover, we are expected to speak only the truth. Thus, we could try to put a meaning-invoking theory of communication to use in formulating a norm of discourse, roughly as follows: we could say that a basic rule of language is that we should utter a declarative sentence only if, in light of the conventions of our language, it does express a propositional content that is the content of some belief that we actually have and which is true in the actual world.

This is not obviously the wrong way to think about the norms of discourse, but if we try, we might come up with some alternatives. A very different approach might begin with the fact that, as I said above in the section on speech acts, a conversation typically has a goal. An alternative approach to formulating the norms of discourse might be to speak of what promotes the achievement of the goals of a conversation. Roughly, what one should say is only what can be expected to promote the achievement of the goal of the conversation one is engaged in (in view of the conventions of the language and the actual arrangement of things in the pertinent region of space and time).

HOW WE CAN THINK IN LANGUAGE

Still, the question remains: how *could* spoken language literally be a medium of thought? Whenever we speak out loud, the *thinking* that is going on is the thinking that underlies and motivates the act of speech. So wherever we might be tempted to say that someone is "thinking in language," will we not find that the real thinking is this other process that underlies and motivates the acts of inner speech?

When we learn to use a language, we acquire an ability to coordinate our affairs with other people in a way that would be completely impossible without language. Having acquired this ability, we can apply it in imagination as well. We can literally imagine having conversations. We can imagine the various things that an interlocutor would say, and we can imagine the various things that we would say in response. In that way we can prepare ourselves for the conversations that we are liable to encounter and can solve problems in the way that conversation itself makes possible. My hypothesis is that there is nothing more to the process of peculiarly *conceptual* thought beyond this process of imagining conversations.

This is not to say that conceptual thought consists in verbal imagery. An actual conversation between two people does not consist in the auditory imagery it causes in the interlocutors. Likewise, a conversation conducted in imagination is not to be identified with verbal imagery. A conversation in imagination may not even be accompanied by verbal imagery. Sometimes we may be aware of a tone of a voice, at other times not. Most of the neurological processing that undergirds the process of imagistic thinking may remain in place even if the perceptual qualities (which themselves have a neurological nature) entirely fall away.

In identifying conceptual thought with imagined conversation, I am supposing that we wish to confine the term "thought" to inner conversations that cannot be heard. But in fact the distinction between covert and overt conversation draws no natural boundary. We might just as well identify conceptual thought with conversation *tout court*, including not only the silent conversations that a person has with himself or herself but also an individual's perceptible contributions to interpersonal verbal exchange.

NOTES

1 See, for instance, page 1 of Stalnaker's *Context and Content* (1999). Stalnaker begins by quoting Dummett, who says that a fundamental axiom of analytic philosophy is the priority of language over thought. Stalnaker then remarks: "I hadn't realized before I read this that the diverse strains of analytic philosophy were held together by such an explicit article of faith, but my discomfort in discovering that I was a heretic was tempered somewhat by recognition that I was in good company in my apostasy," and then he lists five other prominent philosophers who he thinks share in his apostasy.

2 Actually, on the basis of a conception of beliefs and desires very different from Searle's, I agree that they cannot be identified with particular neuro-physiological states (see Gauker 2003: chs. 10–12). But Searle might have formulated his argument just as well in terms of occurrent thoughts and volitions, which I *would* identify with neurophysiological events; so there is still good reason for me to challenge his asymmetry claim.

3 For a defense of this approach to the typology of speech acts, see Kölbel (ms). Kölbel proposes to explicate the constitutive norms in terms of intentional states. That is not the route I would take.

4 For my published discussions of some of the experimental literature, see Gauker (1990, 1991, 1994a, 1994b: chs. 8–10, and 2005a).

5 For an account of translation, see Gauker (1994b: ch. 13). For a treatment of belief-sentences, see Gauker (2003: ch. 12). For an alternative treatment of logical validity, see Gauker (2005b).

Chapter 7

Rule skepticism: Searle's criticism of Kripke's Wittgenstein

MARTIN KUSCH

1 INTRODUCTION

For almost fifty years now, Ludwig Wittgenstein's reflections on rule-following (Wittgenstein 1953: §§138–242) have been one of the most controversial topics in analytic philosophy. Saul Kripke's book *Wittgenstein on Rules and Private Language* (Kripke 1982, subsequently *WRPL*) is the best-known and most provocative interpretation of this difficult material. Almost all leading analytic philosophers working in philosophy of mind and language have commented on Kripke's interpretation (cf. Kusch 2006). In this chapter I shall assess John Searle's contribution to this ongoing discussion. The key text is Searle's "Skepticism about Rules and Intentionality" (Searle 2002: ch. 14, subsequently *SRI*), an essay in which Searle attacks Kripke's book head on. Although *SRI* was written in the early 1980s, it was not published until 2002. The time of writing explains why *SRI* makes no reference to any other contribution in the extensive "Kripkenstein debate." Searle charges Kripke with misunderstanding Wittgenstein's ideas and he maintains that Kripke's interpretation leaves Wittgenstein with a weak and unconvincing position. I shall seek to defend Kripke on both scores.

2 KRIPKE'S WITTGENSTEIN

The basic problem of *WRPL* can be summarized as follows, and independently of conflicting interpretations. Suppose you are calculating an instance of the scheme $x + y = z$ where x and y are larger than in any instance of the scheme that you have calculated so far. Assume for the sake of simplicity that such x and y are 57 and 68 respectively. Allow that you are near infallible in your arithmetical skills, and that hence you calculate that $68 + 57 = 125$. This is the correct answer. Or, rather, it is the correct answer provided you mean *addition* by "+"; it is the correct answer provided you intend to follow the rule for *addition*; it is the correct answer, provided you are committed to using "+" in accordance with the addition function. Imagine a skeptic who challenges you to justify your belief that you are so committed. The skeptic wants you to justify your belief that by "+" you mean *addition* rather than some other function, say *quaddition*. (The quaddition function coincides with the addition function if both x and y are smaller than 57. Otherwise the quaddition function gives the result of 5.) The skeptic insists that your justification take the form of your identifying a fact about yourself, a fact in virtue of which you meant and mean *addition* (rather than *quaddition*) by "+," a fact in virtue of which you were and are following the rule for *addition*. The "skeptical challenge" is thus *ontological* rather than *epistemic*; the skeptic seeks to show not that you are somehow unable to track the facts of what you mean, but that there are no such facts for you to track.

This skeptical challenge, Kripke suggests, is central to Wittgenstein's rule-following considerations. Moreover, Kripke argues that Wittgenstein was right to think that the challenge cannot be met: there is no "straight solution" to the skeptical challenge. The best we can do is to offer a "skeptical solution." According to the skeptical solution, meaning it is to be understood in terms of communal "assertability conditions." The meaning of, say, "Jones means *addition* by '+,'" is not given by the conditions under which this (type of) statement is true; the meaning of "Jones means *addition* by '+'" is captured by our rough and ready understanding of when it is appropriate to utter this statement. The "our" is important: Kripke's Wittgenstein insists that meaning and rules are essentially social phenomena, and that we cannot make sense of *private* rule-following.

3 SEARLE'S INTERPRETATION OF KRIPKE'S WITTGENSTEIN

Searle's *SRI* offers an interpretation and a critique of Kripke's *WRPL*. As far as the interpretation goes, the most interesting suggestion is that *WRPL* concerns two different forms of skepticism; I shall distinguish them as "skepticism$_1$" and "skepticism$_2$." Skepticism$_1$ is "about the presence of mental phenomena sufficient to mediate the relation between expressions on the one hand and concepts on the other" (*SRI*: 253). But skepticism$_1$ treats rules, concepts, and meanings as

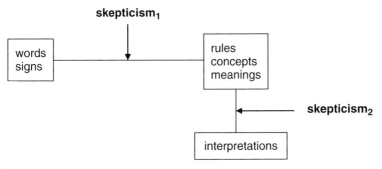

Figure 7.1

"absolutely clear, unambiguous, and unproblematic" (*SRI*: 257). In this regard skepticism$_1$ differs from skepticism$_2$. Skepticism$_2$ concerns "the traditional notions of rules, concepts, meanings and mental states" (*SRI*: 257). Skepticism$_2$ argues that these intentional phenomena can always be interpreted in many different ways. The difference between skepticism$_1$ and skepticism$_2$ is perhaps best captured in diagram form (figure 7.1).

As Searle sees it, the skeptical challenge of *WRPL* – "what makes it so that by '+' you mean *addition* rather than *quaddition*?" – betrays a one-sided preoccupation with skepticism$_1$. Skepticism$_2$ enters only once we consider the problem of meaning skepticism in general and drop the special restrictions of the initial example. Assume, for instance, that we drop the restriction according to which you have never calculated $68 + 57$ before. In order to block your drawing on the results of your previous calculations, the skeptic has to question the interpretation of rules learnt in the past. And this introduces skepticism$_2$ with its suggestion that rules do not have single and fixed interpretations.

Searle seeks to throw new light on the dialectic of *WRPL* also in a second way. While acknowledging that Kripke's analogy between meaning skepticism and Hume's views on causation is helpful, Searle finds another parallel even more striking: the parallel with Russell's skepticism about the past. The latter presents us with the challenge of ruling out the skeptical possibility that the world came into "existence thirty seconds ago with all of our fossils, memories, libraries, and photographs intact" (*SRI*: 255). Searle recognizes that Russell originally formulated this skepticism in an epistemic guise, but he believes that an ontological rendering is straightforward. The ontological form of Russell's skepticism can be couched in this form: "what fact about the present makes it the case that present objects existed in the past?" (*SRI*: 255).

Finally, Searle offers a distinctive reading of the skeptical solution of *WRPL*. According to Searle the skeptical solution is meant to "show how I can be justified in my use of a word, even while accepting the original skeptical argument" (*SRI*: 261). *WRPL*'s answer lies, in Searle's view, with the switch from truth conditions to assertability conditions. Assertability conditions provide me with the possibility of justifying my use of expressions. And they are not affected by the skeptic's critical arguments. Assertability conditions "depend on public agreement": "Any application of a word or symbol necessarily involves reference to a community and depends on there being general agreement within the community about the correct use of the word or symbol" (*SRI*: 252). A speaker who wishes to apply an expression correctly must speak in ways which others would agree with (*SRI*: 260).

4 SEARLE'S CRITICISM OF *WRPL*

Searle contends that Kripke's reading of Wittgenstein constitutes a "misinterpretation" (*SRI*: 251). Kripke not only fails to see the difference between skepticism$_1$ and skepticism$_2$, he also misses the fact that Wittgenstein's primary interest is with skepticism$_2$ (*SRI*: 253, 257). Skepticism$_1$ is much less radical than Kripke leads us to believe. It is unable to challenge even "the most naive Fregean view about the explanatory power of concepts"; for instance, it does nothing to undermine the claims that "the concept of addition explains the results of addition" or that "Jones's grasp of the concept of addition explains his results in adding" (*SRI*: 253). Searle defends his interpretation of Wittgenstein as a commentator on skepticism$_2$ by reminding his readers of a well-known example in the *Philosophical Investigations*. Consider the child who continues the series *2, 4, 6, 8* ... beyond *1,000* as *1,004, 1,008, 1,012* (Wittgenstein 1953: §185). Searle proposes that Wittgenstein is here highlighting the fact that rules are not self-interpreting. The child thinks that *1,000* marks an important arithmetical boundary after which the rule "add 2" must always be applied twice. What this shows, Searle submits, is that for Wittgenstein "there are facts of the matter [concerning rules and meaning], but [that] any facts of the matter about meanings are subject to alternative interpretations" (*SRI*: 257).

A further important objection raised by Searle concerns the skeptical solution. Searle maintains that the skeptical solution begs the question against the skeptical challenge. If we grant the meaning skeptic that there is no fact of the matter as to whether you are an adder or a "quadder," then we must also concede that there is no fact of the matter as to whether you have the concept of *agreement* rather than the concept of *quagreement*. And yet, if *agreement* walks the plank with *addition*, then the skeptical solution is rendered unworkable. After all, the skeptical solution is based on the idea that speakers make judgments about whether their verbal behavior agrees with that of others.

As Searle would have it, Kripke recognizes the force of this objection himself but fails to produce an appropriate rejoinder. Kripke grants that members of another form of life might apply terms like "agreement" in a "quus-like" way. But for Kripke this is no objection to Wittgenstein's project: "This cannot be an objection to Wittgenstein's solution unless he is to be prohibited from any use of language at all" (*WRPL*: 146; *SRI*: 260–1). Searle remains unconvinced; Kripke's agreement-based solution fails to introduce a relevant difference between truth conditions and assertability conditions: "The problem is not, as Kripke suggests, a difficulty in the attempt to get truth conditions as opposed to assertibility conditions. The problem is to get any rational constraint at all on our use of words, and Kripke's proposed solution does not show how this is possible" (*SRI*: 261).

Searle's discussion is not merely negative, however. He puts forward his own way of answering the meaning skeptic. As far as skepticism$_1$ is concerned, Searle's anti-skepticism is inspired by G. E. Moore who famously held that we can answer skepticism by relying on our common-sense knowledge of ordinary objects (1925; 1939; cf. Malcolm 1942). Skepticism about the external world is false since here is one hand, and here is another. Skepticism about time is false since I started writing this paragraph two minutes ago. Skepticism about space is false since I am sitting in front of my computer. And so on. Searle first tries out the maneuver on Russell's skepticism about the past:

There isn't any fact about the present that makes it the case that present objects existed in the past other than the fact that many existed in the past . . . The facts about this watch that makes it the case that it existed in the past are such things as that it was manufactured in Switzerland about forty-five years ago. (*SRI*: 262)

And since Searle deems this response successful he repeats it – *mutatis mutandis* – against the meaning skeptic:

if we take seriously the question "What fact about me makes it the case that by '+' I mean addition and not quaddition?" we would get facts like the following: I was taught to use the "+" sign for addition in school; and finally I got the hang of it. I simply learned addition . . . The fact about my past that makes it the case

147

that I meant addition and not quaddition is that I learned to use "+" for addition and not for quaddition. Period. And the fact about my present that makes it the case that I now mean addition and not quaddition is simply the fact that I mean addition and not quaddition. Period. (*SRI*: 262–3)

Searle recognizes of course that the skeptic will not be impressed by this reply. Searle's response is to shift the burden of proof. The onus is on the skeptic to force us out of our common-sense attitude – and Searle declares himself unable to find any consideration that would be up to the task (*SRI*: 262).

Against skepticism$_2$ Searle takes his lead from Wittgenstein's remark that "there is a way of grasping a rule which is *not* an *interpretation*" (1958: §201; *SRI*: 259). Searle develops this idea by drawing on his theory of the "Background." The background to our intentional states are nonintentional "capacities" ("abilities, dispositions, tendencies, and causal structures generally" [Searle 1995: 129]; "a set of skills, stances, pre-intentional assumptions and presuppositions, practices, and habits" [Searle 1983: 154]). The presence of these capacities radically restricts the ways in which rules can be interpreted: "In any given case of applying the rule, my behaviour is fixed by the fact that I have the rule and apply the rule only against a set of Background practices and capacities. I don't have to offer a new interpretation for the rule" (*SRI*: 264).

5 AN ALTERNATIVE READING OF THE SKEPTICAL CHALLENGE AND ARGUMENT

In order to develop a critical perspective on Searle's discussion of *WRPL*, I need to introduce, however briefly, my own take on Kripke's book (cf. Kusch 2006). This is the task of the present section.

In everyday life we occasionally say of other people and ourselves that they, or we, follow a rule, grasp a concept, or mean something by a given word or sign. *WRPL* is a critical study of philosophical analyses of such meaning attributions. Most of these analyses are based on the same "picture" (e.g. *WRPL*: 50). "Picture" here contrasts with "theory" (*WRPL*: 50). A picture of a phenomenon is rough, vague, only in part explicitly formulated, metaphorical, and amenable to different ways of developing it and making it more precise. One and the same picture can therefore underlie different, indeed incompatible, theories. I propose calling the picture under investigation in *WRPL* "meaning determinism." Meaning determinism holds that sentences of the form "person *x* means *Y* by sign '*z*'" (e.g. Jones means *addition* by " + ") are true if, and only if, x has a certain mental state. This mental state *constitutes* x's meaning Y by "z," or, put differently, this mental state is the necessary and sufficient condition for x's meaning Y by "z." Meaning determinism makes several assumptions about this mental state.

A first assumption, call it *Immediate Knowledge (MD-1)*, is that x usually knows this mental state "immediately and with fair certainty" (*WRPL*: 41). Assumption number two is *Privacy (MD-2)*. This is the idea that the meaning-constituting mental state is an *intrinsic* state of x; x could be in this state even if she had never had any contact with other humans: "a person following a given rule is to be analysed simply in terms of facts about the rule follower and the rule follower alone, without reference to his membership in a wider community" (*WRPL*: 109).

The third assumption of meaning determinism is *Grasping (MD-3)*. This introduces time and learning into the picture. Grasping has several aspects. *Grasping as Cause* is the idea that grasping a meaning at one time can be the cause of applying an expression in a certain way at a later time: "instructions I gave myself in the past compel . . . the answer '125' rather than '5'" (*WRPL*: 13). Acts of grasping are *private* (*WRPL*: 68, 79–80). The reason why acts of grasping can be private is that they consist of an individual's forming intentions, and thus giving herself instructions, concerning the future use of a sign (*Grasping as Intending*): "This is the whole point of the notion that in learning to add I grasp a rule: my past intentions regarding addition determine a unique answer for indefinitely many new cases in the future" (*WRPL*: 7–8). According to meaning determinism the sets of examples that are used in teaching are always limited in number. We learnt to add on the basis of a finite number of instances of $m + n = o$; and we were taught the concept *cat* on the basis of a finite number of cats. Because the "learning set" is always and necessarily finite in this way, grasping a meaning or concept has the character of an *extrapolation*. Let us call this claim *Grasping as Extrapolating* (*WRPL*: 7, 8, 82): "in this new instance [the query '68 + 57 = ?'], I should apply the very same function or rule that I applied so many times in the past. But who is to say what function this was? In the past I gave myself only a finite number of examples instantiating this function" (*WRPL*: 8). Closely related to *Grasping as Extrapolating* is *Grasping as Interpreting*. At least it is closely related as long as we just focus on the idea that learning involves an *interpretation* of the learning set: "the skeptic argues, in essence, that I am free to give any new answer to an addition problem, since I can always interpret my previous intentions appropriately" (*WRPL*: 32). "Can we conceive of a finite state which *could* not be interpreted in a quus-like way?" (*WRPL*: 52). Finally, meaning determinism uses the act of grasping also to explain why different speakers apply an expression in highly similar or identical ways. The reason why two persons x_1 and x_2 call the same animal "cat" is that they have grasped the same concept or meaning of *cat* in the past (= *Grasping as Explanation*): "we all respond as we do to '68 + 57' because we all grasp the concept of addition in the same way" (*WRPL*: 97).

The fourth assumption, *Semantic Normativity* (MD-4), is also best understood as a covering term for several specific ideas. These are: (a) *Non-Blindness*: if Jones has grasped the meaning of "+" then his use of "+" is not blind (*WRPL*: 10, 15, 17, 23); (b) *Guidance*: x's meaning-constituting mental state guides and instructs x on how to apply "z": "inner 'ideas' or 'meanings' guide our linguistic behaviour" (*WRPL*: 56); (c) *Justification*: since the meaning-constituting mental state guides x in her use of "z," x can refer to this mental state in order to justify her use of "z" (*WRPL*: 11); (d) *Justification of Unhesitating Application*: "I immediately and unhesitatingly calculate '68 + 57' as I do, and the meaning I assign to '+' is supposed to *justify* this procedure" (*WRPL*: 40); (e) *Left-to-Right Interpretation of Meaning Conditionals*: "If Jones means *addition* by '+,' then if he is asked for '68 + 57,' he will reply '125' ... the conditional as stated makes it appear that some mental state obtains in Jones that guarantees his performance of particular additions such as '68+ 57'" (*WRPL*: 94–5).

Although the fifth key assumption of meaning determinism, *Objectivity* (MD-5), is implicit in what has already been said above, it is useful to formulate it explicitly. The idea is that x's meaning-constituting mental state contains and determines all future, potentially infinite, correct applications of "z." Sometimes meaning determinists despair of explaining what the relevant sense of "contains" or "determines" is; they then qualify these verbs with the adverbial phrase "in a queer way" (*WRPL*: 52).

The sixth key ingredient of meaning determinism is *Classical Realism* (MD-6). Its core is the idea that "a declarative sentence gets its meaning by virtue of its *truth conditions*, by virtue of its correspondence to facts that must obtain if it is true" (*WRPL*: 72). The meaning determinist is committed to the ideas that meaning is given by (contribution to) truth conditions; that truth is to be analyzed according to the correspondence theory; and that propositions play a central explanatory role in the philosophy of language and mind (*WRPL*: 86).

The seventh and final assumption is *Metaphysical Justification* (MD-7). This takes us to the overall motivation of the meaning determinist. His overall goal is to justify our use of meaning attributions. He believes that our meaning attributions demand a philosophical license and that his project can deliver the goods. For the meaning determinist the justification of our meaning attributions must come from ontological considerations; it is an exercise in metaphysics (*WRPL*: 66).

Meaning determinism stands at the centre of *WRPL*. Chapter 2 of *WRPL* tests both the general "picture" and various attempts to give it theoretical precision. All of these positions are tested by confronting them with the skeptical challenge of explaining what makes it so that one means *addition* rather than *quaddition* by "+." The initial target is the picture of meaning determinism. The question is whether it has the resources to pick out a fact that makes it so that someone – Jones, say – means *addition* by "+." Two proposals are first tried out and rejected. According to the first, the "Use Response," it is Jones's use of "+" that determines whether or not by "+" he meant and means *addition* or *quaddition* (*WRPL*: 8). This solution fails. My past use of "+" is necessarily finite and hence it cannot determine a unique function.

The second response is the "Algorithm Response" (*WRPL*: 16–17). It holds that what makes "Jones means *addition* by '+'" true is that Jones is following, and has followed in the past, some algorithm for calculations with the sign "+." One such algorithmic procedure is the counting of marbles. Jones determines the result of $57 + 68$ by forming two heaps of marbles, with 57 and 68 marbles respectively, by combining the two heaps into one, and by counting the overall number of marbles. This response fails as well. Trying to identify the mental state that constitutes Jones's meaning *addition* by "+," the meaning determinist invokes other of Jones's mental states; to wit, the mental state that constitutes his possession of the concepts of *counting* and *heap*. And thus the real question, namely what makes it so that Jones has one concept or meaning rather than another, has not been answered.

It is at this point in the dialectic that more theoretically refined versions of meaning determinism enter the ring. A first such refinement is "reductive semantic dispositionalism." In its most sophisticated form it maintains that Jones now means *addition* by "+" since, *ceteris paribus*, he has the disposition to give sums in answer to queries of the form $m + n = ?$. Here the *ceteris paribus* clause involves an idealization of Jones's abilities. The skeptic argues that this cannot be right. Amongst other things, dispositionalism fails to capture *Semantic Normativity*. If

Jones produces "z" as a manifestation of his disposition to produce "z" under circumstances C, then he is not guided by the disposition. Compare: the sugar cube has the disposition to dissolve in water, but in manifesting this disposition on a given occasion the sugar cube is not guided by the disposition.

The second version of refined meaning determinism is the suggestion that "Jones means *addition* by '+'" is true if, and only if, it is the simplest explanation of Jones's operating with the "+" sign. The skeptic points out that this proposal violates *Immediate Knowledge*: if x means Y by "z," then x usually knows his meaning-constituting mental state "immediately and with fair certainty." The simplicity proposal cannot honour this condition since it makes knowledge of meaning inferential rather than direct.

The next step of the skeptical argument attacks a nonreductive form of meaning determinism, which submits that to be in one and the same type of meaning-constituting mental state is, first, to have one and the same type of qualitative "feel" or quale, and second, to know of this quale directly on the basis of introspection (*WRPL*: 41–51). Of course it takes little reflection to realize that this classical empiricist proposal is unsatisfactory: it fails to do justice to *Semantic Normativity*. This is most obvious in the case of *Guidance*: on the meaning-determinist picture, the mental state that constitutes Jones's meaning *addition* by "+," guides Jones on how to use "+," that is, guides him on how to answer plus-queries. It can do so – always on the meaning-determinist picture! – because it has intentional content; to mean *addition* by "+" is to intend *that* one use the "+" sign in certain specifiable ways. Unfortunately for the theory tested here, qualia do not have such content. And hence, on their own, they can provide neither guidance nor justification.

The next meaning-determinist proposal insists that meaning-constituting mental states are *primitive* states. *WRPL* prefaces its criticism of this proposal with two noteworthy qualifications: that the proposal "may in a sense be irrefutable," and that "if it is taken in an appropriate way Wittgenstein may even accept it" (*WRPL*: 51). Nevertheless, there is a "logical difficulty" about the idea that there could be "a state of 'meaning addition by "plus"' at all." The problem is that such a state would be a finite state of a finite mind. And yet, in order to be the state of meaning addition by "plus," the state would have to determine the results for an infinite number of plus-queries. The advocate of semantic primitivism owes us an explanation of how any finite mental state could possibly have this capacity (*WRPL*: 52–3). Otherwise the meaning determinist fails to remain true to *Objectivity*.

Finally, Platonism constitutes a different sort of semantic primitivism. With respect to the addition function the Platonist claims that it is primitive or objective in the sense of being fully mind-independent. The same goes for the objective senses *addition* or *plus*. As nonspatial and nontemporal objects, Platonic senses are not constrained by finitude. There is thus – *prima facie!* – no problem with them determining an infinite number of cases. Little reflection is needed to see that Platonism does not solve the problems of meaning determinism. Mental states are finite, but the addition function is infinite. How then can a mental state grasp the latter? The Platonist thinks he is in a better position to answer this question since between mental states and the addition function he places the objective sense. The latter is thought of as having both a finite and an infinite side: it is finite – one sense – and yet determines an infinite number of truths. But the advance is dubious: if we do not understand how a finite mental state can grasp an infinity, then we do not understand how a finite mental state can grasp a finite objective entity that determines an infinity.

6 ARE THERE TWO FORMS OF SKEPTICISM IN *WRPL*?

I now have outlined enough of my own understanding of *WRPL* to take on Searle's interpretation of the skeptical challenge and argument. First and foremost I am puzzled by Searle's distinction between two forms of skepticism in *WRPL*. Searle bases his interpretation upon the very formulation of the skeptical challenge: "what makes it so that by '+' you mean *addition* rather than *quaddition*?" Searle here reads *addition* and *quaddition* as referring to Fregean senses or concepts. But this cannot be right. Remember that Fregean Platonism is just one of seven different meaning-determinist answers to the skeptical challenge. If Searle's interpretation were correct, Fregean senses (or other intensional entities) would have to figure in each and every meaning-determinist proposal. And they do not. Thus we must read the skeptical challenge differently. When the skeptical challenge speaks of *addition* and *quaddition* it refers to concepts (or rules, functions, or meanings) "in extension" rather than concepts (or rules, functions, or meanings) "in intension." Addition-in-intension is an abstract (Fregean) object, while addition-in-extension is the set of all sums (cf. Pettit 1990). The skeptical challenge asks us to bridge the (assumed) gap between signs and concepts-in-extension. Concepts-in-intension are part and parcel of *some* answers to this challenge. If we read the skeptical challenge in this way, then Searle's distinction between the two forms of skepticism collapses. Meaning skepticism challenges us to provide a link between the two ends of Searle's picture – Searle's "interpretations" being our "concepts-in-extension." And there is no suggestion in Kripke's text that this skepticism can be subdivided into two distinct stages or challenges.

Second, what the skeptic shows to be multiply interpretable are not only, as Searle's skepticism$_2$ would have it, rules *qua intentional phenomena*, but various nonintentional mental contents and physical entities: past usage and learning sets, signs and algorithms, dispositions to produce sounds or scribbles, and qualia. Does this mean that Kripke's argument is in an even worse state than Searle alleges? I do not think so. I rather suspect that Searle misunderstands the main theme of *WRPL*. The ultimate interest of Kripke's Wittgenstein is to understand intentionality and intentional content; his study of philosophical accounts of meaning attributions is merely a step along the way. The question "under what circumstances is it correct to attribute the concept of *addition* to Jones?" is just a special case of the question "under what circumstances is it correct to attribute *any* intentional content?" Now since intentional phenomena are the central *explananda* of the whole investigation, the question cannot be whether they have unique interpretations; the question is rather whether a given intentional phenomenon – for example, that I mean *addition* by "+" – can ever be the unique interpretation of a given set of nonintentional contents. Put differently, the challenge is to show how we get from the nonintentional to the intentional phenomena; the challenge is *not* to show how we establish unique interpretations of intentional entities.

Third, assume that Searle were right about the two forms of skepticism. Even in this case he would be wrong to say that the skeptical argument leaves even "the most naive Fregean view about the explanatory power of concepts (meanings, rules, functions, etc.) ... entirely untouched" (*SRI*: 253). Assume the skeptic were to succeed in his attempts to show that we (*qua* meaning determinists) are unable to explain how any rule (concept, meaning, function) could ever be grasped. Surely this would throw doubt not only on the mental acts of grasping, it would also put the very existence of abstract entities like rules and concepts into serious question. These abstract entities and acts of grasping are part and parcel of the same general explanatory (folk) theory for making causal and normative sense of human behavior. We are accustomed to explaining people's calculations such as "$68 + 57 = 125$" by invoking their grasp of the rule of addition. Should that explanation break down because no sense can be made of the grasping, then the rule will inevitably be a second casualty. The inference to the best explanation that underwrites the assumption of abstract rules will have lost its basis.

Fourth, this leaves the question how Kripke's Wittgenstein relates to Wittgenstein himself. As we saw above, Searle does not find much in common between the two philosophers. My arguments in this section have made this issue even more pressing. If Searle is right to say that the real Wittgenstein is interested only in skepticism$_2$, and if I am right to say that skepticism$_2$ makes no appearance in *WRPL*, then Kripke really must have produced a "misinterpretation of Wittgenstein" (*SRI*: 251). But Searle is *not* right. It can be shown that "Wittgenstein's patient" is very close to the meaning determinist targeted in *WRPL*. Let me explain. Chapter 2 of *WRPL* is naturally treated as a dialogue between the meaning skeptic and the meaning determinist. The *Philosophical Investigations* can also be looked upon as a dialogue. Picking up on a familiar Wittgensteinian idea, we might label the two characters "the patient" and "the therapist." The patient holds and defends certain general philosophical views. These views change under the argumentative pressure exerted by the therapist. Now, the best way to address the question whether the key problem of *WRPL* is sufficiently similar to the central concerns of (parts of) the *Philosophical Investigations* is to ask how Wittgenstein's patient compares with Kripkenstein's meaning-determinist interlocutor. I believe that the two figures are fairly close to each other – close enough for Kripke's interpretation to be judged adequate. In order to see this, consider the following central pronouncements of the patient in the rule-following considerations (Wittgenstein 1953):

139. What really comes before our mind when we *understand* a word ... [is] something like a picture ...
146. The understanding itself is a state which is the *source* of the correct use.
147. "... In my own case at all events I surely know that I mean such-and-such a series; it doesn't matter how far I have actually developed it."
152. ... "He understands" must have more in it than: the formula occurs to him. And equally, more than any of those more or less characteristic *accompaniments* or manifestations of understanding.
153. ... the mental process of understanding ... seems to be hidden behind those coarser and therefore more readily visible accompaniments.

154. ... I employ the sentence "Now I understand ..." or "Now I can go on" as a description of a process occurring behind or side by side with that of saying the formula ...

184. I want to remember a tune and it escapes me; suddenly I say "Now I know it" and I sing it. What was it like to suddenly know it? ... "It's a particular feeling, as if it were *there*" ...

186. ... "The right step is the one that accords with the order – as it was *meant*." – ... [When I gave him the order + 2 ...] "... what I meant was, that he should write the next but one number after *every* number that he wrote; and from this all those propositions follow in turn."

188. [The] act of meaning the order had in its own way already traversed all those steps ... And it seemed as if they were in some *unique* way predetermined, anticipated – as only the act of meaning can anticipate reality.

191. "It is as if we could grasp the whole use of the word in a flash." ...

194. ... the possible movements of a machine are already there in it in some mysterious way ...

195. "But I don't mean that what I do now (in grasping a sense) determines the future use *causally* and as a matter of experience, but that in a *queer* way, the use itself is in some sense present."

198. "But how can a rule shew me what I have to do at *this* point? Whatever I do is, on some interpretation, in accord with the rule." ...

205. "But it is just the queer thing about *intention*, about the mental process, that the existence of a custom, of a technique, is not necessary to it." ...

209. "But then doesn't our understanding reach beyond all the examples?"

210. "But do you really explain to the other person what you yourself understand? Don't you get him to *guess* the essential thing? You give him examples, – but he has to guess their drift, to guess your intention." ...

213. "But this initial segment of a series obviously admitted of various interpretations (e.g. by means of algebraic expressions) and so you must first have chosen *one* such interpretation." – ... it must have been intuition that removed this doubt ...

218. ... the beginning of a series is a visible section of rails invisibly laid to infinity ...

219. ... The rule, once stamped with a particular meaning, traces the lines along which it is to be followed through the whole of space ...

238. The rule ... produce[s] all its consequences in advance ...

These statements characterize a viewpoint that is broadly meaning determinist. First of all, the patient analyzes meaning, rule-following, and understanding in terms of intentions (§§186, 210), and mental states more generally (§§139, 146, 152, 153, 154, 205, 210). Second, the patient adheres to *Privacy* in conceiving of understanding-constituting mental states as independent of social contexts, customs, and techniques

(§§147, 205). Third, the patient assumes *Immediate Knowledge*: mental states that constitute meaning and understanding are directly accessible and immediately known (§§147, 184). *Grasping* a meaning or rule appears in a number of ways: *as Cause* (§146), *as Intending* (§§205, 210), *as Extrapolating* (§§191, 209, 210), and *as Interpreting* (§§198, 213). Fourth, the patient believes that acts of meaning and understanding a rule determine how the rule *ought* to be applied. In other words, the patient is committed to *Semantic Normativity* (§§146, 186, 238). *Objectivity* surfaces in many places, culminating in the idea that meaning determines application "in a *queer* way" (§§184, 186, 188, 191, 195, 209, 218, 219, 238). *Classical Realism* and *Metaphysical Justification* are not mentioned in these passages most closely associated with the rule-following considerations, though the former is at least alluded to in §154. However, *Classical Realism* and *Metaphysical Justification* are themes that – as Kripke documents (*WRPL*: 72–86) – surface throughout the *Philosophical Investigations*.

It is true of course that Wittgenstein does not couch the problem in precisely the skeptical way Kripke does; we do not find the exact Kripkean skeptical challenge in the *Philosophical Investigations*. But this much deviation seems tolerable enough: after all, Kripke is offering us an *interpretation* of the original text, not a repetition or paraphrase. In any case, the adequacy of Kripke's interpretation should be judged on other grounds. The question should be whether the *targets* of Wittgenstein's therapist and Kripke's skeptic are sufficiently similar. And this question clearly demands a positive answer. The patient is a meaning determinist, and hence he must accept the skeptical challenge. To ask, as Kripke's Wittgenstein does, "How do my past intentions regarding the use of '+' relate to my current intentions?," is not to change the topic; it is to pick up on facets of the position of Wittgenstein's patient. Indeed it is to follow the patient's suggestions on how to approach the question of how a rule determines its application.

7 AN ALTERNATIVE READING OF THE SKEPTICAL SOLUTION

I also disagree with Searle's interpretation and critique of the skeptical solution. Again I shall begin by outlining my own reading. In the literature on epistemological skepticism it is customary to distinguish between two forms of anti-skepticism: "direct" and "diagnostic" (e.g. Williams 1999). Whereas the direct anti-skeptic *accepts* the terms of a given skeptical challenge, the diagnostic anti-skeptic *rejects* them.

It seems to me that Kripke's own distinction between "straight" and "skeptical" solutions to the meaning-skeptical challenge (*WRPL*: 66) is best understood as a special case of the direct-diagnostic dichotomy. Meaning-determinist responses all qualify as "straight," and only Wittgenstein's solution is called "skeptical." Meaning determinist answers accept the skeptical challenge and its presuppositions; in particular they accept the idea that meaning is given by (realistically conceived) truth conditions. Wittgenstein's reaction is different; he rejects that crucial presupposition (as well as other elements of meaning determinism). And in so doing, he develops a position against which the skeptical challenge is powerless. Wittgenstein is thus a "diagnostic anti-skeptic" (cf. Wilson 1994).

Chapter 2 of *WRPL* is entitled "The Wittgensteinian Paradox." What is this paradox, or rather, what exactly is paradoxical for whom? The correct answer is that the paradox exists first and foremost for the meaning determinist. Consider his position in light of the skeptical argument. For him, the meaning of sentences of the type (A) "*x* means *Y* by '*z*'" is given by truth conditions. Central amongst these truth conditions is a meaning-constituting mental state of *x*, a mental state that fits with the conditions of the meaning determinist picture. Let us call this fact a "meaning determining fact." Chapter 2 of *WRPL* shows that there can be no such meaning-determining fact. There can be no such fact because the conditions imposed by meaning determinism do not form a coherent whole. And thus the meaning determinist is in a quandary. He believes that (A) can be true only if there is a meaning-determining fact, and he believes, on the basis of the arguments given in chapter 2 of *WRPL*, that there cannot be such a meaning-determining fact. He thus has to conclude that (A) is false, and false for all its instantiations. Alas, to conclude that (A) is false is to conclude that (B) "[t]here can be no such thing as meaning anything by any word" (*WRPL*: 54). And this is obviously paradoxical.

Kripke's Wittgenstein accepts the skeptical paradox as a natural consequence of meaning determinism. Accept the latter, and you have to accept the former. But Kripke's Wittgenstein does not view the skeptical paradox as the correct view of meaning per se – for him the skeptical paradox merely shows that the meaning-determinist way of handling meaning attributions and meaning conditionals is hopeless (*WRPL*: 60, 71).

There are alternatives to accepting meaning determinism (as formulated in *WRPL*) and (therewith) the skeptical paradox. These alternatives fall into the three categories of "revision," "reform," and "revolution." The revisionist aims to improve particular theoretical renderings of the meaning-determinist picture without changing the picture itself in any way. This might, for instance, take the form of suggesting a more complex interplay of dispositions in order to protect dispositionalism from the normativity considerations. Reformers and revolutionaries go further and change key ingredients of the meaning-determinist picture. The contrast between reform and revolution is that between changing at most one or two of the elements of the meaning-determinist picture, and abandoning almost all of them. The first path is that of reform, the second that of revolution.

Kripke's Wittgenstein is a revolutionary by my standards: he accepts none of the central elements of meaning determinism; each one is replaced with a successor concept. Such a successor contains "all we can salvage of" the meaning-determinist notions (*WRPL*: 68). Here is a summary of the resulting position, as I understand it (Kusch 2006):

(W-1) *Confidence* (successor to *Immediate Knowledge*): subject to correction by others, we are entitled to ascribe meanings to ourselves.

(W-2) *Intersubjectivity* (successor to *Privacy*): attributions of meaning make sense only in a social setting. Assertability conditions essentially involve communities.

(W-3) *Primitiveness* (successor to *Grasping*): our inclinations to use our words, our feeling that we have "got it," and our first-person and third-person meaning attributions, are all primitive. That is, they cannot be explained by the grasp of concepts, or interpretations of our past uses or past or present intentions.

(W-4) *Intersubjective Normativity* (successor to *Semantic Normativity*): there is no special form of normativity based upon meaning-constituting mental states. We are guided by others; we justify our applications of terms, as well as our meaning attributions, on the basis of publicly available criteria.

(W-5) *Finiteness* (successor to *Objectivity*): the attribution of infinitary concepts to others is legitimate. But we attribute infinitary concepts on the basis of finite, surveyable, evidence. What makes this possible is that "our eyes are shut" in similar ways.

(W-6) *Assertability* (successor to *Classical Realism*): the meaning of declarative sentences is given by rough and ready assertability conditions, not by (meaning-determinist) truth conditions.

(W-7) *Functional Justification* (successor to *Metaphysical Justification*): our practices of meaning attribution are justified on the basis of social-functional considerations. To say that "Jones means addition by '+' " is not just a description; it is also to give Jones a certain social status.

Here I cannot discuss all of the successor concepts in detail; I shall focus on those that are relevant for a critical assessment of Searle's interpretation of the skeptical solution. Consider first the move from *Privacy* to *Intersubjectivity*. Meaning determinism assumed that meaning-constituting mental states are intrinsic states of the individual who has them. But if the skeptical argument is right, then meaning determinism fails: "having meaning-constituting mental states" cannot denote an *intrinsic property* since it cannot denote a *property* at all. Hence the skeptical solution discards *Privacy* and replaces it with *Intersubjectivity*. *Intersubjectivity* has to be understood in the context of *Assertability*. Rather than look for (possible) explanatory social facts that correspond to meaning attributions, we must appreciate that correction by, and comparison with, others is essential to all meaning attributions – even to meaning attributions in the first person. The very possibility of meaningful meaning attributions hinges upon this: since *Privacy cum Classical Realism* ends in paradox, *Intersubjectivity cum Assertability* is the only option. And of course, if *Intersubjectivity cum Assertability* is the only option then meaning and rule-following cannot be understood outside of a social setting.

The Wittgensteinian alternative to *Grasping* is to see linguistic inclinations as "primitive." When we give the answer "125" to "68 + 57 = ?," we do so neither on the basis of an interpretation of previous linguistic intentions, nor on the basis of having grasped the concept of addition. Our inclination to give particular answers to particular addition problems is "to be regarded as primitive" (*WRPL*: 91). That is to say, we are entitled to say that Jones has grasped the concept of addition because he has passed our tests, amongst which, say, is that he answers "125" to "68 + 57." We cannot further explain Jones's inclinations regarding plus-queries by drawing on concepts like meaning, intention, grasping, or interpretation. To give up meaning determinism is to recognize that none of these concepts can be used to explain linguistic behavior.

It is not just Jones's (or our) inclination to give particular answers to particular addition problems that is to be regarded as primitive. Equally primitive is his inclination to say "I have got it" when being taught how to apply a (for him) new word, and his inclination to self-ascribe meaning addition by "+." Here too the inclination is prior to, not dependent upon, any interpretation of previous practice, previous intention, or previous grasp of a concept.

Moreover, *Primitiveness* is important also as a phenomenon of *Intersubjective Normativity*. Consider the case where Smith tests whether it would be appropriate to assert that Jones means addition by "+." In doing so, Smith compares his primitive inclination to give particular answers to particular plus-queries with Jones's primitive inclination. And no less primitive is Smith's inclination to judge that Jones is an adder. None of the three phenomena involved – Jones's giving his answers to plus-queries, Smith producing his own answers, and Smith comparing the two – is based on the interpretation of intentions or concepts. As Kripke puts it: "In all this, Smith's inclinations are regarded as just as primitive as Jones's. In no way does Smith test directly whether Jones may have in his head some rule agreeing with the one in Smith's head. Rather the point is that if, in enough concrete cases, Jones's inclinations agree with Smith's, Smith will judge that Jones is indeed following the rule for addition" (*WRPL*: 91).

Finally, *Primitiveness* also concerns agreement amongst ourselves. The practice of attributing meanings to others could not exist if we did not usually agree in our responses and inclinations. If Jones's and Smith's inclinations to answer plus-queries differed radically, then Jones could never arrive at meaning attributions for Smith. And so for all concepts. We would be reduced to a "babble of disagreement" (*WRPL*: 92), and would lack a common "form of life": "The set of responses in which we agree, and the way they interweave with our activities, is our *form of life*. Beings who agreed in consistently giving bizarre quus-like responses would share in another form of life" (*WRPL*: 97).

Meaning determinism is committed to (the) *Objectivity* (of meaning). How does Kripke's Wittgenstein deal with the infinity involved in attributing addition (and other mathematical functions) to someone? Statements like "Jones means addition by '+'" have important functions in our language games of meaning attribution. We are inclined to produce these statements on the basis of a finite number of tests and comparisons with our own inclinations. This *Finiteness* is not a regrettable shortcoming that would introduce uncertainty and underdetermination. To believe that it is a shortcoming is to contrast it with an ideal, meaning determinism, that has proven untenable. At this point *Finiteness* links up with *Primitiveness*: *Finiteness* is not "a problem" or "shortcoming" since our inclinations are always already broadly in agreement. As Wittgenstein put it in the *Investigations*: our "eyes . . . are shut" in similar ways (1953: §224). This makes it unlikely, empirically unlikely, that our inclinations will deviate in the future. And it is this probability that makes it natural for us to always say more, in and with our meaning ascriptions, than is covered by our finite number of tests.

8 WHY THE SKEPTICAL SOLUTION DOES NOT BEG THE SKEPTICAL CHALLENGE

Searle claims that the skeptical solution begs the question against the skeptical challenge. First, if grasping truth conditions cannot explain how the use of expressions is rationally constrained, then neither can grasping assertability conditions. Second, the skeptical solution presupposes that we grasp the concept of *agreement*. But no such presupposition is legitimate. (Similar objections have been voiced e.g. by Blackburn 1990: 20; Cavell 1990: 75; Loar 1985: 278; and Wright 1984: 770–1.)

I beg to differ. The first thing to emphasize here is that assertability conditions are not supposed to play the exact same role as truth conditions. Assertability conditions are *not* there to be grasped (in the sense of *Grasping*). We cannot keep the overall meaning-determinist picture and merely replace truth by assertability conditions. Recall that *Classical Realism* goes hand in hand with *Grasping*, whereas *Assertability* is inseparable from *Finiteness* and *Primitiveness*. Assertability conditions are rough and ready glosses on practices, not necessary and sufficient conditions in order for an expression to have a specific meaning. Assertability conditions are not rules to which we commit ourselves in order to speak correctly. I calculate that $57 + 68 = 125$ not because I somehow have grasped my previous commitments to rules concerning the use of "+"; I calculate the way I do because I have been *trained* to operate with "+" in certain ways. Likewise, my judgment according to which my toddler-daughter means *addition* by "+" is also a primitive phenomenon. I do not arrive at my judgment by relating her behavior to my explicit interpretations of the assertability conditions governing meaning or concept attributions. Again, I have been *trained* to make meaning attributions, and to make such attributions is no less "primitive" a phenomenon than is my adding of two numbers. Both types of actions are primitive in that they do not involve intentional acts of grasping and interpreting rules and other commitments. Moreover, as creatures sharing the same "form of life," we tend to agree in our responses both to addition tasks and to the arithmetical behavior of others. And it is only because we so agree that assertability conditions *qua glosses on our practices* can be formulated and understood.

Searle accuses Kripke of making illegitimate use of the category of agreement. But here he conflates the empirical phenomenon of our agreement in (primitive) responses with possession and application of (the concept of) *agreement*. Kripke insists that there cannot be a solution to the skeptical problems unless members of the same form of life agree (more or less) in their responses. But Kripke does not demand that for two people to agree in their responses they have to make use of (the concept of) *agreement*. *Agreement* is just another concept or meaning; and thus it too presupposes our primitive agreement in responses. The dependence runs only one way, however; while *agreement* presupposes agreement, agreement does not presuppose *agreement*. In sketching the skeptical solution, Kripke's Wittgenstein does of course make explicit use of both the concept *agreement* and the expression "agreement." This would be question-begging only if the philosophical description of the skeptical solution were part and parcel of the skeptical solution itself – which of course it is not.

How do Searle's own anti-skeptical proposals fit with the skeptical solution, properly understood? What should we say about the neo-Moorean response according to which I am an adder because "I was taught to use the '+' sign for addition in school; and finally I got the hang of it. I simply learned addition" (*SRI*: 262)? To begin with, note that this response clearly cannot be taken as a defense of meaning determinism. The meaning determinist is committed to the possibility of *explaining* what makes claims like "By '+' I mean *addition*" true and meaningful. And this commitment to explanation surely extends to offering an *analysis* of what makes it so that I was taught addition rather than quaddition. Should we read Searle's neo-Moorean reply as simply a rejection of the whole explanatory project of meaning determinism? In some respects this might seem to move Searle close to the Wittgenstein of the skeptical solution. But then the worry must arise whether Searle does not go too far: his response is so minimalist that it does not even seem to leave room for the skeptical solution. Put differently, if Searle's response were satisfactory, there would be no need for a skeptical solution. Lest this begin to seem an attractive option, it is imperative to register that the whole skeptical setting of *WRPL* is really just a dramatic way of calling for an account of attributions of meaning and intentional content. In other words, to demand an explanation for why you mean *addition rather than quaddition* is just a dramatic way of pressing for an analysis of what it is to have the concept *addition*. If this is correct, then Searle's proposal is obviously inadequate: to say that Jones means addition by "+" because addition is what he was taught, is not much of an answer.

Searle's second, Wittgenstein-inspired reply to the meaning skeptic is more substantive. This is the idea that "there is a way of grasping a rule which is *not* an *interpretation*" (Wittgenstein 1953: §201). Searle puts flesh on this programmatic statement by linking it to his work on the "Background." Now, the first thing to say about this suggestion is that – contrary to a popular belief amongst Kripke critics (e.g. McDowell 1984b) – it does not run counter to the skeptical solution of Kripke's Wittgenstein. To see this we just have to remember that to grasp a rule without interpreting it is simply to adopt and follow the rule "blindly," without further reflection. And the role of such blindness is stressed repeatedly in *WRPL*. For example:

Even the very first section of the *Investigations* can be read, with hindsight, as anticipating the problem ... See: "But how does he know where and how he is to look up the word 'red' and what he is to do with the word 'five'? – Well, I assume that he *acts* as I described. Explanations come to an end somewhere." [Wittgenstein 1953: §1] In hindsight, this is a statement of the basic point that I follow rules "blindly", without any justification for the choice I make. The suggestion in the section that nothing is wrong with this situation, provided that my use of "five", "red", etc. fits into a proper system of activities in the community, anticipates Wittgenstein's skeptical solution.   (*WRPL*: 81)

In this passage we find not only the idea of "acting blindly" but also the further insistence that blind action *qua* rule-following is part of a communal custom or practice. Kripke develops the same idea in greater detail six pages later. He first emphasizes the importance of acting blindly: "The entire point of the skeptical argument is that ultimately we reach a level where we act without any reason in terms of which we can justify our action. We act unhesitatingly but *blindly*" (*WRPL*: 87). Subsequently Kripke goes on to remind us that there must be more to rule-following than acting blindly – there must be more for there to be normativity, for there to be a distinction between "is right" and "seems right." And this distinction plays a role when we assess the performances of others who are engaged in more or less ordinary practices (like going to the grocer). No regress threatens here, since our assessments of others are ultimately "unhesitating but blind" as well (*WRPL*: 90–1).

This brings us, finally, to Searle's emphasis on the "Background" as a way to flesh out Wittgenstein's "no-interpretation" thesis. Here too there is much agreement between Searle and the skeptical solution. Searle's insistence that intentionality presupposes a network of nonintentional capacities contradicts *no* element of the skeptical solution. This is not to say, however, that the Wittgenstein of Searle and the Wittgenstein of Kripke are indistinguishable. Some deep-seated differences remain. Perhaps the most important difference concerns Searle's willingness to speak of the "Background" in individualistic terms: "Even if I am a brain in a vat ... nonetheless, I do have the Intentional content that I have, and thus I necessarily have exactly the same Background that I would have if I were not a brain in a vat and had that particular Intentional content" (Searle 1983: 154). Although Searle adds that my Background is the empirical product of a "specific biological history and a specific set of social relations to other people" (*ibid.*), he shows little interest in the possibility that my Background functions the way it does only in and through my *continuous* interaction with others. But such continuous interaction is central to the skeptical solution.

9 CONCLUSION

In this chapter I have tried to defend Kripke's *Wittgenstein on Rules and Private Language* against Searle's criticism in his paper "Skepticism about Rules and Intentionality." I have sought to show that Searle's interpretation of Kripke's book is not adequate and that accordingly his criticism is not on target. In particular, Searle is mistaken in alleging that Kripke conflates two distinct forms of rule skepticism; he errs in maintaining that Kripke misinterprets Wittgenstein; he is wrong to suggest that the skeptical solution begs the question of the skeptical challenge; and he is not right to suppose that his own anti-skeptical arguments are sufficient for the task.

It might seem as if my argument has been exclusively negative – as if I could see nothing of value in Searle's criticism. This would be a misunderstanding. Not only do I regard Searle's discussion as a very important test-case for my reading of Kripke, I also believe the critical engagement between Kripke's Wittgenstein and Searle must not end here. On the contrary, I would like to think that this chapter is merely a preliminary to such an encounter. To my mind the really important question is how we should think of Searle's overall position in the philosophy of mind, language, and society in relation to *WRPL* and the positions distinguished there. To what extent is the position developed in *Speech Acts, Intentionality, The Construction of Social Reality*, and *Rationality in Action* committed to meaning determinism?

To what extent is Searle a reformer or revolutionary with respect to meaning determinism? And to what extent can he avoid the arguments of the meaning skeptic? These to me are the issues that really matter – but in order to pave a way towards them I here had to argue for setting aside Searle's own first attempt at addressing them.

NOTE

For comments and corrections I am grateful to Lorenzo Bernasconi, Jeff Kochan, Nigel Pleasants, Savas Tsohatzidis, and Marcel Weber.

PART II

From meaning to force

Chapter 8

How to say things with words

KEPA KORTA AND JOHN PERRY

1 INTRODUCTION

You really do not need us to tell you how to *say* things with words, any more than you (or your ancestors) needed J. L. Austin or his student John Searle to tell you how to *do* things with words. Austin's *How to Do Things with Words* (1961) and Searle's *Speech Acts* (1969) offered a theory to explain how we do things that go *beyond saying*: that is, how we perform illocutionary and perlocutionary acts in and by saying things.

In this chapter, we develop Austin's concept of a locutionary act, using the "reflexive-referential theory" of meaning and cognitive significance as developed in Perry's *Reference and Reflexivity* (2001).[1] We distinguish the locutionary content of an act both from what a speaker says and what a speaker intends to say. These three concepts often coincide, but keeping them separate is important in reconstructing the plans of speakers and the inferences of hearers, for those cases in which the concepts diverge are often of great theoretical interest.

Our plan is as follows. In section 2 we give an overview of our reasons for distinguishing locutionary content from what is said. In section 3 we explain locutionary content in the context of speakers' plans. In section 4 we look at a number of examples to show how locutionary content can diverge from what is said. In section 5 we compare our concepts to Austin's, and consider Searle's misgivings about locutionary acts. (We should emphasize that, although there are some differences between our concept of a locutionary act and Austin's, and although we disagree with Searle's rejection of locutionary acts, we see our concept of locutionary content as a friendly amendment to the basic ideas of the Austin–Searle theory of speech acts.)

2 LOCUTIONARY CONTENT VERSUS "WHAT IS SAID"

Pragmatics and the philosophy of language have put a number of pressures on the concept of what is said by (the speaker of) an utterance. First, David Kaplan and others grounded the concept of "the proposition expressed" in intuitions about what is said, to support arguments that the contribution names, indexicals, and demonstratives make to the proposition expressed is the object referred to, rather than some identifying condition that the referent meets.[2]

Kaplan distinguishes between the character and content of a sentence in a context. The character of the sentence, together with the context, determines the content; semantics spells this out. Since the content of a sentence is the proposition expressed, which is explained in terms of what is said, it creates a second pressure: *what is said* is (more or less) equated with what semantics provides.

A third pressure comes from Grice's (1975) distinction between what is said and what is implicated by an utterance. In the standard case, the hearer takes what is said as the starting point in inferring implicatures. So what is said has another role to fill, serving as the starting point of Gricean reasoning about implicatures.

These combined roles for "what is said" give rise to what we will call the "classic" picture of the relation between semantics and pragmatics. Semantics provides what is said as the input to pragmatics. In both speech act theory and Gricean pragmatics, as originally developed, pragmatics is focused on what is done with language *beyond saying*.

We do not think the ordinary concept of saying is quite up to meeting all of these pressures, and that this has obscured some issues about the interface between semantics and pragmatics. There are (at least) the following two difficulties.

On the one hand, as we argued in "Three demonstrations and a funeral" (Korta and Perry 2006), it is not always the *referential* content of an utterance that provides the input to Gricean reasoning about implicatures. Often it is some kind of *utterance-bound* or *reflexive* content. In section 5 we extend this point to speech act theory. Information that is required to determine the illocutionary force of an utterance is sometimes lost at the level of referential content, but available at the level of reflexive content.

On the other hand, and our main point in this chapter, it is necessary to distinguish between acts of saying and locutionary acts. Our locutionary content is, like the classical picture of "what is said," a form of referential content, and is intended to give grounding to the ubiquitous concept of "the proposition expressed." The problem is that the ordinary concept of saying is shaped by the everyday needs of folk psychology and folk linguistics, and does not quite carve phenomena at their theoretical joints, in the following ways.

First, saying is naturally taken to be an illocutionary act, of the same species as asserting, with perhaps somewhat weaker connotations. A speaker is committed to the truth of what she says. But propositions are expressed in the antecedents and consequents of conditionals, as disjuncts, and in many other cases without being asserted.

Second, the concept of saying is to a certain extent a *forensic* concept. One is responsible for the way one's remarks are taken by reasonably competent listeners. But locutionary content is not sensitive to the actual and hypothetical mental states of the audience.

Finally, what we take as having been said is sensitive to the information that the speaker is trying to convey. Intuitively, Joana does not say the same thing when she says "I am Joana," as she does when she says "Joana is Joana" or "I am I." An utterance of "I am I" would not commit her to having the name "Joana," but this might be the main information she is trying to convey when she says "I am Joana." Locutionary content does not have this sensitivity to the information the speaker is trying to convey to sort this out. Our theory is quite sensitive to such matters, but we do not handle this by stretching the concept of what is said to cover all needs, but replace it, for theoretical purposes, with a number of other concepts.

These three differences we illustrate and discuss by going through a number of examples in section 4.

3 LOCUTIONARY ACTS AND LOCUTIONARY CONTENT

The central concept in our approach is that of a *speaker's plan*. This is a natural outgrowth of the Austin–Searle concept of language as action, and of Grice's concept of speaker's meaning. Paradigmatically, a speaker utters a sentence with the intention of producing an utterance with certain truth conditions, and thereby achieving further results, such as conveying information to a hearer, and perhaps thereby getting the hearer to do something. So, for example, Kepa might say the words "I'm hungry" with the intention of uttering the English sentence "I'm hungry," so that his utterance is true if and only if he, the speaker, is hungry, and so informing John that he is hungry, implicating that he'd like to break off work to go to lunch, and eliciting John's response as to whether that seems like a good idea.

We take an *act* to be a specific occurrence, an *action* to be a type of act. In analyzing any species of action, one takes certain actions that can be performed at will, at least in circumstances taken as normal for the analysis, as basic.[3] These actions are *executions*; usually they can be thought of as bodily movements. By executing movements, the agent brings about results, depending on the circumstances. These actions, what the agent brings about, are *accomplishments*. Accomplishments can be thought of as nested, each action being *a way of* bringing about further accomplishments in wider and wider circumstances. We use "accomplishment" in such a way that accomplishments need not be intended. By moving his arms in certain ways, in certain circumstances, John may pick up the coffee cup; by doing that he may spill the coffee on his lap; by doing that he may burn himself. Kepa may say, using "accomplish" in the way we have in mind, "My, look at what you have accomplished."

For our purposes, we assume that we are dealing with competent speakers who can utter (speak, type, write, or sign) meaningful words, phrases, and sentences of English at will, as a part of a plan that marshals the requisite intentions to perform locutionary acts. This involves:

(1) Producing grammatical phrases of English, by speaking, writing, typing, signing, or other means;
(2) Doing so with appropriate intentions that resolve:
    a. which words, of those consistent with the sounds uttered (or letters typed), are being used;
    b. which meanings of those permitted by the conventions of English for the words and phrases being used, are being employed;
    c. which of the syntactic forms consistent with the order of words, intonations, etc. are being employed;
    d. nambiguities; that is, issues about the reference of names which various persons, things, or places share;
    e. the primary reference of demonstratives and other deictic words and issues relevant to the reference of indexicals;
    f. anaphoric relations;
    g. the values of various other parameters that are determined by the speaker's intentions.

(3) Having (possibly quite minimal) beliefs about the facts that resolve the semantic values of indexicals;

(4) Having the intention of producing an utterance that will have certain reflexive truth conditions, and of thereby producing an utterance with certain referential truth conditions, in accord with the beliefs in (3);

(5) Having (possibly quite minimal) intentions to accomplish other results by producing his utterance: conveying implicatures, performing illocutionary and perlocutionary acts, and the like;

(6) Accomplishing other results by doing all of this: conveying implicatures, performing illocutionary and perlocutionary acts, and the like.

In determining the locutionary content, the speaker's intentions (1) and (2) are determinative; actual and possible misunderstandings, however easily the speaker could have foreseen and prevented them, are not relevant. Thus the intended reflexive truth conditions will be what the speaker intends them to be, so long as the meanings and structures the speaker intends are allowed by the conventions of English. The speaker's beliefs in (3) are *not* determinative for locutionary content, however. The *intended* locutionary content will be the referential content of his utterance *given* his beliefs in (3). But the *actual* locutionary content will be determined by the facts, not by the speaker's beliefs about them.

Suppose, for example, that John is in the philosophy lounge, but thinks that he is in the CSLI lounge. "Kepa is supposed to meet me here," he says. He intends to use "here" indexically rather that deictically, and intends the range of "here" to mean the room he is in, not, say, the campus he is at or the nation in which he resides. These intentions are determinative. The locutionary content of his utterance is that Kepa was to meet him in the philosophy lounge, the actual referent of his use of "here." The intended locutionary content, however, is that Kepa was to meet him in the CSLI lounge, the place he thought would be the referent of his use of "here."

4 'LOCUTED' BUT NOT SAID: SOME EXAMPLES

Grice's main distinction in his analysis of utterance meaning is between what is said and what is implicated. Grice also remarked that there are implicatures in cases in which the speaker says nothing, but only "makes as if to say." Irony is a case in point. Let us assume that X, with whom John has been on close terms until now, has betrayed a delicate secret of John's to an academic rival. John and Kepa both know this and they both see X passing by. John utters:

(4.1) He is a fine friend[4]

Mere reflexive content will not do:

(4.1.1) That *the person that* **John** *is referring to by his use of "he"* is a fine friend [the reflexive content of (4.1)].

Kepa must go through sentence meaning to the locutionary content of (3).

(4.1.2) **X** is a fine friend [the referential content, and hence the locutionary content, of (4.1)].

Independently of what John might intend to communicate – typically, the opposite, or something implying the opposite, of (4.1.2) – and how the understanding process exactly works, it seems clear that for Kepa to take the utterance as ironic he has to identify the referent of "he" and the property of "being a fine friend," i.e. the locutionary content. Without identifying **X** and the property ascribed to him in the locutionary content of John's utterance, and as the **X** that has betrayed John's confidence in him, Kepa will not grasp John's utterance as ironic, and will miss the point. John may be *making as if to say* (Grice 1975), *pretending* (Clark and Gerrig 1984) or *echoing* (Sperber and Wilson 1986) a proposition, but definitely he is not saying it; he is not committing himself in any way to the truth of the locutionary content. However, this content has a role to play in the understanding of John's ironic utterance.

However the difference between saying and just making as if to say should be characterized, it seems clear that when a speaker is being ironic she refers to objects and predicates properties so as to provide content for her utterance that the hearer is intended to grasp. From the perspective of the speaker, this content plays a role in her utterance plan; from the perspective of the addressee, it plays a role in understanding the utterance. This content does not count as what she said because, possibly among other things, she is overtly not committed to its truth, and she expects the hearer to understand that she is not so committed, but it is a content anyway: a content that is locuted but not said.

In the case of many logical operators and other sentence embedding constructions, propositions are locuted but not said, as Frege pointed out, and Geach reminded a generation of ordinary language philosophers.[5] When someone says, "If Hillary is elected, Bill will enjoy his return to the White House," she does not say either that Hillary will be elected, or that Bill will return to the White House. These seem to us sufficient reasons for keeping a place for locutionary content in a theory of utterance content.

(4.2) *John is turning red*

In a discussion with alumni about politics on campus, Kepa says, "John is turning red." He means that JP's face is turning red, perhaps from anger, or eating a hot chilli pepper. The alumni take him to say that JP is becoming a communist. Kepa should have seen that people were likely to interpret his remark that way. Later he may protest, "I didn't say that." John might retort, "You didn't mean to say it, but you did, and I had to do a lot of explaining." Perhaps this retort is not correct. But the fact that the issue is debatable suggests that our ordinary concept of what is said is to some extent responsive to uptake on the part of the audience. What is said seems to have both illocutionary and perlocutionary aspects. In contrast, our concept of locutionary content will not depend on effects on the listener.

(4.3) *Flying planes can be dangerous*

Kepa produces the sounds necessary to say "Flying planes can be dangerous" [(1)].[6] He intends to be producing a token of "planes," not of "plains" [(2a)]. He intends to be using "plane" with the sense of airplane, not flat surface [(2b)]. He intends to use "Flying planes" as a verb phrase, rather than a noun phrase [(2c)]. These intentions are all determinative for the locutionary act.

They might not be determinative for what is said. Suppose Kepa and John are flying kites on a hill near the airport with some other folks. People have been discussing the dangers that birds, power lines, electrical storms, and other phenomena pose for kite flyers. Kepa has not really been paying attention, but is daydreaming about being a pilot. He utters, "Flying planes can be dangerous," somewhat loudly, to remind himself of the reasons for forgoing his dreams. Everyone takes him to have used "flying planes" as a noun phrase, and to have added a warning to the list generated by the conversation about the dangers of flying kites on the hill. Any semantically competent listener who had been listening to the conversation would have taken Kepa that way, and Kepa himself would have realized this if he had not been daydreaming.

When Kepa realizes how he has been taken he can surely protest, "I didn't *mean* to say that." But it is at least arguable that he *did* say it. Our ordinary concept of saying has a forensic element; Kepa would be responsible if a member of the group, frightened by his observation, quit flying kites. A discussion of whether he *did* say what he meant to, or said what he did not mean to, would likely devolve into a discussion about his responsibility for the effects of his remarks on others. But, to repeat, with respect to our theoretically defined concept of locutionary content, there is no room for debate. There are no "uptake" conditions, no forensic dimension, to consider.

(4.4) Aristotle enjoyed philosophy

Graduate students are discussing the life and times of Jackie Kennedy and Aristotle Onassis in the lounge. John comes in, and hears a debate about whether Aristotle Onassis enjoyed philosophy. What he hears is a loud assertion: "Aristotle despised philosophy and philosophers." He thinks the conversation is about the philosopher, and says, "That is the stupidest thing I have ever heard. Aristotle enjoyed philosophy." His intention in using the name "Aristotle" is to refer to the philosopher, and this is determinative for the locutionary content [(2d)]. The locutionary content of John's remark is a true proposition about the ancient philosopher. But it is at least not totally clear that this is what he has said.

One might object at this point that we are abusing the concept of reference. We are assuming that one could consistently say that John *locuted* (for we will now allow ourselves this verb) truly that one fellow liked philosophy, while, in the very same act, *saying* falsely that another fellow did. But surely he referred to one or the other, or perhaps neither, but not both.

Two points are in order here. First, the reflexive-referential theory sees propositions as abstract objects that are used to *classify* events of certain types (cognitive states and utterances, paradigmatically) by conditions of truth (or other relevant forms of success) – used explicitly by theorists such as ourselves, and implicitly in the practice of those who have mastered the propositional attitudes and similar constructions. We do not see propositions as denizens of a third realm to which some quasi-causal relation relates us, but as devices by which we can classify events along different dimensions of similarity and difference. Different propositions can be used to classify the same act, relative to different frameworks for associating success conditions of various sorts.

A normal assertive utterance will express a belief on the part of the speaker, it will have a locutionary content, it will count as saying something, it will be taken a certain way by listeners. When things go right, the same proposition will get at the truth conditions of the belief, of the locutionary act, of the saying, and of the resulting beliefs. But not when things go wrong. John's assertion expressed his belief that the philosopher enjoyed philosophy, locuted the same thing, but conveyed something different.

There are two quite intelligible routes from John's utterance of "Aristotle" to potential referents. One proceeds through his own system of mental files, back through centuries of commentary, to an ancient Greek philosopher. The other proceeds through the ongoing use of "Aristotle" in the conversation of which his remark is a part, back through the minds of the other participants, to decades of commentary in various supermarket tabloids, to the shipping magnate. While our ordinary concepts of reference and "what is said" are keyed to the successful cases, our theoretical concepts need to be more flexible. In a case like this, one choice of referents is suitable for understanding the utterance as the production of a person with John's beliefs; another is more suitable for understanding the effects of his utterance on the other conversants.

An analogy from the philosophy of action may be helpful by way of our second point. Indeed, given the Austin–Searle perspective of language use as a type of action, it is more than a mere analogy. We can classify the results of action propositionally, as is done with the concept of accomplishment explained above. By spilling his coffee in his lap, John accomplished a number of different things. He dampened his pants: that is, brought it about that his pants were damp. He wasted the coffee: that is, brought it about that his coffee was wasted. And he brought it about that Kepa was amused. And so on. Each of these accomplishments is used to characterize the act given various circumstances and connections.

We can also characterize acts by accomplishments they were intended to have, or would have had in various counterfactual conditions.

John wanted to bring it about that he got a drink of coffee; he might have brought it about that he had a seriously burned lap, or that Kepa laughed so hard he had a stroke.

Our practice of saying, and our concepts for classifying what we do in speaking, have the feature that, when things go right, a great number of different aspects of the act will be classifiable by the same proposition: the conditions under which the belief that motivates the utterance is true, the conditions under which the intended locutionary content is true, the conditions under which the locutionary content is true, the conditions under which what is said is true, and the conditions under which the beliefs that the utterance leads the audience to adopt or consider are true. This gives rise to the picture of a single proposition that is passed along, from a speaker's belief, to his utterance, to the mind of his audience. But the picture breaks down when things do not go right, and we need different propositions to classify different aspects of the act, relative to different circumstances and interests.

(4.5) You are late

Here is the situation. Kepa and John were supposed to meet at 10:30 at their office at CSLI. It is 10:35. Kepa hears the door handle turn, and hears the door begin to open. He looks toward the door and sees the shoulder of the person who is coming in, whom he takes to be John. He utters the words, "You are late."

Kepa's plan is as follows. He intends to produce a certain string of sounds that count as a token of the English sentence "You are late" [(1), (2a)]. He intends to produce these sounds as words and phrases with certain of the meanings permitted by English: "you" as a the second-person singular pronoun, which refers to the person the speaker addresses; "are late" as a verb phrase that is truly predicated of a person if that person, at the time of the utterance, is late for an event, which event being determined by the speaker's intentions [(2b)]. He intends to be referring with "you" to the person entering the room, whom he is addressing [(2e)], and he intends to predicate being late for the meeting they had scheduled, which is the event he has in mind [(2g)]. So he intends to produce an utterance **u** that has the reflexive truth conditions:

(4.5.1) That *the person the speaker of* **(4.1)** *is addressing* is late for *the event that the speaker of* **(4.1)** *has in mind*.

Given that Kepa is the speaker and the event he has in mind is the appointment, the incremental truth conditions are:

(4.5.2) That *the person **Kepa** is addressing* is late for **Kepa's 10:30 appointment with John** [truth conditions with speaker and (2g) parameters fixed].

Kepa takes it that the person he is addressing is John [(3)], and so intends to produce an utterance with these referential truth conditions:

(4.5.3) That **John** is late for **the 10:30 meeting between Kepa and John**.

This is the *intended locutionary content*. If Kepa had been right about whom he was addressing, it would also be the locutionary content. But given that it is not John, but Tomasz, whose shoulder Kepa sees, the actual locutionary content of his act is

(4.5.4) That **Tomasz** is late for **the 10:30 meeting between Kepa and John**.

In this case, Kepa produced an utterance with the reflexive content that he intended, but not with the locutionary content he intended. The locutionary content depends on the actual features of context relevant to indexical features of language.

We need to use the concept of the speaker's plan to approach concepts like "intended referent" or "speaker's referent" with the needed delicacy. Did Kepa refer to the person he intended to refer to? Yes, because he referred to the person he was addressing, just as he intended? Or no, because he referred to Tomasz, when he meant to refer to John? The answer is that Kepa intended to refer to whomever was playing a certain role vis-à-vis the utterance, and in this he succeeded, and he intended by doing that to refer to John, and in this he failed. Because his belief was false, his utterance did not have the locutionary content he intended it to have.

The conventions of English permit one to use "is late" to predicate being late for an appointment or other event, which need not be articulated, and it is in this way that Kepa intended to use the phrase [(2g)]. The conventions also permit one to predicate the property of arriving later than one usually arrives. Perhaps, independently of appointments, John usually shows up by eight, and is in the office before Kepa arrives after his train trip from the city. John might take Kepa to have used "late" in this sense and to convey not criticism in hopes of producing chagrin, but curiosity in hopes of obtaining information about what happened to get John off to a late start on this particular day.

For the locutionary act, however, Kepa's intentions in the matter are determinative. Even if John understands Kepa to have used "are late" in the second way, it does not matter. Even if any fair-minded observer would have taken Kepa to have used them in that sense, it does not matter for the locutionary content.

(4.6) I am Joana

With identity statements what is said seldom coincides with locutionary content. When Joana says (4.6) to John, the locutionary content of her utterance is:

(4.6.1) That **Joana** is **Joana**.

If this were what she said, she would have said the same thing by saying

(4.7) Joana is Joana

or

(4.8) I am I.

But only those with intuitions twisted by theoretical commitments would suppose that this is correct. So what is going on?

There are many people in the world who share the name "Joana," a number of whom Joana knows, and uses the name to refer to. The issue of which Joana she refers to is settled by her intention [(2d)]. In this case, of course, she refers to herself. So Joana intends to produce an utterance (**4.6**) with the reflexive content

(4.6.2) That *the speaker of* (**4.6**) is *the person the speaker of* (**4.6**) *is referring to with the name "Joana."*

Joana realizes that she is the speaker, and that she intends to use "Joana" to refer to herself, and so intends, by producing an utterance with (4.6.2) as its reflexive truth conditions, to produce one with (4.6.1) as its referential truth conditions. She succeeds in this, and so (4.6.1) is the locutionary content of her remark.

But our ordinary concept of "what is said" is responsive to the information the speaker is attempting to convey, which may be lost at the level of referential content. In this case, Joana might be trying to convey that her name is "Joana." This would be likely if she were talking to someone for a while, whom she did not have any reason to believe had ever heard of Joana Garmendia, but had obtained a concept of her, and would like to know her name. The relevant information might be identified as the truth conditions with the context and the meanings, other than the referent of "Joana," fixed:

(4.6.3) That **I** am *the person with the name "Joana" to whom the speaker of* **(4.6)** *intends to refer.*

Or perhaps Joana's interlocutor has been waiting for Joana Garmendia to show up to give a talk, but does not recognize her. Then the information she manages to convey is that the person he is looking at, and whose utterance (4.6) he hears, is Joana. She conveys this information by conveying the truth conditions of her utterance with the meanings fixed, including that of "Joana," but the context allowed to vary, so what the interlocutor grasps is:

(4.6.4) That *the speaker of* **(4.6)** is **Joana**.

Since the interlocutor identifies (4.6) as "the utterance I am hearing," and the speaker of it as "the woman in front of me," he learns that the person he has been waiting for is now in front of him, something he would not have learned had Joana said (4.7) or (4.8).

5 LOCUTIONARY VS. PROPOSITIONAL CONTENT

Our concept of a locutionary act is intended to be similar to Austin's. His definition was: "The utterance of certain noises, the utterance of certain words in a certain construction, and the utterance of them with a certain 'meaning' in the favourite philosophical sense of that word, i.e. with a certain sense and with a certain reference" (Austin 1961: 94). According to Austin, locutionary acts are what saying consists in, when taken in its full general sense. They are the acts *of* saying something in contrast with the acts performed *in* saying something. We formulate it as the difference between the act of "locuting" something (with a certain content, in our favored sense of the word) and the act of "saying" it (telling it, asking it) to someone. How faithful to Austin this is depends on just what he had in mind, which has been a matter of debate (cf. Searle [1968]; Strawson [1973]; Forguson [1973], for an early discussion).[7]

Surprisingly, Searle rejected Austin's distinction between locutionary acts and acts of (illocutionary) saying, arguing that "it cannot be completely general, in the sense of marking off two mutually exclusive classes of acts" (Searle 1968: 407).[8] From our point of view, this would mean that the same act could be an instance of two different actions, locuting and saying, and would not constitute a problem. Setting this argument aside, it seems that Searle followed Austin's lead, and offered a concept of locutionary act under a different label: the *propositional* act.

So, in order to clarify our concept of locutionary content, a comparison with Searle's propositional content will help. In (5.1)–(5.5) Kepa is talking to John; John is the speaker in (5.3), Kepa in the others, and all occur on Monday, May 14, 2006.

(5.1) Will I finish the paper by tomorrow?
(5.2) I will finish the paper by tomorrow.
(5.3) Kepa, finish the paper by tomorrow!
(5.4) [I hope] to finish the paper by tomorrow.
(5.5) If I finish the paper by tomorrow, [John will be pleased].

According to Searle, the same propositional content is expressed by the unbracketed parts of all of these utterances.

Within the reflexive-referential theory, there is more than one candidate for this content. For each utterance except (5.3) we can identify a reflexive content:

(5.x.1) That *the speaker of* (5.x) finish *the paper referred to by the speaker of* (5.x) *before the day after* (5.x) *is uttered.*

But this will not do. First of all, since the reflexive truth conditions are conditions on the utterance itself, the reflexive truth conditions for each utterance are different. Second, a proposition of this sort will not do for (5.3), where John is the speaker. So it seems our candidate for the common propositional content must be the referential content:

(5.x.2) That **Kepa** finishes **the paper** by **May 15, 2006**.

That seems to work for all of the utterances. They are all about a person and his finishing a certain paper by a particular date. They use this content in different ways but all locute or express it. It fits well our intuitions that, on Wednesday, May 16, Kepa could express it by uttering:

(5.8) I finished the paper by yesterday,

or John by addressing Kepa,

(5.9) You finished the paper by yesterday [as you promised].

It seems, then, that our locutionary content is just another label for Searle's propositional content. But there are some points where Searle's propositional content diverges from our locutionary content.

First of all, according to Searle's original view, there would be no difference in the propositional content of utterances (5.1)–(5.5) on the one hand, and (5.10), on the other:

(5.10) I promise to finish the paper by tomorrow.

Thus, the content of the (sub-)utterance of "I promise" would vanish from the content of (5.10) because its meaning, he thought, determines the illocutionary force and that is what we are trying to contrast the proposition with.

On our view the locutionary content of the subordinate clause in (5.10) is the proposition (5.x.2), but the whole of (5.10) has a more complex locutionary content:

(5.11) That **Kepa** promises at **the time of (5.10)** to bring it about that **Kepa** finishes **the paper** before **the day after the time of (5.10)**.

However, Searle changed his view on this point in his later essay, "How performatives work" (1989), where the propositional content does include the content of the "performative verb" and its subject, so this is a moot point.

There is a second and more important difference between propositional content and locutionary content, however. An important concept in Searle's theory is the concept of the propositional content conditions of a speech act. Some of these conditions are determined, according to the theory, by the illocutionary point. The commissive illocutionary point, for instance, establishes that the propositional content of a speech act with that point – e.g. a promise – must represent a future act of the speaker. The directive illocutionary point, in contrast, determines that the propositional content of a speech act with that point – e.g. a request – must represent a future act by the addressee.

We think that the locutionary content (or Searle's propositional content) is not the content that could satisfy the "propositional content" conditions of the speech act. Recall our basic picture: a speaker plans to produce an utterance with certain reflexive truth conditions, and intends to thereby produce an utterance with certain referential truth conditions, i.e. locutionary content. The level of reflexive content is crucial, because many of the effects that a speaker will intend his utterance to have will depend on the hearer's recognition of the reflexive content. This was illustrated by the discussion of identity statements in section 4. Joana's plan for conveying the various bits of information she wants to convey involves the hearer hearing the utterance and grasping its reflexive contents. The hearer can combine this content with what he already knows, and infer the information she is trying to convey. In one case, this was the name of the person he is talking to; in another, it was the whereabouts of someone whom he already had a "file" on, namely, that Joana is the person talking to him.

We call the constituents of the locutionary content, the places, things and people that are constituents of the proposition expressed, the *subject matter* of the utterance. So Joana is the subject matter of her utterance, "I am Joana." Often, the elements of the subject matter play a role in the utterance situation. Indexicals, of course, are the most explicit means of conveying this information. When Joana says "I am Joana," she conveys not only the trivial locutionary content, but the important fact that the person in the subject matter of the locutionary content is also playing the role of the speaker of the utterance itself. When John says to Kepa, "You must finish the paper," Kepa is an element of the subject matter, the paper-finisher, but also a part of the utterance situation, the addressee. This information is conveyed by "you." This sort of information is lost at the level of locutionary content. If the speaker does not get the reflexive content right, even if the locutionary content is grasped, important information will be lost.

We agree with Searle that the illocutionary point of an utterance is not part of the locutionary content or propositional content. It is a fact about the utterance that it is important for the listener to grasp, but it is not part of the proposition expressed. And we agree that certain illocutionary points (and forces) of utterances put conditions on the content. But it is up to the reflexive content, not the locutionary content, to satisfy these conditions.

It is in grasping the reflexive content that the hearer understands the intended relationships between the speaker and the utterance, including the time of the utterance and the addressee.

Consider again

(5.2) I will finish the paper by tomorrow.

and now compare it with

(5.12) Kepa finishes the paper by May 15, 2006.

Both of these utterances could arguably be uttered as commissives: that is, with that intended illocutionary point on the same locutionary content. But (5.12) puts a greater cognitive burden on the listener. To understand (5.12) as a commissive, the hearer has to have at least the information that the speaker is Kepa and the time of utterance is prior to May 15, for one can only commit to future actions, and one can only commit *oneself*. (5.8), on the other hand, cannot be understood as a commissive. The reflexive content of (5.2) imposes the right utterance roles on the finisher of the paper and the time of finishing; the reflexive content of (5.12) is *consistent* with them having the right roles in the utterance, and the reflexive content of (5.8) is *inconsistent* with them playing the appropriate roles; the finishing has to be in the *past*. Similar remarks apply to (5.3), uttered as a directive.

Searle's theory of speech acts poses two different tasks for the concept of propositional contents. On the one hand, it represents the basic content on which the diverse illocutionary forces operate. On the other hand, it is the content that meets the conditions imposed by certain illocutionary points and forces. But, as we argued for the case of the ordinary concept of what is said, these two tasks cannot be accomplished by a single content. The locutionary or referential content of an utterance can be taken as that basic shared content of different speech acts but, instead of locutionary content, reflexive content is needed to serve as the content fulfilling Searle's "propositional content conditions." The theory of speech acts, as well as the theory of implicatures as we showed in "Three demonstrations and a funeral" (Korta and Perry 2006), and the theory of meaning, content, and communication in general, would benefit if they adopted a pluralistic view of utterance content in terms of locutionary and reflexive contents such as the one we sketch here. They all are too demanding on a single content, whatever it is called: "what is said," "propositional content," "proposition expressed," or "truth conditions of an utterance."

6 CONCLUSION

The main focus of this chapter is the development of the concept of locutionary content, as a theoretical concept that is better suited than the ordinary concept of *what is said* for some of the theoretical purposes to which the latter has been put, especially that of grounding the concept of *the proposition expressed by an utterance*.

What does this tell us about how to say things with words? The important lesson, we believe, is that the intentions involved in saying something are not simply a matter of choosing a proposition to serve as locutionary content, and hoping that the uptake circumstances are such that one manages to convey the information one wishes; instead one has to focus on the reflexive truth conditions of the utterance one plans to produce, for only at this level can much of the crucial information, necessary to producing the intended cognitive and noncognitive effects, including the grasping of the intended illocutionary force, be found. The reflexive-referential theory allows us to incorporate this point of view into a theory that ties the pragmatics of an utterance closely to the semantics of an utterance, conceived (more or less) traditionally as a matter of its truth conditions.

APPENDIX: THE REFLEXIVE-REFERENTIAL THEORY

The reflexive-referential theory of meaning and content (RRT) has the following basic tenets and uses the following notation:

1. The basic subject matter of semantics and pragmatics are the *contents* of utterances, where utterances are taken to be intentional acts, at least typically involving the use of language. Utterances are assumed to occur at a time, in a place, and to have a speaker.

2. The paradigm is the use of a declarative sentence. For such utterances, the contents of utterances are *propositions*. Propositions are abstract objects that are assigned *truth conditions*. Propositions are conceived as classificatory tools rather than denizens of a third realm. Theorists use propositions to classify utterances by the conditions under which the utterances are true. This use of propositions is a development of a capacity of ordinary speakers, who classify not only utterances but also other cognitive states and activities by their truth conditions, typically, in English, with the use of "that"-clauses.

3. We adopt a notation for propositions that is compatible with a number of different theories of what propositions are, and choices of abstract objects to model them. The proposition that **Elwood** lives in **Dallas** can be thought of as the set of worlds in which Elwood lives in Dallas, or the function that yields truth for worlds in which he does and falsity for worlds in which he does not, or as a sequence of the relation of living, Elwood and Dallas, or in a number of other ways.

Now suppose that Elwood is in fact the shortest podiatrist. The proposition that **the shortest podiatrist** lives in **Dallas** will be the same proposition as that **Elwood** lives in **Dallas.** The roman bold-face in our language for specifying propositions indicates that the constituents of the proposition are the objects designated (named or described) by the boldface term, rather than any identifying condition that may be associated with that term.

On the other hand, the proposition that *the shortest podiatrist* lives in **Dallas** does not have Elwood as a constituent, but the identifying condition of being the shortest podiatrist; this is what is indicated by the boldface italic. This proposition will be true in worlds in which, whoever the shortest podiatrist is, he or she lives in Dallas. The proposition that *the shortest podiatrist* lives in *the city in which* **John F. Kennedy** *was shot* is true in a world in which whoever the shortest podiatrist is, he or she lives in whatever city Kennedy was shot in. This will be the same proposition as that *the shortest podiatrist* lives in *the city in which* the **thirty-fifth President** *was shot*. The boldface roman indicates that Kennedy himself, the person described by "the thirty-fifth President," is a constituent of the condition that identifies the city. On the other hand, the proposition that *the shortest podiatrist* lives in *the city in which the thirty-fifth President was shot* is true in worlds in which whoever is the shortest podiatrist lives in the same city in which whoever was the thirty-fifth President was shot.

4. RRT assigns *contents* to utterances based on the idea of *relative truth conditions*: given certain facts, what *else* has to be the case for the utterance to be true? We illustrate the idea with an example. Let **u** be an utterance of "You are irritating David," by Kepa, addressed to John, and expressing the proposition that John is getting on David Israel's nerves.

   a. Given that **u** is uttered by Kepa in English, and given the meanings of the words, etc., and that Kepa is addressing John, and that Kepa is using "irritate" with its meaning of "get on the nerves of," and that Kepa is using "David" to refer to David Israel, **u** is true iff **John** is getting on the nerves of **David Israel.**

   The proposition that **John** is getting on the nerves of **David Israel** is called, at various times, the *referential* content of **u**, the *official content* of **u**, and the content of **u** with the facts of meaning and context fixed and nambiguities resolved, notated "Content$_C$."

187

("Nambiguity" is the phenomenon of more than one person, place or thing having the same name.)

b. Given *only* that **u** is uttered in English, and given the meanings of the words, but none of the other facts listed above, **u** is true iff there are x, y, and z such that x is the speaker of **u**, x is addressing y, x is exploiting a convention that assigns "David" as a name of z to refer to z, and either (i) x is using "irritate" with its meaning of "get on the nerves of" and y is getting on z's nerves, or (ii) x is using "irritate" with its meaning of "cause inflammation" and y is causing the inflammation of some part of z.

The proposition identified by the sentence to the right of the "iff" is what the RRT calls *a* reflexive content of **u**. The word "reflexive" honors the fact that the proposition in question has **u** itself as a constituent; it gives us the truth conditions for **u** in terms of conditions on **u** itself.

c. Given everything in (b), plus the fact that the speaker of **u** is using "irritate" to mean "get on the nerves of," and is using "David" to refer to David Israel, **u** is true iff there are x, and y such that x is the speaker of **u**, x is addressing y, and y is getting on **David**'s nerves. This is also a reflexive content; it is what we call *indexical content* or Content$_M$ – content with the meanings fixed and ambiguities resolved, but not the contextual facts.

d. Given everything in (b), plus the fact that Kepa is the speaker, he is speaking to John, and is using "irritate" to mean "get on the nerves of," **u** is true iff there is a z such that **Kepa** is using "David" to refer to z and **John** is getting on z's nerves. Here the context is given, and the meanings that are being exploited, but the nambiguity is not resolved. Notice that the proposition expressed by the sentence to the right of the "iff" is not reflexive in our official sense; its constituents are Kepa and John, and do not include the utterance. However, it is not fully referential either, since it involves an identifying condition of David, and not David himself. Sometimes such contents, which no longer have the utterance itself as a constituent, are called "incremental," and the referential content is called "fully incremental."

5. The official or referential content is what is ordinarily taken as the proposition expressed, or *what is said*; that is the basis of the account of locutionary content in this chapter. But the other contents are available to describe the various communicative intentions and uptakes that occur, as is also illustrated by examples in the chapter.

NOTES

We are grateful to Savas L. Tsohatzidis for inviting us to collaborate in this volume, for his enormous patience with our delays, and for his helpful comments and corrections. We would also like to thank Joana Garmendia and Genoveva Martí for comments and criticisms, and the Center for the Study of Language and Information (CSLI) and the Institute for Logic, Cognition, Language, and Information (ILCLI) for support.

1 See the appendix for a brief introduction to this theory.

2 See the Peter–Paul argument in Kaplan (1989: 512ff).

3 See Goldman (1970) and Perry, Israel, and Tutiya (1993).

4 We will use citations such as "(4.1)" to refer to sentence types and also to hypothesized utterances involving those types; context should make it clear which.

5 Frege (1879), Geach (1965).

6 Bracketed items refer to the list of elements of a speaker's plan given in section 3.

7 Our locutionary content would probably be closer to Strawson's B-meaning, but we are not interested in exegetical issues here.

8 Searle does not distinguish between meaning and content, and this makes him sound quite a literalist, i.e. as defending that sentence meaning determines utterance content. That would contrast with his better-known contextualist views as exposed in Searle (1980b), for example.

Chapter 9

Semantics without the distinction between sense and force

STEPHEN J. BARKER

INTRODUCTION

At the heart of semantics in the twentieth century is Frege's distinction between *sense* and *force*. This is the idea that the content of a self-standing utterance of a sentence S can be divided into two components. One part, the sense, is the proposition that S's linguistic meaning and context associate with it as its semantic interpretation. The second component is S's illocutionary force. Illocutionary forces correspond to the three basic kinds of sentential speech acts: assertions, orders, and questions. Forces are then kinds of acts in which propositions are deployed with certain purposes.

There are at least five reasons for positing Frege's distinction, which we can discern in Searle's *Speech Acts* (1969) and other writings:

R1: It seems we ought to analyze assertion in terms of belief: assertions are acts in which we utter sentences aiming to manifest our commitment to belief states. Belief states are truth-apt. Therefore, the primary truth-bearers are prior to assertion. Furthermore, beliefs are propositional attitudes, states that comprise an attitude component – characteristic of belief – and a content. It seems reasonable then to equate the primary bearers of truth with the contents of belief states, and to claim that these contents are propositions. Thus the content of an assertion involves two components: a propositional content – the object of the belief that the assertion is a manifestation of – and a force – the act type which is that of committing oneself to a certain belief.

R2: To assert that P is to utter a sentence S with the intention of manifesting one's commitment to belief that P. But assertion must involve more than this. In uttering *I hereby commit myself to P*, I utter a sentence and commit myself to P, but do not assert

190

that P – Pagin (2004). The extra distinguishing characteristic of asserting that P is that the speaker utters a sentence S that *means* that P. To assert that P is to utter S, meaning P, and committing oneself to P. Here we have the idea of a sentence *meaning* or *saying* something that is distinguishable in its nature from the illocutionary act in which the sentence is performed. But that means a sentence has a component of content not captured by its assertoric use. That, it would appear, is its encoded propositional content.

R3: Part of doing semantics is providing a compositional account of how the meaning of a sentence depends on the meaning of its parts and their mode of composition. Compositional semantics can be divided into several parts. One part concerns subsentential constituents, such as names and predicates, and how they combine to form meaningful simple sentences. For example, one might think that a name introduces an object and a predicate a property. They get together somehow to form the content of a subject–predicate sentence. Propositions beckon as an explanation of such basic compositional facts since objects and properties have nothing to do with speech acts as such.

R4: A second aspect of compositional semantics concerns sentential compounds. In (i) below, *Fred is sick* is asserted as a premise of an argument, but in (ii) it is not asserted, yet these two instances of *Fred is sick* must, in some sense, have the same meaning if the validity of the argument here displayed is to be affirmed:

(i) *Fred is sick.*
(ii) *If Fred is sick, he will die.*
(iii) *Therefore, he will die.*

The common content that *Fred is sick* has must be assertion-independent. What else would this assertion-independent content be if not propositional content? Thus we should analyze (i) as a sentence with a propositional content plus something else, i.e. an assertoric force.

R5: A third aspect of compositionality concerns grammatical mood. The three mood-modified sentences

Fred jumps.
Does Fred jump?
Fred, jump!

all involve the same grammatical elements but combined differently. The content that *Fred jumps* shares with the other sentences cannot be anything that depends on its assertoric use, since the other sentences are not associated with assertion. Thus the common content must be assertion-independent. What is this assertion-independent content if not a propositional content? Denote it by <Fred jumps>. Structurally the content of the three sentences is given thus, where A, Q, and O correspond to three distinct forces:

Fred jumps $\qquad$ A <Fred jumps>
Does Fred jump? $\qquad$ Q <Fred jumps>
Fred, jump! $\qquad$ O <Fred jumps>

That there is a common content seems to be confirmed by the fact that the truth conditions for the declarative sentence, affirmative-answer conditions for the interrogative, and compliance conditions for the imperative can all be specified by the same condition: that Fred jumps.

With the sense/force distinction in place – reasonably secured, one might hope, by $R1$ to $R5$ – the problem of meaning is divided into two parts: *Pragmatics*, the study of speech acts and communicative structures, and *Semantics* – with a big S – the study of propositional content. The dominant form that theories of Semantic content take is theories of truth conditions – Davidson (1984) and Lewis (1972). Truth conditional Semantics has its detractors: Dummett (1976), Horwich (1998), Brandom (1994), who dispute that truth explains propositional content. They recommend that we look to other kinds of properties of sentences to explain their senses, such as verification conditions, certain use properties, or conceptual roles. Such critics of truth conditional semantics accept the force/sense distinction: the issue for them is how to understand propositional content as conceptualized within that distinction.

There is, however, a second more radical way of rejecting truth conditional semantics. This involves abandoning the distinction within which the idea of proposition lives: the force/sense distinction. The form that this more radical approach takes is the speech-act-theoretic semantics – STA – developed in Barker (2004). In STA, there is no distinction between Semantics and Pragmatics. The study of how sentences gain their truth conditions – *semantics* – is a kind of formal pragmatics, which is developed without the concept of a proposition. In what follows I block the five arguments, $R1$ to $R5$, for the force/sense distinction, constructing as I go the alternative STA: semantics without the distinction between sense and force.

1 ASSERTION AND BELIEF – *R1*

What is that peculiar activity we call assertion? Grice (1957) argued for a perlocutionary effect theory of assertion, according to which, in asserting that *P*, a speaker U utters a sentence intending to get an audience to have a belief that *P*, or a belief that U has a belief that *P*. Such *perlocutionary effect* theories have big problems – see Alston (2000). I offer instead a non-perlocutionary-effect theory. Assertion is an act in which a speaker utters a sentence and *defends* a state of mind. To defend a state of mind is to take epistemic authority for tokening a property Π, where Π is a mental property – or state of mind type. To take epistemic authority for a tokened mental state is to represent oneself as able to offer reasons for that state: sufficient reasons. So in asserting that the sky is blue, U defends a mental property Π of some kind, representing herself as possessing reasons for that state. If she is sincere and clear-headed, she has the state, if she is insincere, or muddled, she does not. U's audience H will consider U's assertion right, just in case she too is willing to make the assertion, that is, defend the state of mind Π concerned. Given that assertions are defenses of Π-properties, as we might call them, truth evaluation has the following *Intersubjective Dimension*, **ID**:

ID: H judges true an assertion of *S* uttered by U conveying that she, U, defends Π iff H judges that she, H, defends Π in her own case.[1]

ID is not an account of what truth consists in; it is no invitation to anti-realism or idealism. **ID** simply follows from the fact that an assertion of *S* commits U to an assertion of *S is true*, and vice versa, and assertion is the defense of a Π-property.

What is the state of mind Π that is defended? Those wedded to Frege's distinction between sense and force answer that this state Π is a belief state. Assertion is analyzed in terms of belief as outlined in *R1*. And that means truth is prior to assertion, and the primary truth-bearers are certain nonassertions. To block *R1* we need, it seems, to deny that the Π-properties defended in assertion are belief states. The general thought I propose is this: although broadly specifiable as cognitive or conative properties, Π-properties are not truth-apt states. Π-properties are functional states of various kinds; they can cause

Table 9.1

		Orthodox Semantics	STA
Act	Assertion: Production of *S* defending Π.	Truth-apt (Secondary)	Truth-apt (Primary)
State	Π	Truth-apt (Primary). Belief state ontologically prior to assertion.	Not a belief state. Non-truth-apt.

behavior, and be caused by and cause other instantiations of Π-properties. But they are not beliefs. Assertion, judgment, and belief are all found on a level of cognition above that of Π-properties. This is a level of cognition that involves symbol manipulation that presupposes instantiation of Π-properties. Assertion and judgment are the production of symbols, either public or private, involving defense of a certain Π-property. Belief is a disposition to perform that kind of defensive act; it is a disposition to produce symbols, either public or private, defending a certain Π-property, where that Π-property is actually possessed.[2] The Π-property itself is not the belief state; the belief is rather the disposition to defend the Π-property through symbol production. Truth-aptness then is not a feature of states that preexist assertion; rather it only arises with assertion. The primary truth-bearers are assertions. Structurally we can represent this approach, which is the basic move of STA distinguishing it from orthodox semantics, in table 9.1. STA is a dialectical conception of truth-bearers, since according to it, truth-aptness only arises at the domain in which reason operates. It might be objected that reason presupposes truth-apt states. Reason is about relations between truth-apt states or contents. Thus if reason is brought in to explain assertion we are back to commitment to truth-apt states that are ontologically prior to assertion. *R1* reasserts itself.

My response here is to deny that reason is fundamentally grounded in relations between truth-apt states. Reason is associated with inference, and the correlates of inferences on the level of intentional systems are *transitional states*: causal regularities of an intentional system that link instantiation of one Π-property Ψ to instantiation of another Σ. I call such transitional states *commitment laws* or *C-laws*, which we represent thus: Ψ → Σ. Think of U's intentional system, at one level, as a web of instantiated Π-properties bound together in part by C-laws, which are themselves Π-properties. What makes the relation → a relation of reason is a certain functional role in relation to inputs and outputs.

Even if some such natural characterization of the reason relation were available, a further critical question would remain: what makes an instance of Ψ → Σ right or valid? One answer is that Ψ → Σ is a valid relation of reason because if Ψ is true then the state Σ must be true. Another is that Ψ → Σ is valid if and only if a warrant for Ψ provides a warrant for Σ. Both these analyses assume that the states Ψ and Σ are truth-apt or doxastic states. Thus, short of treating validity as a primitive fact – surely an unattractive option – it would appear that the need to assign normative status to C-laws as right drives us back to viewing Π-properties as already belief states, and thus into the arms of *R1*.

Fortunately there is a way out. This is to embrace *expressivism* about reason and norms. In order to understand the notion of validity as it applies to C-laws we should not frame the issue in terms of what constitutes the rightness of a certain C-law. Rather we should ask: what goes on when we assert the rightness of a C-law, or more generally, what goes on when we assert that something is a reason for something else? I deal with this question now and show how judgments about the rightness of Ψ → Σ do not imply that Ψ and Σ are truth-apt.

1.1 *Reason and normative expressivism*

Suppose that to assert P is to defend Ψ and that to assert S is to defend Σ. Our concern is what Π-property is defended in asserting R:

R: Asserting/believing that P is a reason for asserting/believing that S.

The answer is that U utters R defending her acceptance of the state: Ψ → Σ. Sentences of the form R have the Π-property specification given in table 9.2 – this is the kind of Π-property that is associated with such assertions by virtue of meaning and context.[3]

In accordance with **ID**, an audience H will judge assertions of R true if and only if she herself experiences the C-law as something compelling in

Table 9.2

Assertion (of reason)	Π-Property specification
Believing P is a reason for believing S	Π-[P] → Π-[S]

her case; she instantiates the state and feels compelled to defend it. Thus, in terms of **ID**, the following holds:

ID-Reason: H judges true an assertion of R uttered by U defending possession of $\Psi \rightarrow \Sigma$ iff H judges that she, H, defends commitment to $\Psi \rightarrow \Sigma$ in her own case.

In asserting R, U is not making an autobiographical claim about her possession of $\Psi \rightarrow \Sigma$. U's statement is not true in virtue of her possession of the state. U is not claiming that members of some class of intentional systems possess the state. Rather, assertions of R are *expressive assertions* in the sense that what U defends is the state itself, not some commitment about her possession of the state. U's utterance is not *about* her instantiating the state Π-$[P] \rightarrow \Pi$-$[S]$. To assume that it must be is to embrace orthodox semantics which treats contents as propositions. U's statement is an expressive commitment to the state.

C-laws are then simply causal facts about particular speakers; it is our attitude in relation to them – which involves our willingness to defend or reject them, through assertions like R – that allows for the emergence of normative judgment. Of course defending a C-law $\Psi \rightarrow \Sigma$ may mean invoking other C-laws. But that is not in itself problematic.

OBJECTIVITY AND NORMATIVE FACTS. To assert statements of reason then is to utter sentences like R defending Π-properties that are C-laws: $\Psi \rightarrow \Sigma$. Π-properties of the form $\Psi \rightarrow \Sigma$ are not belief states as such. The state $\Psi \rightarrow \Sigma$ is not truth-apt. Only the assertions of defending such states are truth-apt. The states Ψ and Σ do not have to be thought of as truth-apt in explaining how claims of validity of reason function.

The idea then is that we account for the nature of reason statements by describing the natural facts about activities of speakers defending C-law Π-properties. We do not specify truth conditions for statements of reason as a way of capturing their content. One might object that STA's analysis of reason statements is manifestly inadequate for this very reason. By not offering truth conditions, or conditions of correct use, it misses a crucial feature; that there are facts of the matter over and above what people are inclined to believe about what reason statements are true: in short, the objective normative facts. The objectivity of a discourse resides in the sentences of that discourse validating bivalence: *either S is true or S is false*. But, the objection goes, it is because sentences in a domain D represent, or have truth conditions about, possible conditions of a determinate reality, that sentences in D are bivalent.[4] Thus we need propositional content to explain bivalence. STA's purely expressive treatment of reason assertions cannot then work.

Fortunately, this objection, natural in many ways, is without cogency. The explanation of bivalence gestured at invokes the idea of sentences representing reality whose structure is determinate. For this explanation to be nonvacuous, reality's being determinate must involve something more than our readiness to affirm bivalence or excluded middle for sentences about it. If not, the explanation invokes the very principle of bivalence we are trying to explain. However, reflection indicates that determinacy is little more than a commitment to bivalence or excluded middle.[5] So the appeal to representing determinate reality cannot explain our adherence to bivalence and excluded middle. Consequently, *pace* the argument just rehearsed, the fact that assertions of reason do not function in terms of representational content does not undermine a bivalent attitude to such assertions.

What then is the source of our affirmation of bivalence for sentences in a domain *D*? STA proposes that it resides in our attitude to the defense of Π-properties for sentences in *D*. It is our vigorous defense of Π-properties in *D* – the fact that we do not ever agree to disagree about acceptance of Π-properties – that grounds our assertion of bivalence in *D*. If such conditions hold for discourse, there is no *faultless disagreement*. Our robust defense of Π-properties in *D*, however, is not explained by our taking them to represent a determinate reality, since *determinate reality* presupposes excluded middle.[6] The attitudes have natural explanations: it has profited humans to have such attitudes to Π-properties concerning C-laws. In renouncing representation in this way, STA is not committed to an idealism in which objectivity is constituted by our attitudes. Objectivity is not constituted by anything, since *objective*, like *is a reason for*, is an expressive concept. To assert that assertions in *D* are objective is to expressively commit oneself to vigorous defense of Π-properties in *D*. In short, STA rejects the equation of *fact-stating* with *representational* and of *non-fact-stating* with *expressive*.

1.2 *A plurality of Π-properties*

Statements of reason then involve defending functional states or C-laws of the form $\Psi \rightarrow \Sigma$. STA is wedded to normative expressivism, or cognitive irrealism, about reason. It is not required as such that assertors have concepts of reason: defending can involve offering or indicating grounds. A child who asserts that Toby the dog is sleeping can point to a sleeping dog. In that sense we can see that the child is disposed to engage in defense.

What generally are the Π-properties, the states Ψ and Σ linked in C-laws? The question is partially empirical – it depends on the kinds of functional states minds can have – and partially metaphysical – it depends on broad assumptions about the structure of reality. In what follows I look very briefly at two classes of cases. The Π-properties of logically simple sentences and those of logically complex sentences. My main task will be to dispel the idea that we need to look at Π-properties as belief states.

LOGICALLY SIMPLE SENTENCES. Sentences like *Haggis is tasty*, *The Tractatus is interesting*, *Murder is wrong*, which is to say, broadly evaluative sentences, are perfect illustrations of the advantages of not treating Π-properties as belief states. Table 9.3 shows hypotheses about what the Π-properties of such sentences are. They are affective states of various kinds. Again, fitting in with **ID**, we find that evaluation of such sentences – for example, of the Haggis-sentence – has the following form:

ID-Haggis: H judges true an assertion of *Haggis is tasty* uttered by U defending her preference for haggis iff H judges that she, H, defends that preference in her own case.

Thus H finds U's assertion of taste right, just in case, H too defends the state that U defends, that is, just in case, she has good reasons, by her lights, to like haggis. Potential intersubjective engagement releases speakers from the solipsism of their own orientations and preferences. Statements of moral value have exactly the same general discourse structure. The difference is that in the case of moral statements speakers may defend the Π-properties concerned more vigorously. Thus there

Table 9.3

Sentence (value)	Π-Property specification
Haggis is tasty	Possessing a gustatory preference state for haggis
The Tractatus is interesting	Being disposed to find a certain intellectual satisfaction in engaging with *The Tractatus*
Murder is wrong	Being disposed to seriously disapprove of acts of murder

are no properties of tastiness or of interest, *qua* entities, which these statements represent. In such cases, the Π-properties are clearly nothing like belief states. And that is a good thing. To insist on the Frege model here only forces us into the problem of value realism, which is clearly problematic.

REPRESENTATION AND BELIEF. The statements just looked at are nonrepresentational in the sense that their predicates do not denote properties, *qua* world parts. One tempting idea is that some logically simple sentences must involve Π-properties that are representational. And it is here that the Fregean paradigm might reassert itself with the following line of thought: Π-properties that are representational should be equated with belief states since what is a belief state, if not a representational state?

The kinds of cases we might have in mind here are nonevaluative empirical sentences such as *Fred is pink*, *George is a cat*, etc. In these cases one might think that the Π-properties defended are ones in which we represent the pinkness of Fred, or the catishness of George. That means having a mental state that represents Fred being pink and George being a cat. But, goes the charge, such states are, more or less, belief states.

Suppose that we granted that some logically simple sentences need to be construed in this way, though it is not yet clear what the basis of this need is. One could still coherently hold out that these states are not, as such, belief states. There are two reasons for this:

(a) If such representational states were deemed belief states then the class of belief states would become quite heterogeneous. Clearly there are beliefs in the case of evaluative sentences: one can believe that haggis is tasty. But surely we do not want to give up the analysis given above in which preference states are those that are defended in such utterances? Belief must be a disposition to defend a prior state, not the prior state itself. Thus, even if some Π-properties are representational we can resist the idea that the representational states are belief states.

(b) A state can be representational, but that does not make it a belief state. Motivational states can also have representational content. Thus states can be representational but may lack the kind of representationality that we associate with belief. A fairly well-entrenched view – instigated by Searle (1983) – is that what makes a representational state a belief state is *direction of fit*. For a representational

199

state to be a belief state, it must be *right* because it fits the world, the world does not have to fit it. Thus it is not intrinsic to a representational state that it is a belief state. The standard view about direction of fit is that it is a matter arising at a level prior to assertion. But in STA it is not. A belief state, *qua* disposition to defend a state Π, which may be representational or not, has a direction of fit because it is defensive. States that have no defensive component are not belief states even if they have a representational component. Thus it is not representationality that is crucial and distinctive of belief, it is direction of fit, which here is captured by the notion of a defensive stance.[7]

LOGICALLY COMPLEX SENTENCES. The next set of Π-properties are those defended in logically complex sentences. Consider negations. In asserting *not-S*, the speaker defends a state of *rejecting* the Π-property of the assertion of *S*. The Π-property defended is, succinctly, the following: Reject: Π-[*S*]. Rejection is not a speech act; it is a mental state. Rejection is a specific functional state that a mind can have towards a Π-property. This is a kind of constraint on not being disposed to token Π – write that as ¬*Disposed-token* Π-[*S*] – which is distinguished from that in which we lack evidence for tokening Π. Rather than being produced by lack of evidence, the state ¬*Disposed-token* Π-[*S*] is produced by evidence. To reject Π is to instantiate some state Ψ such that there is a C-law Ψ → ¬Disposed-token Π-[*S*]. Thus rejection is the state:

 (i) U tokens some Ψ.
(ii) In U, Ψ → ¬Disposed-token Π-[*S*].

Rejective states are in themselves subjective. I emphasize again that in asserting *not-S*, a dialectical stance is taken with respect to U's tokening the rejective state, which, in terms of the intersubjective dimension **ID**, means that truth evaluation works in these terms:

ID-Not: H judges true an assertion of *Not-S* uttered by U defending Reject: Π-[*S*] iff H judges that she, H, defends Reject: Π-[*S*] in her own case.

In short, evaluators are not concerned with whether or not U instantiates any such state but with their own willingness to defend a comparable state in their own case. It is this intersubjectivity of **ID-Not** that drags U and H out of their respective solipsisms.

It should not be thought for one moment that *Not-S* is equivalent in any way to *I reject Π-[S]*, or any sentence used to make a claim about

Table 9.4

Sentence (logical)	Π-Property specification
Not-S	Reject: Π-[*S*]
Either P or Q	Reject: [Reject: Π-[*P*], Reject: Π - [*Q*]]
If P, Q	D{Π-[*Q*], Π-[*P*]}
Every F is G	D{Π-[*T is G*], Π-[*T is F*]}

possession of a subjective state. The Π-property associated with *I reject* Π-*[S]* is distinct from that for *Not-S*. For that reason, one cannot substitute, *Not-S* for *I reject* Π-*[S]* in, say, assertions of the form: *either S or not-S*, to produce *Either S or I reject* Π-*[S]*.

The expressivist proposal is that for all logically complex assertions the Π-properties defended are nonrepresentational. The Π-property specifications for negation, disjunction, indicative conditional, and universal statements are as shown in table 9.4.

The case of disjunction is a translation of de Morgan. The conditional corresponds roughly to a translation of a Ramsey belief-update analysis. Thus in uttering *if P, Q*, U defends a disposition to token Π-[*Q*] given her defense of Π-[*P*]. That disposition would reflect actual background beliefs, or further suppositions, possessed by the agent. In the case of the universal, *Every F is G*, we find a generic disposition: being disposed to assert/infer a sentence of the form *T is G* based on assertion/supposition of a sentence of the form *T is F*. This disposition can be analyzed as a disposition to token Π-[*T is G*], given tokening of Π-[*T is F*].

Again, we should see the evaluation of acts involving defense of such Π-properties in terms of **ID**. In asserting logically complex sentences speakers are not making claims about their subjective states, but defending those states. This expressive treatment of logically complex sentences is neither a truth conditional analysis nor an assertability, or inferential analysis. And again we can assert with some confidence that the Π-properties involved here are not belief states.

TRUTH. On the conception of semantics unfolding, STA, truth-bearers are acts: assertions. But what of the very assertions of truth and falsity? Truth ascriptions and falsity ascriptions are assertions in which we defend Π-properties. But what are these Π-properties? The minimal assumption that explains the intersubjective engagements outlined above is simply the following:

That S is true: Π-property: commitment to Π-[*S*].
That S is false: Π-property: commitment to rejecting Π-[*S*].

Truth and falsity ascriptions are expressive commitments to either accepting the Π-property defended in asserting *S*, or rejecting it. Truth and falsity ascriptions are not assertions about the speaker's acceptance or rejection of Π-properties. Such an interpretation would construe them as claims about subjective states, which would not get the dialectical effect we want. They are not reports that certain parties agree. That would be to collapse into a kind of relativism. They are not assertions about what we should ideally believe. That is a speculative assertion about the ideal. Rather they are expressive assertions and thus conform in terms of **ID** to:

ID-True: H judges true an assertion of *S is true* uttered by U defending Π-[*S*] iff H judges that she, H, defends Π-[*S*] in her own case.

Utterance of *S is true* simply has the normative force of assertion of *S*. Whatever dialectical obligation is imposed by assertion of *S* on others to respond to the state Π defended, will be imposed by *S is true*. Likewise, *mutatis mutandis*, for *Not-S* and *S is false*.

The truth and falsity predicates are then our means to carry on our defense or rejection of Π-properties. This treatment is not a theory of what truth resides in. Rather, the whole semantics of *is true* concerns the act the speaker performs in using *is true*. Again, it might be objected that this theory only tells us about how speakers engage in agreement and dispute about truth and falsity attribution. But what about the facts about what is true? In such debates there is a fact of the matter. How does the expressive theory account for this fixation of truth by something outside of practice? This is, of course, the same question posed above that led us to note the need to refer to our metatheoretic, factive attitudes, in particular our commitment, in some areas of discourse, to bivalence. We do not, however, need to explain this commitment by appealing to representational and ontic structures; the Π-properties that underpin assertion of bivalence are not representational.

2 COMPOSITIONALITY: JUMPING TO *R3*

That completes my response to reason *R1* for postulating the force/sense distinction. Dealing with *R1* has been quite an involved business. Giving up on the idea of belief as an explanatory concept in pragmatics has wide-ranging ramifications. As I have urged, it implies a general kind of expressivism about the logical and the normative. Our next reason for the sense/force distinction is *R2*. However, it is expositionally useful to deal with *R3* and *R4* first, and return to *R2*. Reason *R3* for the sense/force distinction invokes considerations of compositionality, as do *R4* and *R5*. *R3* focused on atomic sentences where a name introduces an object and a predicate a property. Name and predicate get together somehow to form the content of a subject–predicate assertion. Propositions beckon as an explanation of such basic compositional facts.

This charge is entirely false. It has been assumed that the meanings of names and predicates are kinds of objects. But in maintaining that propositions are not the contents of assertions we have to renounce the idea that the meanings of subsentential units such as names and predicates are objects and properties, etc. What are the meanings of names and predicates? The answer is: speech-act types – see Barker (2004). Consider names first. STA begins by asking what we do when we use a name. We might answer: utter a term, *N*, and intend to denote something. We can say a bit more than this. Names involve using a technique of denotation of some kind. When we intend to use a name to denote something, we do so by relying upon the fact that tokens of it have already denoted. In using *Bush* to denote, I intend to denote whatever I, or someone else, denoted last time they used certain tokens of the orthographic-phonological type *Bush-bʊʃ*. The rules for name use are basically anaphoric. So names have rules of use associated with them that are to do with denotative techniques.

But is this the basic speech-act U performs in uttering a name: uttering *N* and intending to denote an object using such techniques? No, it is not. Consider communication. In communicating, a speaker U engages in verbal behavior with the intention of getting an audience to make certain inferences about what her, U's, intentions are. In using a name to sincerely refer, U utters an expression with the syntax of a referring term and intends to denote, in the manner of a name, an object with certain properties.[8] But if U communicates, U also wants her audience H to recognize that she has this intention. How does U get H to do this? Simply by acting in the manner of someone who, following certain rules, known to both U and H, has that sort of intention. So what is basic to name use is that we intentionally engage in the behavior characteristic of someone who, following the rules determining name

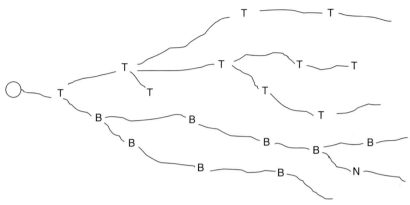

Figure 9.1

use, intends to denote something. Call this *advertising intentions*. And call advertising an intention to denote something, a *proto-referring act*.

The basic speech act I perform in using a name is not a referring act, but a proto-referring act. Communication, as we have seen, shows this, but so does another fact. It is not essential when using a name that I believe that it denotes. Perhaps I believe that I am denoting. But perhaps I do not. So what is common to name use? It is advertising an intention to denote: proto-referring. In uttering *Pegasus* U advertises an intention to denote a certain object, namely, something denoted by earlier uses of *Pegasus*. This means U engages in the behaviour characteristic of a speaker, who, following certain rules, has such an intention. Again U may or may nor have the intention. Advertising an intention to represent is the common element in sincere, insincere, and fictional uses of the name.

The next fact about names to note is that they naturally form referential trees, such as figure 9.1. Each letter is a tokening of a name – the performance of a (nominal) proto-referring act. The letters differ since the same source, origin of the practice, may spawn different phonemic types. We have a complex causal–social–intentional structure. It is basically a convergence of very specialized anaphoric chains. The source of the name is where it begins whether or not it may issue in an object. If it is the tree for *George Bush*, it does issue in an object; that name denotes. But the tree for *Pegasus* does not issue in an object.

But at this stage, having described all these structures, what do we say is the meaning of the name? Why opt for the object, or descriptions? The best idea is that the meaning of the name is the speech-act types defined by the tree. That gives us a theory of names that is neutral between empty and full names. The semantic contribution of a name is the speech-act type all of whose tokens are nodes on a certain referential tree. That is, acts, Ref(N)$_{\text{pro}}$, in which speakers advertise intentions to use some name N to denote an object using the denotative techniques of names.

Predicates have similar kinds of speech-act structure. Predicates have their meanings fixed by Π-property types: which is to say, speech-act types that, combining with proto-referring-act types, generate acts in which Π-properties are defended. A simple assertion A($T\ V\_\_$), where T is a referring term and $V\_\_$ a predicate, has the structure:

A: Ref(T)$_{\text{pro}}$ $\frown$ Pred($V\_\_$)$_{\text{pro}}$

That is, we find the concatenation of two speech-act types. The nominal proto-act Ref(T)$_{\text{pro}}$ and the predicative proto-act Pred($V\_\_$)$_{\text{pro}}$. This is the constituent structure of the thought encoded by a sentence $T\ V\_\_$.

3 PROTO-ASSERTING AND SENTENTIAL EMBEDDING – R4

There is another aspect of compositionality that also needs to be addressed. *R4* sets out the charge that to explain the embedding of sentences in sentential compounds we need to invoke propositions as the contents of embedded sentences. There is a simple reply to this line of argument. Clearly assertions cannot embed. But we do not have to turn to propositions to explain embedding. We can appeal to a concept we already have: *proto-acting*. I suggested above that the basic facts about name use boil down to performing proto-referring acts. Something similar holds for sentences. The basic act U performs with declarative sentences is proto-assertion. U utters S and advertises defense of a Π-property. This is a proto-assertion, which I symbolize thus: A(S)$_{\text{pro}}$. To proto-act is to utter an expression – or produce it mentally – with the intention of engaging in a behavior characteristic of someone who, following certain rules, defends a certain Π-property.

So in uttering "Snowy is black," U advertises defense of an intention to represent with *Snowy is black* a complex of the form <Snowy, black>. If U sincerely asserts that Snowy is black, U really has the defensive state she advertises herself as having. And if U is engaging in fictional make-believe, she lacks the intention she advertises, and intends her audience to recognize this fact. When U has the defensive state she advertises herself as having, I say that the proto-assertion is doxasti-cally grounded. The proto-assertion is part of an assertion.

It is proto-assertions that embed logical compounds. Although fall-ing short of a full-fledged assertion, proto-assertions, nevertheless, determinately indicate assertions. So in *Either S or R*, U performs a proto-assertion with S and R, and indicates a commitment to the Π-properties of the corresponding assertions. Of course, in uttering S embedded, she lacks the state she advertises herself as having and it is clear to her audience H that she lacks that state. Thus in a compound *Either S or R*, U performs a proto-assertion with S and R and expresses her commitment to a Π-property that concerns the status of assertions A(S) and A(R), corresponding to the proto-assertions A(S)$_{\text{pro}}$ and A(R)$_{\text{pro}}$. The state Π in the case of disjunctions was given in section 2.

One might ask: does the embedding not simply cancel the advertis-ing? A characteristic behavior of someone defending Π is to utter S free standing and not flanked by *either ... or*, or *if*, etc. But embedded, S is flanked by *either ... or*, so U cannot advertise defense of Π. This objec-tion flows from an understandable misunderstanding of *advertising*. There are a number of ways we might rectify this misunderstanding. Here is one that works through a causal account of what constitutes being an assertion and proto-assertion. Let us begin with assertion. Assertions are utterances of sentences S that have a specific kind of cause. The cause is U's desire to defend a certain Π in combination with a dispositional state Δ. Δ is the dispositional state that underpins U's use of S; we might say Δ is a linguistic production disposition which is guided by U's grasp of the syntactic and semantic properties of words in the language U speaks. Roughly, Δ is triggered by U's desire to defend Π, plus other background factors. Thus Δ, U's desire to defend Π, and background conditions issue in production of S. Moreover, since U is conscious, at some level, that her assertions are acts produced by stable linguistic dispositions, we can say that U desires that Δ cause her production of S. In self-conscious linguistic production, U wants her utterance of S to be caused by Δ, the causal system that is triggered by the kind of defensive desire she possesses. (Which is to say, U wants to speak in accordance with the meaning of her terms.) Such is assertion. What is proto-assertion? Proto-assertion is assertion abstracting away from the desire to defend Π (and get others to believe that one so desires). But what is that act? It is the utterance of S caused by the causal factor Δ in combination with U's desire that Δ cause her produc-tion of S. That goes on in assertion, and so assertion also counts as proto-assertion. But it also goes on in embedded utterances of *S*. With embedded *S*, the same causal factor Δ is behind the production of *S*. It is just that here U's utterance of *S* is not the manifestation of Δ triggered by a desire to defend Π, but rather an act caused by Δ in combination with a desire that Δ be a cause of her behavior. That is what constitutes U's advertising a defensive stance with *S* embedded.

To conclude: a speech-act semantics faces no insuperable problem of embedding. Proto-assertions indicate clearly enough assertions, or assertion types. Logical compounds are used to express commitments about assertion types corresponding to the proto-assertions displayed. This is a compositional semantics without the force/sense distinction. Rather the work done by that distinction in orthodox semantics in explaining embedding is taken over by the assertion/proto-assertion distinction. Proto-assertions are nothing like propositions: they are *force-y* in a way that propositions are force-less. How one supplements a proto-assertion to produce an assertion is nothing like how one supplements a proposition to produce an assertion.

4 BACK TO ASSERTION AND SAYING – *R2*

We can now return to reason *R2* for the sense/force distinction. *R2* is the claim that analyzing assertion requires reference to the notion of *saying* and this means introducing propositions. The resources that enable us to tackle *R1*, *R3*, and *R4* allow us to defuse *R2*.

An assertion involves the production of a sentence with the defense of a Π-property. The Π-property of an assertion A(*S*) is ontologically prior to A(*S*). On the other hand, in a literal assertion of *S*, the Π-property defended in asserting *S* is one that is fixed compositionally by the linguistic meaning of *S* and the context of utterance. Indeed, we can think of the linguistic meaning of the sentence as a Π-property specification, that is, a specification of the kind of Π-property correlated with that sentence, which, supplemented by context, can fix a Π-property token.

With this idea we can give a simple account of the saying component of assertion, or at least of literal assertion. We can analyze attributions of literally asserted content thus:

U literally asserts that P by uttering S as uttered by an attributor *A* is true if and only if the Π-property specification Π-[*S*] in the context of utterance in which *S* is produced by U fixes a token Ψ, where Ψ is the Π-property defended in an assertion of *P* by *A*.

This is an account of literal assertion. It will not do as an account of nonliteral assertion. In asserting as a metaphor *George is a rock*, U makes an assertion. In asserting ironically *George is a real genius*, U makes an assertion. And in asserting *I think that George should go*, U can assert that George should go. In these cases what is literally said is not what is asserted. It might seem that we need the notion of proposition here to account for the said but nonasserted contents. But again the notion of proto-assertion does all the work we need. In these cases the speaker performs a literal proto-assertion, but lacks the state she advertises, having instead some other state. So in asserting ironically *George is a real genius*, U performs: A (*George is a real genius*)$_{pro}$ – so she says that George is a real genius – but U lacks the defensive state she advertises, and indicates that what she defends is the rejection of the state correlated with this proto-assertion.

5 MOOD – R5

The final reason to accept the force/sense distinction – R5 – was an appeal to mood. Our three mood modified sentences, *Fred jumps*, *Does Fred jump?*, and *Fred, jump!*, it seems, should be analyzed in terms of a common propositional content combining with distinct force operators. That is the argument, but it does not work.

According to STA, the illocutionary acts that are conventionally associated with the three kinds of sentences are given below:

Assertion:
(i) U utters *Fred jumps* and advertises defense of a commitment to the state Π.
(ii) U really defends the state.

Question:
(i) U utters *Does Fred jump?* advertising a state of representing herself as having an intention that H provide information regarding the status of A(*Fred jumps*).
(ii) U really represents herself thus.

Order:
(i) U utters *Jump, Fred!* advertising a state of representing herself as having an intention that H make true A(*Fred jumps*).
(ii) U really represents herself thus.

There are three distinct kinds of speech acts here. The (i)-components in each case are the proto-acts. The (ii)-components are the states advertised actually being possessed by the speaker. Assertions are democratic in that they involve defenses of mental states that invite a response from audiences. Orders and questions are autocratic in the sense that social intentions are manifested and audiences are expected to act accordingly.

It will be noted that the speech-act specifications for the orders and questions make reference to the assertion: A(*Fred jumps*), which involves a proto-assertion. Thus, given that the speaker performs such a proto-assertion in **Assertion** (i), there is, one might argue, a common content between all three acts. But this admission does not in any way move us towards accepting the sense/force distinction. This is so for two reasons.

(a) It is not part of the analysis of orders and questions in STA that in performing an order or question U performs a constituent proto-assertion. U may have a commitment about a proto-assertion. So nothing comparable to the structure articulated above in my original discussion of *R*5 holds in this analysis.

(b) Nothing in the given analysis implies that there is an entity that is *force-less* in the makeup of an order or question. Proto-assertions, we have already noted, are *force-y*. Thus, even if we admit that the proto-assertion A(*Fred jumps*)$_{pro}$ is somehow a content common to all three illocutionary acts, it is not a content that fits into the model of the distinction between sense and force.

CONCLUSIONS

There is no compelling set of reasons – such as *R1* to *R5* – to accept the distinction between sense and force. In adopting the speech-act-theoretic approach to semantics – STA – we provide a semantics without that distinction. But, unsurprisingly, STA takes us far from reaches chartered by orthodox truth conditional semantics. Whether we should follow STA into these reaches is another matter.

NOTES

1 I do not require that U and H are different people. The intersubjectivity may be intra-subjective, as it were. I note that for literal assertions to take place, Π must be conventionally associated with S. Sincerity means U not only defends the state, but has the state. Falsity evaluation requires more than merely that

H lacks the state. She must reject the state, or be in a position to defend the Π-property of *Not-S*. I define rejection below.

2 Assertion is a kind of disposition to (privately or publicly) assert. The sincerity condition required is that the speaker actually have the state defended. Unlike for other sincere assertion accounts of belief developed within the Frege approach, this is not circular, since sincerity is not explained in terms of belief.

3 In what follows Π-*[S]* is used to designate the Π-property associated by context and meaning with a sentence *S*.

4 Wright (1992) defends the idea that the objectivity of a domain of assertion functions in terms of representation with his notion of *cognitive command*. Dummett (1963) equates realism with bivalence, indicating that he thinks that bivalence is ultimately explained by representation of determinate reality.

5 We might understand determinacy in terms of properties: for every property π, either *O* has π or lacks π. But if *property* here just means *set qua* extension of a predicate, then our explanation of bivalence is vacuous, since we think predicates fix sets because bivalence holds for sentences featuring the predicates. By properties we might mean universals. So our claim of determinacy is: for every universal υ, either *O* instantiates υ or it does not. But now we should ask: why are universals determinate? Why do we assert for any particular object *O*, either *O* has υ or not? There is nothing built into the concept of a universal that makes them determinate. Nor will it do any explanatory work here to reply: *Because "O has υ" represents a state of affairs and reality in this domain is determinate.*

6 Thus Wright (1992) takes faultless disagreement to be a sign of non-representationality.

7 On the other hand, it is quite possible that an expressivist analysis of such predicates is available, in which case no reference to representational states is required at all.

8 I use "denotes" for the relation that holds between a referring term and an object, if it has a denotation, and "refers" for the act the speaker performs in uttering a referring term.

Chapter 10

Dynamic discourse semantics
for embedded speech acts

NICHOLAS ASHER

1 INTRODUCTION

A traditional separation of pragmatics and semantics has it that speech acts are computed at the level of the entire sentence and that their illocutionary force cannot be embedded under various truth conditional operators. To quote from David Lewis (1972: 209):

the entire apparatus of referential semantics pertains to sentence radicals and constituents thereof. The semantics of mood is something entirely different. It consists of rules of language use such as ... React to a sentence representing the mood *imperative* with an S-meaning m, by acting in such a way as to make m true.

Since speech acts other than assertions do not classically have truth values as extensions (Searle 1969; Vanderveken 1990), they cannot possibly combine with truth-functional operators like the propositional connectives in standard logic. This much is right. But when we look at the behavior of natural language conjunctions such as *and, or*, or *if... then*, speech acts such as directives and questions clearly embed under some of these operators. As Krifka (2001, 2002) has argued, considerable evidence has amassed over the years that most types of speech acts do embed within conjunctions and conditionals, and imperatives clearly embed under disjunctions. The problematic question for truth conditional semantics is then: what is the uniform account of the meaning of natural language sentential connectives that captures their behavior with interrogatives, imperatives, and indicatives?

Several decades of research have shown that this question is difficult if not impossible to answer within the confines of standard truth conditional semantics. However, if the meaning of directives, questions, commissives, and other speech acts is given dynamically, we open the way to give a uniform account of the meaning of connectives. The reason why this is so is roughly that in dynamic semantics all well-formed clauses in natural language are actions that change the input context in some way. Assertions, questions, requests, etc. are all alike in this respect, although the ways in which they change the input context can differ considerably.

Treating all speech acts dynamically, however, gives rise to a different but equally perplexing puzzle: if all speech acts are actions and operators such as conjunction and implication combine with actions, why do not all speech acts embed equally well in all contexts? Dynamic semantics is not by itself enough to explain the embedding behavior of various speech acts. To give a satisfactory account of this embedding behavior, we need to resort to discourse structure. Some embeddings cannot work because they make impossible a coherent discourse.

To develop this claim, I will use Segmented Discourse Representation Theory or SDRT (Asher 1993; Asher and Lascarides 2003). SDRT builds a formal theory of discourse structure and discourse coherence on top of a dynamic semantics. But SDRT is especially useful for my purposes here because it explicitly connects the formalism of discourse structure with the system of speech acts. SDRT's account of speech acts begins with Searle's typology of speech acts and refines it considerably by adding many types of relational speech acts. These relational speech acts are the discourse relations that bind discourse constituents together in discourse structure. Attendant formalizations of Searle's ideas use in effect a pre- and post-condition analysis, which lends itself naturally to the dynamic concept of update conditions. (Perhaps Searle did not realize that he was in fact doing dynamic semantics or dynamic pragmatics!) We can easily incorporate the outlines of the traditional analyses of speech acts into the dynamic view of contexts by enriching information states with information about the commitments *à la* Hamblin (1987) of the speaker and the addressee, but I will not go into details here. The main problem for the traditional analyses of speech acts, and a problem that SDRT (Asher and Lascarides 2003) attempts to address in detail, is the alignment of speech acts with surface forms of utterances. Without this question we cannot begin to address the idea of embedded speech acts, which is after all an issue about compositionality.

2 EMBEDDINGS OF VARIOUS SPEECH ACTS

The data concerning the embedding behavior of speech acts is rather complex. I will here only consider the embedding under various truth conditional, modal, and tense operators of those speech acts with a grammatically determined, different mood.[1] For instance, Krifka (2002), following Merin (1992), has doubted whether disjunctions have scope over imperatives, and he has also claimed that we cannot quantifiy into directives in the imperative mood with other than universal quantifiers, which for finite domains reduce to unproblematic conjunctions. Krifka notes that only questions with universal quantification get pair list readings. That is, with a question like *which dish did every guest make?*, we can get an answer like: *Paul made the lasagne, Mary the quiche* … But we cannot give the same sort of pair list answer to *which dish did several guests make?* or *which dish did some guest make?*

Nevertheless, Krifka's and Merin's observations are not entirely compelling. First there are some very interesting examples from Mastop (2005) in which apparently imperatives or something similar to them embed under tense in languages like Dutch and Cheyenne.

(1) Was toch naar huis gegann toen Jan het foto-album. (You should have gone home before Jan opened the photo album.)
(2) Had die appel can ook obgegeten. (You should have eaten that apple.)

These can be considered to be imperatives because they share the same form (verb first, implicit second-person subject) and have a closely related use.

Here are some examples of future imperatives from Cheyenne (again quoting from Mastop 2005):

(3) méseestse (eat!)
(4) méseheoʔo (eat later on!)

With regard to quantification, the picture is also complex. Mastop also shows that at least for subject position we can easily quantify into directives expressed in the imperatival mood.

(5) a. Somebody get this table off the set.
   b. Whoever stole this television bring it back.
   c. Nobody move a muscle.

Whatever one wants to say about these examples, it is clear that they do not express a directive to some individual addressee. As Portner (2004) suggests, this is a directive to a group such that nobody in that group move a muscle. Nevertheless, this still implies that something like (5c) must be understood as a quantification into the scope of the imperatival operator; that is, they have the logical form:

(6) Quant(x)[x ∈ C Imp [ϕ(x)]]

These provide counterexamples to Krifka's claim.

Quantification into the object position of the clause within the verb phrase of the imperatival is not in general possible with any determiners using the *DP such that* construction:

(7) a. *Every bottle you find such that confiscate it!
   b. *Someone is such that give him a present!
   c. Someone is such that Mary gave him a present.

However, variables can be bound from without if we use an anaphoric construction:

(8) a. Those students must have a bottle of liquor. Confiscate it.
   b. For every bottle that you find, confiscate it.
   c. For at least three bottles that you discover, confiscate them.

This sort of data suggests that the limitations on quantifying into imperatival contexts may not be a matter of semantics, but rather of syntax. But the lack of pair list readings for questions with quantifiers other than universal ones is quite striking.

Like quantifiers, conditionals also exhibit particularities with interrogatives and imperativals. Conditionals are perfectly felicitous with imperativals or interrogatives in the consequent.

(9) a. Let me take your bags, if you've finished shopping.
   b. And if I buy into the plan, what returns can I expect?
   c. If I do my homework now, can I go shopping later?
   d. Go home, if you're feeling sick.
   e. If there's beer in the fridge, have one.

And there are also conditional readings of conjunctions (from Asher and Lascarides 2003):

(10) Come home by 5p.m. and we will finish the shelves tonight.
(11) Smoke a pack of cigarettes a day and you'll die before you're thirty.

Some of these conditionals have an interpretation where they embed a speech act: for example, (9d, e) contain a directive that only takes effect if the antecedent of the conditional holds. As such, it is similar to what in programming languages is called a guarded action, which is of the form *if p, do A*. Thus, for those examples, it is reasonable to speak of embedded speech acts. One can understand the optative speech act in (9a) similarly. However, imperatives do not always issue in directives. (10) has an interpretation according to which there is a directive to come home by 5p.m., which, if carried out, will have the result that the speaker and addressee can finish the shelves. (11), on the other hand, has a conditional reading but no embedded directive: it certainly does not mean that if the speaker directs the addressee to smoke a packet of cigarettes a day, the addressee will die before he is thirty; rather, it means that if the addressee smokes a packet of cigarettes a day, he will die before he is thirty. In (11), we have an imperative that does not express a directive.

The conditionals with embedded questions can be understood in some cases as having scope over an embedded question. For example, (9b) expresses a Wh-question whose answers depend on the satisfaction of the antecedent of the conditional. The direct answers to this question may, however, be of the form *if you buy into the plan, you can expect at least $1.5 K returns per year*. This would suggest that the question actually has wide scope over the conditional (simliarly for (9c)). This might be amenable to some sort of a syntactic solution of raising the Wh-element to an appropriate node so that when interpreted it has scope over the entire sentence. However, we can reformulate (9b–c) so that the conditional reading is distributed over several sentences, in which case we no longer have recourse to a syntactic solution.

(9b′) Suppose I buy into the plan. What will my returns be?
(9c′) Suppose I go do my homework now. Can I go shopping later?

There is of course a *discourse relation* similar to the conditional that links the clauses of (9b′–c′), but this still leads the question to be understood as linked to the other clauses via some sort of operator similar to a conditional. Thus, these would count as embedded questions; and if that is right, then since they are basically synonymous with (9b–c), we might as well understand those as conditionally embedded questions as well.

I think the evidence strongly suggests that questions and directives do embed within the scope of conditionals. But conditionals with embedded questions and directives are only good when those speech acts occur in the consequent – when directives and questions occur in the antecedents, the conditionals are fully ungrammatical:

(12) a. *If let me take your bags, I'll be very honored.
    b. *If did you go to dinner, I'd be very interested to know.

The conditionals in (12) are simply ungrammatical, as well as uninterpretable.

Next, let us turn to data about embeddings with disjunction. Disjunctions also occur with imperatives and interrogatives and appear to have interpretations where they sometimes take scope over various speech acts like directives, optatives, and questions. But these interpretations are sometimes quite difficult to get.

(13) a. Get out of here or I'll call the police.
    b. Open a window or turn on the fan. It's so hot in here!
    c. Take her to Knightsbridge or to Bond Street.
    d. Oh, that I were a king or (oh) that I were at least a prince.

(13a) conveys a conditional proposition, the one expressed by *if you don't get out of here, I'll call the police*. There is also a conveyed request, however: the request is for the addressee to get out of here. (13a) in effect provides two alternatives for the addressee to consider: the first is that he accede to the request to leave, while the second is that he not accede and that the speaker call the police. (13b) plainly involves a disjunction taking scope over two requests; one of these must be performed, but perhaps it is up to the addressee to choose which request to satisfy. This is known as the free-choice reading of the disjunction. (13c) is somewhat different. Hamblin says there are two readings of this sentence – one is that I have not decided which and the other is the free-choice reading. Krifka (2002) and Merin (1992) find Hamblin's intuitions dubious; they claim that the non-free-choice reading of (13c) does not exist. But Hamblin's intuitions seem to me to be the right ones.

Disjunction can also take scope over interrogatives though such readings must be distinguished from so-called "alternative questions":

(14) a. Did Pat or did Sue find the solution?
    b. Does Chris have a Mercedes, or does he have at least a nice car?
    c. What kind of fancy car does John own, or is he the guy who had the wreck last night? (due to Josh Dever, personal communication)

When disjunction takes narrow scope with respect to the question operator as is plausibly the case with (14a), we have an alternative question. It has a distinctive set of direct answers consisting of three or four propositions – the proposition that Pat found the solution, the proposition that Sue did, the proposition that both did, and perhaps also the proposition that neither did.[2] When disjunction takes wide scope over the question operator, it is much less clear what is going on. It seems conceivable that some such disjunctions can be read as a revision of the question being asked as in (14b, c). Another possible interpretation of a disjunction between two interrogatives is that the speaker has a list of actions that he has not decided upon yet. For instance, someone who is interested in Chris and wants to find out about his/her affluence might say the following to a friend:

(14c′) Does Chris own a nice car, or does he have a second home? I'm not sure which question I should ask first.

Thus, it seems that disjunction can have scope over interrogatives and that various interpretations of these are possible.

Finally I examine briefly the embedding of questions and directives under the scope of negation. They are largely impossible with imperatives and optatives. There do seem to exist wide scope negations over interrogatives as in (15a) but they are marked and trigger a particular discourse bias. The fact that one can use a positive polarity item like *too* suggests that the negation must have scope outside the question operator:

(15) a. Isn't John coming too?
     b. Isn't John coming either?

There are also corrective uses of negation on questions, and these also appear to be genuine examples of speech acts embedded under negation:

(16) a. A: What did this?
     b. B: Not what did this, but who?

3 A DISCOURSE-BASED SEMANTICS FOR INTERROGATIVES AND IMPERATIVES

3.1 *Interrogatives*

While there is good evidence that various sorts of speech acts embed within the scope of different operators, there is also clear evidence that clauses in the imperative and interrogative mood have differing interpretations within these embeddings. Not all imperative clauses issue in commands or directives when embedded. That is, the *alignment* of speech acts with moods is not a trivial matter. The analysis of embedded speech acts poses three related problems: (1) the compositional interpretation of clauses with imperatival, indicative, and interrogative mood within various discourse contexts and within the scope of varying operators; (2) the determination of what speech acts are expressed by clauses in a given mood; and (3) how those speech acts themselves are to be interpreted with respect to operators that have scope over them, given that there do appear to be such. I will look at these three problems for both interrogatives and imperatives.

Some sorts of embedded speech acts, like conditional directives, have attracted considerable attention within traditional truth conditional semantics. But most of the other phenomena surveyed in the previous section have not, and for good reason. For truth conditional semantics, some embedded speech acts would seem to pose intractable difficulties, like conditional questions. However, if questions and requests are actions on an information state in a way similar to that already understood for assertions in standard dynamic semantics, then conditional questions and conditional requests have a natural semantics.

Before starting on the dynamic analysis of questions and requests, let me briefly remind the reader of how dynamic semantics works. In dynamic semantics the meaning of a sentence is a relation between information states or discourse contexts. If we understand a discourse context as a set of pairs of possible worlds and assignment functions, then the meaning of a sentence converts an "input" discourse context into an output set of world assignment pairs. Assertions typically act on such information states *distributively*; that is, they modify or test the elements of the input context one at a time.[3] An illustration of this approach is the theory of Groenendijk and Stokhof (1991) which describes the meaning of a sentence as a relation between world assignment pairs. However, we can lift the relational version of dynamic semantics to a relation between sets of world assignment pairs or information states following Asher and Wang (2003) so that we can analyze the effects of speech acts that may not have a distributive meaning.

With this in mind, let us consider the case of interrogatives and questions. What could be an action corresponding to a question? Groenendijk (1999) suggests that we think of a question as the act of partitioning the information state created by the discourse into a set of exhaustive direct answers to the question. Thus questions, like epistemic modals in Veltman's (1996) analysis, act on information states *non-distributively*.[4] A question sets out a set of epistemic possibilities for the discourse, which answers can sometimes identify exactly (that would be an exhaustive answer) or more likely identify a set of such epistemic possibilities. Thus, answers in general select out subsets of the input partition. Assertions update various parts of the partition distributively as is usual in dynamic semantics. The combination of distributive and nondistributive actions on an input information state creates certain complexities for the semantics that have been studied to some extent in the literature on epistemic modals and plurals.[5] But luckily most of these complexities can be avoided if we just stick to the interaction between questions, assertions, imperatives, and their embeddings using conditionals and disjunctions.

But assigning such a dynamic interpretation to a question is only the beginning. We now have to address the alignment problem: when do interrogatives issue in questions? How are interrogatives to be interpreted in various discourse contexts and with respect to various operators that take scope over them? I propose the simple approach to the alignment question that Asher and Lascarides (2003) and Asher and Reese (2005) adopt: interrogative mood always yields a question, but it may also sometimes yield in conjunction with other information a complex speech act – e.g. in the case of biased questions, the interrogative yields a complex speech act that is both a question and an assertion (Asher and Reese 2005). Such complex speech acts can be understood in SDRT along the lines of Asher and Lascarides (2003).

If the correlation between interrogatives and the type of speech acts they express is relatively straightforward, the interactions between context and interrogatives is not. SDRT postulates that there are many different types of relational speech acts: a clause that conveys an assertion may have many other functions; it may be an explanation, or form part of a narrative sequence or constitute an elaboration of some topic, among other things. Each type of relational speech act corresponds to a discourse relation between constituents. Discourse relations link basic discourse constituents – which SDRT takes to be logical forms for clauses – together in a discourse structure. A discourse structure itself is a pair consisting of a set of labels of discourse constituents and a function that assigns to each label an appropriate logical form, some of which may involve formulas that predicate a type of relational speech act or discourse relation to two or more discourse constituents. SDRT provides a *glue logic* for inferring what sort of type of relational speech act a clause gives rise to in a particular discourse context. The logic is a nonmonotonic one for making defeasible inferences about what is conveyed in context. The logic contains axioms of the form $A > B$, which is glossed as *if A, then normally B* (for details see Asher and Lascarides 2003).

Interrogatives like indicatives give rise to many different relational speech acts within the SDRT glue logic. While all interrogatives give rise to questions, there are many ways in which a question can relate to a discourse context. Questions may elaborate on other questions, in the sense that the second question can ask about something that may help pick out the right answer to the first question. They may link to other discourse components so that an answer to the question forms a narrative sequence with the other components – an example of such a question would be *and then what happened?* Pairs of questions can also form narrative sequences as in:

(17) Did Sue teach her class? And then did she leave for the conference?

Asher and Lascarides (2003) study a wide variety of such relational speech acts.

Here I shall just concentrate on the relation between a question and its answer, the *Question-Answer-Pair* relation or QAP. This is important in understanding how questions act as actions on an information state. I thus propose the following for a dynamic semantics of interrogatives. We will first raise dynamic semantic clauses for standard assertions to the level of sets of world assignment pairs, where the clauses determine a distributive semantics over elements of these sets. Thus, if $[\![.]\!]$ is the basic relational semantics for indicatives, we will raise this to a bisimulation relation $||.||$ between sets of world assignment pairs as follows:

- $\varepsilon ||\psi|| \varepsilon'$ iff $\forall (w,f) \in \varepsilon \exists (w', g) \in \varepsilon'$ and $\forall (w', g) \in \varepsilon' \exists (w, f) \in \varepsilon$ such that $(w, f)[\![\psi]\!] (w', g)$.

Given our informal semantics for questions, however, the basic inputs and outputs of evaluation dynamically speaking are sets of sets of world assignment pairs, or more precisely partitions over the set of all world assignment pairs. So we need to raise our semantics one more level; the meaning of a sentence is now a relation between partitions or sets of sets of world assignment pairs. We cannot say how formulas in general will interact with a partition independently of its discourse function. As a simplification, I will let formulas other than questions simply act distributively over the elements of the partition. Some world assignment pairs will be eliminated, others modified, and still others passed on without change. For all formulas ϕ other than questions, which are of the form $?\psi$, we define the meaning of $\phi ||\phi||$ as follows:

- $\sigma ||\phi|| \sigma'$ iff $\sigma' = \{\varepsilon' : \exists \varepsilon \in \sigma \text{ such that } \varepsilon' = \{(w',g) : \exists (w,f) \in \varepsilon \ (w,f)[\![\phi]\!](w',g)\}\}$.

Questions transform one partition into another:

- $\sigma \ ||?\phi\ || \ \sigma'$ iff σ' is a refinement of the partition given in σ such that every element $\varepsilon \in \sigma'$ is a direct answer to $?\phi$.
- $\sigma \ || \ \phi \rightarrow? \ \psi \ || \ \sigma'$ iff $\forall \sigma' \ (\sigma \ ||\phi|| \ \sigma' \rightarrow \exists \sigma'' \ ||?\psi||\sigma'')$.

A relation like QAP between two discourse constituents π and π' with associated logical forms ϕ_π and $\phi_{\pi'}$ will have the following semantics:

- $\sigma \ ||QAP(\pi,\ \pi')|| \ \sigma'$ iff $\exists \sigma'' \ (\sigma \ ||\phi_\pi|| \ \sigma'' \wedge \{\varepsilon' : \exists \varepsilon \in \sigma''$ such that $\varepsilon \ ||\phi_{\pi'}|| \ \varepsilon'\} = \sigma')$.

In words, $QAP(\pi,\pi')$ will hold just in case the partition P induced by the question associated with π is a partition that is a result of updating with the answer all those elements in P that are compatible with the answer. Note that on this semantics an answer may also update those elements of the input partition that satisfy it, as it may not only be nonexhaustive but may also be overinformative and throw out elements of the partition by bringing in other information not countenanced in the meaning of the question. Thus, an answer very naturally provides information that is modeled in the standard way by the elimination of possibilities raised by the question it answers.

What about the other relations that interrogatives can bear to discourse contexts? Those who are familiar with SDRT will know that the relation IQAP or Indirect Question Answer Pair, subsumes QAP. On this new semantics: indirect answers will "normally" select a subset of the input partition. We can in this framework give a completely model theoretic characterization of the IQAP relation. Another discourse relation that is important in the analysis of discourse is Q-elab, where the second question's answers help determine the answer to the first question. Without going into details, one can impose constraints on partitions to model such a relation too.

On this semantics, questions can embed within many contexts. Conditional questions are not themselves questions; they are tests on the input information state that yield partitions of those elements that satisfy the antecedent. Thus, if the antecedent of the conditional is true then conditional questions do issue in a question, i.e. a further partition of the elements of the input partition that satisfy the antecedent. Negations with scope over a question do make a certain kind of semantic sense, but only in certain situations. Our semantics predicts that for a negated question, $\sigma \ ||\neg? \ \phi|| \ \sigma$ iff there is no refinement of σ that is the result of taking the pairwise intersection of elements of σ with the epistemic possibilities that give the semantics of the question $?\phi$. This condition would hold, for instance, if ϕ had a presupposition that is incompatible with the global discourse state σ. But if the question already has been answered in a particular discourse context as in (18) or if an answer has not been ruled out, then such negated questions should lead the information state to inconsistency. This would suggest then that negated questions are highly marked and have a special discourse meaning.

(18) a. A: Samantha isn't coming, so there will be no syntacticians at the conference.
  b. B: Isn't the syntactician Jane coming too?

Such threatened inconsistency would force a coercion in meaning – e.g. the negation could be understood metalinguistically. One might expect in such a case a special discourse meaning for such negated polar questions, which seems to be the case (Reese 2006).

With respect to disjunction, this semantics allows $?\phi \vee ?\psi$ as a meaningful construction. But once again its semantics is rather special. The meaning of disjunction in dynamic semantics is a nondeterministic choice over two possible actions – in the case of questions between making one partition of the information state or making another. This is a strange semantic instruction. What is the point of giving the addressee an option between two partitions of the input information state? It may be that the speaker is wanting the addressee to pick out one of the questions and then answer it, as in:

(14b) Does John have a Mercedes, or does he have at least a nice car?
(14c) What kind of fancy car does John own, or is he the guy who had the wreck last night?

If we look at the responses to such disjunctions of questions in discourse, we do see that speakers do often pick one of the questions to answer. Sometimes they answer both questions.

This semantics, finally, is quite liberal with respect to quantification into question speech acts. So let us look in detail at some examples.

(19) a. Which dish did every guest make?

With the wide scope reading, this becomes

(19b) $\forall x(\text{Guest}(x)) \rightarrow ? \lambda y(\text{made}(x, y) \wedge \text{dish}(y))$

Now consider:

(19c) Which dish did most guests make?
(19d) Which dish did a certain guest make?

With the wide scope reading, these become respectively:

(19e) For most(x)(Guest(x)), ? λy(made$(x, y) \wedge$ dish(y))
(19f) $\exists x$(Guest(x)) $\wedge$? λy(made$(x, y) \wedge$ dish(y))

Recall that the problem was that questions with quantifiers scoping over the Wh-elements or question operators were supposed to yield pair list readings. But only (19a) has a pair list reading. For (19a), it is clear that the pair list reading can give an exhaustive correct answer to the question. But for (19c), a simple "dish" answer will give a correct and exhaustive answer to the question. No pair list reading is needed or else it is trivially equivalent in a dynamic setting to one where we reset the variable to some guest and then pair that guest with the dish. For example, when we give a bit of context, a "pair list reading" is a perfectly acceptable answer to (19d).

(19d') Oh you must mean Peter. He made the pasta.

With (19c) it is just unclear what a pair list reading could give us. You could say: "Well let's see: John made pasta, Mary made pasta, Jim made pasta, Julie made moussaka, Tijana made holupci. I guess most guests made pasta." In some sense that description of the pairs is equivalent to the direct answer that most guests made pasta. But the latter is so much more economical; and so the pair list reading might well be precluded on pragmatic grounds. If that is right, then there is nothing special about conjunctions of speech acts semantically, contrary to what most have supposed. The difference must lie in the pragmatics. List answers for (19c–d) are possible in certain pragmatic contexts.

3.2 *Imperatives: propositional dynamic logic + dynamic semantics*

The dynamic semantics of interrogatives is quite simple, and the alignment between speech acts and mood forms appears to be also quite simple, complicated only by the fact that interrogatives can express other types of speech acts besides questions when they are marked in certain ways.[6] The situation is different with clauses in imperatival mood. For one thing, we have many counterexamples to the claim that imperativals always issue in directives. The alignment problem for imperatives and the speech acts they give rise to appears to be quite complex.

If imperativals do not always issue in directives, what should the semantics for imperatives be? I will propose and defend here the view of Asher and Lascarides (2003) that imperatives express actions that reset the world components of the elements of the input context. The general semantics of actions expressed by imperativals is that they change the world of evaluation in some way, and are thus *transitions* between worlds in a dynamic semantics. It is then up to the sort of rules found in SDRT's glue logic to supplement the basic semantics of imperatives and allow us to infer the appropriate type of speech act expressed by an imperatival in a particular discourse context. The glue logic will interpret imperatives in certain contexts as issuing in directives, while in other contexts the actions denoted by imperatives will issue in different sorts of speech acts. Directives, like most types of speech acts inferred in the glue logic, have a different semantics from the basic semantics for imperatives; a directive concerns a *discourse action* with respect to the commitments of the addressee. Following Hamblin (1987), most researchers have analyzed this action in terms of commitment slates. Commitment slates are a distinguished element of information states, just like worlds, times, and assignment functions. Updating a discourse with a directive to do an action α amounts on those semantics to adding to the commitment slate of the addressee the action α. It should be noted, however, that the semantics proposed for imperatives here is compatible with a number of other interpretations of directives.

Asher and Lascarides (2003) extend the dynamic semantics for indicatives to a dynamic semantics for requests as action terms. These are like other formulas in dynamic semantics in that they can affect an input information context; and like formulas derived from indicatives, they operate on the basic building blocks of information states, world assignment pairs. Unlike formulas derived from indicatives, however, which never change the world component of an input world assignment pair, action formulas can change both the world and the assignment components. The language introduced in Asher and Lascarides (2003) builds on the basic idea that one can convert any formula that describes a situation into an action by an operator δ (in an analogy to the *Stit* operator of Belnap, Horty, and Xu 1995); $\delta\phi$ denotes an action whereby ϕ is achieved. The rest of the language is a straightforward importation from propositional dynamic logic (e.g. Harel 1984).

1. *Seeing to it that p*, where p is a normal formula or *state formula*, i.e. if ϕ is a state formula (a typical assertion), then $\delta\phi$ is an action term.
2. If a_1 and a_2 are action terms, then so are $a_1 ; a_2$ (this stands for action sequence) and $a_1 + a_2$ (this stands for choice).

3. If a is an action term and ϕ is a state formula, then $[a]\phi$ is a DRS condition (this will mean that once a is performed ϕ is true).

4. If ϕ is a state formula and a is an action term, then $\phi \rightarrow a$ is a state formula (this describes guarded action).

5. If ϕ is a state formula and a is an action term, then $\phi > a$ is a state formula (this describes defeasibly guarded action).

However, if we build too much into the semantics and *identify* the meanings of natural language conjunctions with these operators, we will not be able to give a uniform account of the connectives. General clauses for conjunctions and disjunctions of imperatives look especially hopeless from this perspective. There is no way, for instance, to give (10) and (11) their very different logical forms, solely on the basis of a dynamic semantics for conjunction; the same thing goes for the interpretation of the other connectives. We need a pragmatics and a discourse level to get a good account of the connectives. In effect, we will turn out to need only the minimum of the action language – viz. atomic clauses and sequences.

3.3 *Extending the semantics*

I give now the clauses for interpreting the language expanded with action denoting terms using the δ (see to it that) operator and generalized conjunction as sequence. All of the formulas are interpreted with respect to an information state distributively. Perhaps the easiest way to do this is to define a separate satisfaction relation on elements of elements of information states – recall that here we are taking information states, the basic parameter relative to which dynamic evaluation is given, to be partitions. Each element of the partition is a set of world-assignment pairs. Let $[\![.]\!]$ be the interpretation relation on world assignment pairs, which we can then lift up in a straightforward way to the operation $||.||$ on information states. We extend the usual $[\![.]\!]$ relation for formulas of dynamic semantics to action formulas as follows:

1. $(w, f)\, [\![\delta\phi]\!]_M\, (w', g)$ iff $(w', f)[\![\phi]\!]_M\, (w', g)$

2. $[\![a_1 ; a_2]\!]_M = [\![a_1]\!]_M \circ [\![a_2]\!]_M$
   (i.e. $(w , f)[\![a_1 ; a_2]\!]_M\, (w'', h)$ iff there is a pair (w' , g) such that $(w, f)[\![a_1]\!]_M\, (w', g)$ and $(w', g)[\![a_2]\!]_M\, (w'', h))$.

3. $(w, f)\, [\![\phi \rightarrow a]\!]_M\, (w', g)$ iff $(w, f) = (w', g)$ and for all w'' and h such that $(w, f)\, [\![\phi]\!]_M\, (w'', h)$ there is a w''' and k such that $(w'', h)\, [\![a]\!]_M\, (w''', k)$.[7]

4. $(w, f)\ [\![\phi > a]\!]_M\ (w', g)$ iff $(w, f) = (w', g)$ and for all w'' and h such that $(w'', h) \in *\ ([\![\phi]\!]_M, w)$, $\exists w'''$, h' such that $(w'', h)\ [\![a]\!]_M\ (w''', k)$.

5. $(w, f)\ [\![[a]\phi]\!]_M\ (w', g)$ iff $(w, f) = (w', g)$ and for every h and w'' such that $(w, f)\ [\![a]\!]_M\ (w'', h)$, there exists w''' and k such that $(w'', h)\ [\![\phi]\!]_M\ (w''', k)$.

Our definition of $||.||$ for information states as sets of sets of world assignment pairs can now apply to action formulas as well as formulas derived from indicatives and interrogatives.

Note that, thanks to condition 2 above, the denotation of the complex action (20) is one where the individual who talks and the individual who walks is one and the same:

(20) $\delta(\exists x, walk(x))$; $\delta(talk(x))$.

Thus, this semantics in principle makes sense of quantifying into imperativals and to embedded commands.

As I said above, it turns out that we cannot make use of many of the operators that are defined in this language directly, if we want a general, compositional account of the connectives. Conjunction, for instance, needs to be much more underspecified than the interpretation given to dynamic sequence ";," because we cannot derive the conditional meaning for the embedded directives in (9) from this meaning. Nor will the dynamic logic rendition of disjunction give us what we want. We need to go through discourse structure to get the right interpretations of the connectives and associated embedded imperativals. To see exactly why, we first have to look more closely at a compositional semantics for imperativals.

3.4 Compositional semantics for imperativals

Let us first look at some of the syntactic facts. Imperativals do not show morphological tense features, like infinitivals. Imperativals also block the use of certain modals, which are admitted in other mood forms. Aspectual auxiliaries *be, have* are possible in imperativals but they do not seem to carry tense information in the way that they do with infinitivals. One piece of evidence for this is that they do not go in front of negation:

(21) To have not finished your homework already is not a good thing.
(22) You were not helping very much.

(23) *Be not working when I get back.
(24) Don't be working when I get back.
(25) *Have not finished the work by the time I get back.
(26) Don't have finished the work by the time I get back.

Most syntacticians take this data to indicate the lack of a tense feature or a clausal head. If that is right, this would immediately explain why we cannot quantify into imperatives using the *DP such that IMP* construction. This might also explain the asymmetries noted with conditionals. If the antecedent of a conditional requires a clausal head so that *if* can go in the head of CP, then the lack of any projections above MoodP for the imperative would explain the ungrammaticality of the imperativals in the antecedents of conditionals as in (12a); there is simply no place for the *if* to go. On the other hand, when we try to put an interrogative in the antecedent of the conditional, the head of CP is already filled by the auxiliary; again there is no place for the *if* to go.[8]

There is also syntactic evidence that even imperatival clauses without an overt subject have a covert one, since reflexives must be bound locally:

(27) Behave yourself.
(28) You behaved yourself.
(29) *You said [John behaved yourself].

These examples make it plausible that there is a covert subject that binds the reflexive in the imperatival clause. Note that the null subject of imperativals can be contextually bound or explicitly introduced as in (5):

(5) a. Somebody get this table off the set.
   b. Whoever stole this television bring it back.
   c. Nobody move a muscle.

If we follow standard compositional semantics for clauses of the sort given in Asher (1993), then we hypothesize that what falls under the scope of the imperatival is at least an eventuality abstract, the event argument not being filled in by tense:

(30) a. Leave
   b. Imp(λe leave(x, e))

The imperative itself then introduces a δ operator as well as an existential closure over the event variable to combine with an event type to yield an action formula of the atomic sort I have outlined above. The imperative must also specify an operator that in the right discourse contexts is capable of being the directive operator Dir_u, where u is the addressee of the directive. As an imperative does not always issue in a directive, the operator introduced must be underspecified – something in SDRT of the form $?_u$ that will be further specified by the discourse context. Whether $?_u$ is specified to Dir_u or not will depend on the discourse contexts in which the imperatival clause occurs; in particular it will depend on how it is attached to other clauses and on the type of speech act the other clauses convey.

The underspecified variable for the addressee u can either be identified with the covert subject of the imperative clause or serve as a contextual restrictor when an overt quantificational subject is given. When an overt subject is given with an imperatival, we seem to have two options. Consider again:

(5a) Somebody get this table off the set.

In (5a) the speaker is directing to everyone in a particular contextually given domain that one of them get the table off the set. On this view, the directive there should be in the nuclear scope of the quantifier binding a variable x, and has something like "$\delta\exists e move(e,x)$" within its scope. In the restrictor of the quantifier there should be a contextual variable which restricts x to a particular set of people.

To have a compositional account of the meaning of imperatives, then, we have to suppose that explicit subject quantifiers scope outside the imperative itself; perhaps the subject quantifier moves to Spec of MoodP, if that is the maximal projection for imperatives. Then an imperative like (5a) has the logical form in (31)

(31) Somebody x $(x \in u)$, $Imp(\lambda e$ get table$(x, e))$.

The quantifier is restricted to some contextually given domain of people, u; the quantifier selects a person of that group and the imperative directs that person to do the moving. This means that the imperative when it is turned into a directive must also have an argument slot that can either be contextually or quantificationally bound. This directive only makes sense when it is addressed to a group which has the joint commitment of realizing "$\exists x \in u; u$ get this table off the set." Someone in the group must be such that they remove the table, though the directive does not specify who is supposed to do that, and similarly for other action statements in which there is a quantification over the subject position.[9]

We now have a compositional story of how to build logical forms with imperativals. But how does this relate in general to dynamic semantics? It is perfectly possible for the δ operator to combine with an event type to yield an action formula of the atomic sort I have outlined above. That will constitute the core semantics of imperatives. These formulas can be quantified into to bind the subject variable or that variable can be contextually bound. But this is not the end of the story; we still need to specify how imperatives or their logical forms align with various types of speech acts, in particular directives. What we are missing is the discourse function of imperatives; that will yield an answer to the question of alignment and provide a compositional account of embedded speech acts.

4 PRAGMATICS AND DISCOURSE

The main question for a theory of embedded imperativals is the alignment of directives and other speech acts to imperatival logical forms. Note that a directive must have a different form from a pure action formula of the sort I have introduced and argued that imperatives have as their logical form. When interpreted the actions denoted by formulas of the form $\delta\phi$ are performed, thus transforming the world, which is the way such formulas are supposed to work, say, in programming languages. But commanding or directing someone to do an action does not make it so! In this directives are different from performatives. How do we account for this?

We have seen some examples already where clauses in imperatival mood do not yield commands – generic sentences like

(11) Smoke a packet of cigarettes a day and you'll die before you're thirty.

But there are many others. Consider, for instance, the discourse type given by recipes or directions for getting to a place, something that has received considerable attention in SDRT (see e.g. Asher and Lascarides 2003).

(32) To make onion soup, heat 10 cups of chicken or beef bouillon to a low boil. Peel and slice two pounds of yellow onions and add to the hot broth. Simmer for 30 minutes.

This recipe involves a topic *making onion soup*, which is then elaborated on by a sequence of imperatives that yield a sort of "narrative." In SDRT, imperatival clauses, just like indicative clauses, can contribute logical forms that enter into a narrative sequence, in which each discourse constituent is linked to the other by the Narration discourse relation. Each one of the imperatival clauses describes an action that is to be performed in a sequence; the action of adding the onions to the *hot* broth should not be carried out if the action of heating the broth has not already occurred. We naturally interpret subsequent imperatival clauses relative to the satisfaction of previous imperatival clauses in such a sequence. And each clause has an effect on the world of evaluation, transforming it via the action described. In this respect, narrative sequences of imperatival clauses and narrative sequences of indicative clauses function similarly.

A narrative sequence of imperatival clauses has a similar semantics to a narrative sequence (*Narration*) between indicative clauses. SDRT signals the difference by linking imperatival clauses with the relation *Narration$_r$*. But the semantics of these two relations is exactly the same! The semantics of Narration is that each action succeeds the next, and just as with Narration between assertions, the post conditions of the *n*th element in the sequence must overlap the preconditions of the $n + 1$st element (Asher and Lascarides 2003). The one difference is that when we have Narration between formulas of the form $\delta\phi$ the sequence of such actions forms a plan rather than a sequence of tests.

Narration(π_1, π_2) entails the truth of the contents of the clauses labeled by π_1 and π_2. Formally, this means that *Narration* is a veridical rhetorical relation and obeys the veridicality axiom of SDRT (ϕ_α below is the logical form associated with the label α and $\phi_{R(\pi_1, \pi_2)}$ is the object language formula providing semantic constraints on R):

- Satisfaction Schema for Veridical Rhetorical Relations:
  $(w, f) \; [\![R \, (\pi_1, \pi_2)]\!]_M \, (w', g)$ iff $(w, f) \; [\![\phi_{\pi_1} \wedge \phi_{\pi_2} \wedge \phi_{R(\pi_1, \pi_2)}]\!]_M \, (w', g)$
- Veridicality*:
  A relation R is veridical iff the following is valid:
  $R \, (\alpha, \beta) \rightarrow (\phi_a \wedge \phi_\beta)$.
  *Many discourse relations including *Narration*, but also *Elaboration* and others that I will introduce soon are veridical relations.

If the *Narration* relation linking the imperatives in (32) is a veridical relation, the relation that links the whole narrative sequence of actions to the topic is not. That is why the actions described in the recipe are not carried out in the actual world of evaluation. The narrative sequence constituted by the clauses linked by *Narration$_r$* constitutes an elaboration of the general plan of making onion soup. The sequence forms a discourse constituent that is itself related via another discourse relation *Plan*

Elaboration to the topic of the recipe, which is given by the first clause. The semantics of *Plan Elaboration* is an intensional one, and it is *not veridical*, unlike its indicative cousin, *Elaboration*. Roughly, *Plan-Elab*(π_1, π_2) says that the elaborating constituent, ϕ_{π_2}, spells out a sequence of actions that if carried out will yield that the topic labeled ϕ_{π_1} is satisfied. But it neither entails ϕ_{π_1} nor ϕ_{π_2}. Refining the view in Asher and Lascarides (2003), a key clue to this relation is the use of the infinitival which is naturally interpreted as being in the antecedent of a conditional. Using our extension of dynamic semantics, the semantics for SDRT formulas involving the discourse relation *Plan-Elaboration* makes plain that no action is being carried out. And no action is directed to the addressee in (32) either. In this case the underspecified operator just resolves to an identity or truth operator that does not affect the content of the discourse. All the content is given by the discourse relations.

- The semantics of *Plan Elaboration*:
  (w, f) $[\![Plan\text{-}Elab(\pi_1, \pi_2)]\!]_M$ (w', g) iff (w, f) $[\![[\phi_{\pi_2}]\phi_{\pi_1}]\!](w, f)$.

As this semantics makes plain, no action is being carried out. And no action is directed to the addressee in (32) either.

The discourse structure changes dramatically if we change (32) just slightly:

(32′) Make onion soup! Heat 10 cups of chicken or beef bouillon to a low boil. Peel and slice two pounds of yellow onions and add to the hot broth. Simmer for 30 minutes.

The command in the "topic" position changes the semantics of the discourse as a whole. Intuitively, the topic now attaches to the discourse context as a directive and the rest of the recipe functions as an Elaboration of that directive, inheriting its directive force. Within the Elaboration of course there is still the narrative sequence containing the details of the recipe.

To spell all this out, we need to attend to the rules of the glue logic of SDRT wherein speech act contributions are calculated. Which speech act a given discourse constituent contributes has as much to do with the discourse context in which it is introduced as with its own content. Let us consider an example already studied in SDRT (Asher and Lascarides 2003):

(33) a. A: How does one catch the 10:20 train to London?
     b. B: Go to the information counter and ask someone.

Note the difference of the meaning of (33b) in this context from its meaning in the 'null' context, or when it is attached to an assertion of some kind as below.

(34) a. A: I'm late.
    b. B: Go to the information counter.

The imperative in (33b) is *not* to be carried out. Rather, its "rhetorical function" is to provide sufficient information so that A can compute an answer to his question. The imperatives that function as "answers" in these contexts are to be understood in the following way: if you perform this action, your question will be answered. In SDRT, we label this relation $IQAP_r$.

SDRT provides a defeasible attachment rule for imperatives when they are attached to questions:

- $IQAP_r$ rule: $(?\ (\alpha, \beta, \lambda) \wedge\ ?\alpha \wedge\ !\beta) > IQAP_r\ (\alpha, \beta, \lambda)$.

In words this rule says that if β is to be attached to α within the scope of some constituent λ, and if α is an interrogative and β is an imperative, then normally one can infer the relation $IQAP_r$ to hold between α and β within the scope of λ.[10] So as long as everything in the context is consistent with inferring this relation, then the glue logic predicts that $IQAP_r$ should hold between an interrogative and an imperative. This glue logic axiom capitalizes on the moods of the clauses to be linked together.

In the case of an $IQAP_r$ relation, again the underspecified operator $?_u$ introduced by the imperative resolves to identity and we specify the covert subject of the imperative to be u. Then the meaning postulate for $IQAP_r$ is:

- $IQAP_r\ ((\alpha, \beta, \lambda) \wedge A: \alpha) \rightarrow (\exists \phi(\exists u(u = A \wedge \phi_\beta) > \phi \wedge \phi$ is an answer to $\phi_\alpha)))$.

In words, the postulate says that there is some proposition ϕ such that whenever the speaker carries out the action specified in β then normally ϕ holds and ϕ constitutes an answer to the question expressed in α. Notice that for examples like (33) that exploit $IQAP_r$, it is crucial that the interpretation of the imperative not be put in terms of putting some action on a commitment slate as in Merin (1992), Portner (2004) or others. For you are not going to get an answer to the question just by putting an action on your commitment slate; just committing yourself to a certain action does not guarantee that the action will get done. It's only the *doing* of the action that will give you an answer to your question – that is the intuitive meaning of the response to the question in (33b).

The point of these examples in discourse is that it is the rhetorical relation that tells us how to interpret the action given by the imperative. And this indicates how we should now finish our interpretation of imperatives, when they are attached to assertions or in out-of-the-blue contexts. I hypothesize that when an imperative occurs in a stand-alone context (rule 1) or is attached to an assertion (rule 2), a rule of the glue logic takes the imperative to be a directive and attaches the imperatival with this form as a request or a directive.

- Rule 1 for Requests: $(\neg \exists \alpha \ ?(\alpha, \beta, \lambda) \wedge \ !\beta) > Dir_u \ (\beta, \lambda)$.
- Rule 2 for Requests: $(?(\alpha, \beta, \lambda) \wedge \ !\beta \wedge \neg \ (!\alpha \vee ?\alpha)) > Dir_u \ (\beta, \lambda)$.

Dir_u is an operator whose semantics is understood in a dynamic way: given an input context in which the referent of u is assigned a commitment slate, then the output context as modified by $Dir_u\phi$ adjusts the commitment slate of the hearer so that ϕ is a commitment of the hearer. What this rule says is that if an imperatival β does not form a sequence of imperatives or form an answer to a question, then defeasibly we can infer that it is a directive to some contextually specified agent u, usually the addressee, which means roughly that the speaker intends to put the content of β on the commitment slate of the addressee.

The addressee, however, need not agree to this commitment. If he or she does not acknowledge or agree to the commitment, then it does not seem as though that commitment can be hers! Because the request is inferred via a rule of the glue logic and is part of the logical form of the discourse structure, it, like any other part of a discourse contribution, can be contested by the addressee or any other discourse participant. A Correction$_r$ may apply that conveys a refusal by the addressee to undertake the request. The rules for the negotiation of standard Corrections (Asher and Lascarides 2003) apply in such cases as well. All that a directive does is imply that the speaker intends to put something on the hearer's commitment slate, which will become an actual commitment of the addressee only when the rules for acceptance are met. It may be that the dialogue "settles" to a point where the request has become moot, as well. SDRT contains a whole theory of settledness which applies to requests as well as assertions.

5 RESULTS AND PREDICTIONS

The semantics for imperatives just proposed makes sense of the liberal quantification into subject position of imperatives. These quantifiers exploit the variable *u* that is associated with the speech act type *Dir* as a contextual restriction. In SDRT, such quantification is novel but poses no problems to the semantics. In cases where the subject of the imperatival is not specified, the contextually specified variable *u* is set to the addressee(s) of the context and $u = x$, where *x* is the variable of the action formula for the subject of the action.

Conditional commands are straightforward. The conditional gives rise to a nonveridical discourse relation in SDRT, Consequence, and our rule for directives yields for (35) the logical form in (35′),

(35) If you want to get an A, study hard.

(35′) $\langle \{\pi_0, \pi_1, \pi, \pi'\}, \pi$: want an $A(u)$, π_1: δ (study hard(u)) $\wedge$ π': Dir_u (π_1) $\wedge$ π_0: Consequence$(\pi, \pi')\rangle$

which corresponds to the formulation of a guarded action in the dynamic semantics, except for the fact that the semantics interprets the consequent as a directive. One might strengthen this further with the pragmatic implicature that a directive that one undertakes is normally carried out, which would simplify the consequent of the conditional to "δ(study hard(u))."

There is probably a syntactic explanation, as I mentioned earlier, as to why conditionals with the imperatival in the antecedent are so bad. If imperativals have no clausal head, then the expression *if* cannot find an appropriate spot in the syntactic tree. There is no room for it. On the other hand, for the consequent which is often signaled by *then*, we can explain the acceptability of imperatives in the consequents of conditionals by noting that *then*, at least in English, is an adverb that can adjoin to VP.

Let us now turn to quantification into directives over arguments other than the subject. As we have seen, anaphoric binding into imperativals is uncontroversial. So the problem is not binding per se into these contexts, but rather quantifying in. On our semantics this should be possible; in fact the anaphoric case and the quantifying in cases are indistinguishable semantically on this semantics. Indeed on most dynamic semantic theories, quantifying in and anaphoric binding with a quantifier are indistinguishable. But since these are indistinguishable semantically, then it seems that there must be either a pragmatic or a syntactic story for ruling out these cases of quantifying in.

Once again our semantics is rather liberal with respect to the standard views. The logical form for (7a) is (playing a little informally with SDRT notation):

(7a′) $\forall x(\text{bottle-found}(x)) \rightarrow Dir_u \; \delta \; (C(x))$

Manfred Krifka denies that

(36) Confiscate most bottles that you find!

has a similar form. I disagree:

(36′) *Most* $x(\text{bottle-found}(x))$, $Dir_u \; \delta \; (C(x))$.

This logical form is perfectly coherent in our dynamic logic; further-more, it is what seems to be verified by speakers' intuitions. Consider that there are five bottles and that you find three of them. (36)'s request is satisfied if you confiscate two of those bottles that you find. And that is precisely what the logical form that is given in (36′) requires. It returns a world that differs from the actual one in that two bottles have been confiscated.

If the standard view is that there is no quantification into directives formulated as imperatives, then there ought to be a truth conditional difference between the wide and narrow scope readings and the wide scope reading should be unavailable. But it appears that it is exactly the wide scope meaning that is intended in (36). To verify this, consider what the quantifier does in dynamic semantics. We take an input state (a world assignment function pair since these operations are all distribu-tive) and (36′) will yield an output just in case most of the objects satisfying the restrictor also satisfy the consequent. Where the antece-dent and consequent are just state formulas, then quantificational for-mulae amount to tests. But when the consequent is a command something else happens: the consequent is "satisfied" just in case the input world is transformed in the required way. Both (36) intuitively and (36′) formally direct the addressee to put on his commitment slate that for most of the bottles that he finds, he must consfiscate them. Crucially what is *not* being said is that he put on his commitment slate that he find most bottles; the commitments are to the acts of confiscation only.

On the other hand, the narrow scope reading of the quantifier is given in the formula (36″).

(36″) Dir_u Most (x) (bottle-found(x), $C(x)$).

What this says is that the addressee is to commit to making true that most of the bottles he finds are confiscated. In English this appears to be equivalent to the meaning of (36′) but formally it depends on the quantifier being interpreted within the scope of the directive. If commitments are understood modally, then this will mean that the quantifier is interpreted with respect to the commitment worlds, and that is not what is at all intended. The commitments are to bottles that one finds in the actual world of evaluation.

This reasoning appears to hold for all positive quantifiers. In particular, we predict wide scope readings for the following:

(7e) Confiscate at least some (three) bottles that you find!

(7f) Confiscate a very nice bottle that I saw them with before.

For negative quantifiers like *no*, there is the matter of the negation of the directive. But note that that is perfectly well defined in dynamic semantics.

The semantics for imperatives and directives extends naturally to a semantics for commissives as well. Further, our semantic account of imperatives applies as it is very nicely to performative speech acts like christening, baptizing, marrying, and so on. These appear to be straightforward action formulas, which are performed when the performatives are uttered in the appropriate circumstances (these appropriate circumstances are taken to be presuppositions of the performative verbs). The proper formulations of speech acts just by occurring transform the world of evaluation in the appropriate way. We can be quite abstract about the details of what actions these particular speech acts make on the world of evaluation. But their analysis can be made quite comfortably within the dynamic discourse semantics proposed here.

5.1 Conjunction revisited

Conjunctions with sentences convey some sort of coordinating discourse relation as noted by Txurruka (2003). This observation proves to be extremely important: a natural language conjunction does not signal a truth conditional connective in SDRT and in any case the dynamic logic does not have such an operation – it has the sequential update operation. The conjunction of an imperatival and an indicative clause seems to give rise to two sorts of discourse relations, Def-Consequence and something like Narration. The former corresponds to the conditional readings of sentences like (11) repeated below, while the second corresponds to the natural interpretation of (37):

(11) Smoke a packet of cigarettes a day and you'll die before you're thirty.

(37) Go to the office, and there you'll find the files I told you about.

The former conveys a sort of generic force, but lest one think that this is a peculiar property of conjunctions involving imperatives, compare (11) with (38) which exhibits the same generic type connection between two *indicative* clauses:

(38) a. John walks two feet, and (normally) he's out of breath.
    b. John has anything to drink and he goes bonkers.

Though one might argue that the generic reading of the first of these clauses is due to the presence of *normally*, at least some speakers find the use of the adverbial completely optional with respect to this interpretation.

    The generic interpretation arises, I think, from a combination of cues that the glue logic of SDRT can exploit. The use of a future tense with the imperative is crucial, because this allows us to interpret the second clause as a consequence that comes after the action performed in the first clause. But clearly that is not sufficient, because (37) has the same sequence of tenses but does not have a readily available generic reading. Perhaps the presence of *there* makes the generic or conditional reading less available. In (38a, b) the use of the present tense or at least the same tense in both clauses is an important clue. Another important clue is the prosody. In all the examples with generic readings there is a prosodic rise at the end of the first clause. There is no intonational break between the first clause and the prosodic contour on the second clause that seems to be also present when such a clause is used in isolation as an assertion. If the intonation is changed so that there is final fall, say, on the first clause of (38a), the generic reading disappears.[11]

    I will not go into formalizations of the appropriate glue logic rules here, since a proper treatment would take us too far afield into matters of prosodic information and how that is handled in SDRT. Suffice it to say that we infer in (11) a relation of Defeasible Consequence between the two clauses, and this automatically gives us the conditional reading of such conjunctions. With (37), we have an episodic reading of the same tense sequence – and so we can conclude that the sequence by itself is not sufficient. We also need a certain connection between the contents of the clauses, but such requirements are familiar from other SDRT examples. Some of the data by Han (2000) might be additional clues for the presence of the generic reading, like the lack of negative polarity items in imperativals except in these antecedents. The same is true of the indicative clauses that are linked by the conjunction and have a generic interpretation. In any case, we see that an SDRT-based account has the wherewithall to account for the varieties of readings when an imperative is conjoined with an assertion. In the glue logic, we will have a more specific default than the rule 1 that will override the defeasible inference to a directive speech act.

I turn now to a discussion of (37) when it lacks the generic reading. This is actually a complex example because the first constituent is interpreted first as a directive in virtue of the SDRT rules given above, but the action it describes is also part of a Narration sequence. Clearly it is going to the office that occasions the finding of the file folder, not the putting of the action of going to the office on one's commitment slate. How do we express that in SDRT? We want something like Narration (π_1, π_2), $\pi_1 : \delta$ (goes$(u, x) \wedge$ office (x)), $\pi_0 : Dir_u (\pi_1)$, but this results in a clash over the status of the action described in π_1. According to Narration it must be performed, but according to *Dir*, that is not the case. So the Maximize Discourse Coherence principle or MDC and SDRT update as defined in Asher and Lascarides (2003) would require that we eliminate this clash by reanalyzing the way the constituents fit together. One way of resolving the clash is to have a discourse structure in which the directive has scope over the constituent which conveys Narration (π_1, π_2), which is not implausible. So the analysis of this discourse would yield the following SDRS.

- π_0, π, π_1, π_2 (these are the speech act discourse referents introduced, while below are the formulas associated with them that give their content).
- $\pi_0 : Dir_u (\pi)$
- π: *Narration* (π_1, π_2)
- $\pi_1 : \delta$ (goes$(u, x) \wedge$ office (x))
- $\pi_2 :$ (find $(u, y) \wedge$ folder (y)).

5.2 *Disjunction Revisited*

Disjunction, unlike conjunction, gives rise typically to a particular discourse relation, Alternation.[12] Alternation conveys a set of epistemic alternatives (cf. Zimmerman 2000); a final ending intonation or rising intonation over the disjunction tells us whether the set of alternatives has been exhaustively specified or not. One additional parameter of variation concerns whether there is a free-choice reading of the disjunction. At present I do not know what are the parameters that influence this reading. But it is obvious that it is present in cases like:

(41) Go or don't go. The choice is yours.

Assuming that the free-choice sense of the disjunction can be expressed via a rule of the glue logic, we would derive the following discourse logical form for (41):

(41′) Alt$_{FC}$ (π, π') $\wedge$ π: go $\wedge$ π': ¬go.

The translation into logical form of (41′) can now proceed easily via the analysis put forward in Asher and Bonevac (2005) and the rules already given:

(41″) Alt (π, π') $\wedge$ π: (Dir_ugo(u) > OK) $\wedge$ π': (Dir_u ¬go(u) > OK).

The other readings of disjoined imperatives besides the free-choice one come from an analysis of Alternation itself. Suppose that the epistemic alternatives given by Alternation are understood as exhaustive. Then we can have either a simple alternation or a conditional reading. The reason for the latter is that an exhaustive alternation of epistemic possibilities has very close connections to the conditional, as Gillies (2004) has pointed out. The inference from (42a) to (42b) seems completely valid when the disjunction is given exhaustive intonation.

(42) a. Either the burglar committed the murder or the cook did it.
     b. So if it wasn't the burglar, it was the cook.

But given this observation, the conditional reading follows immediately for (13a) repeated below,

(13a) Get out of here or I'll call the police.

when this is read with exhaustive intonation, as is natural.

5.3 Negation revisited

We have seen that the dynamic semantic treatment of negation, together with a dynamic treatment of questions, predict that negated questions can exist but they have a very special, metalinguistic meaning. This same dynamic treatment of negation makes it in principle possible that negation should be able to combine with an imperative meaning. But we have observed that negations do not have scope over an operator like *Dir*. That is, sentences like

(43) Don't close the door

simply do not have the reading that a directive to close the door is not being made. This is puzzling from a strictly semantic point of view, but from a discourse point of view this observation falls into place. In general, we do not find negation, in contrast to conditionals, taking scope over discourse relations.[13] There are indeed negative discourse relations that correspond to metalinguistic uses of negation. Corrections and denials, for instance, are the dynamic operation of negation raised into a discourse relation. This relation has determinate truth conditions but its semantics is not anything like that of a truth function. Self-corrections and the retraction of directives is thus sensible from this point of view. But one needs to express the Correction with another clause from that of the directive:

(44) Close the door. Actually, I take that back.

In fact, moving to dynamic semantics where we have actions at different levels allows us to unify metalinguistic uses of negation with the more standard objectual uses. The so-called metalinguistic uses operate not on the content of an utterance but rather on other features of it. But once we have means of referring to these in a dynamic setting, then we can treat them all uniformly.

If negations of speech acts make sense though, then we have to explain the ungrammaticality of sentences like (45) in a different way.

(45) It's not the case that close the door.

I suspect that it is the syntactic structure of imperativals that precludes a wide scope negation over the imperatival mood. If negations take VPs as syntactic arguments or fall into CP, the imperatival mood lacking a clausal head would block the application of negation.

5.4 What does this semantics not claim to be consistent?

Our semantics is very liberal. But there are some sequences of imperativals that do not work without a radical reinterpretation.

(46) Go! Don't go!

This discourse interpreted as a sequence of clauses, i.e. linked via Narration$_r$, is unsatisfiable, because the post-state of the first action is incompatible with the pre-state of the second action and because

Narration$_r$, like simple Narration, requires this compatibility between pre-states and post-states of sequenced actions.

6 CONCLUSIONS

The work presented here on imperatives begins with the intuitions developed in the *Stit* logics of Belnap, Horty and Xu (1995) that Asher and Lascarides (2003) use in a dynamic semantic setting to give a semantics for imperatives. But that semantics had several problems: it failed to capture the directive force of imperatives in certain contexts. For that we needed SDRT's view about speech acts and discourse relations. The point about imperatives is that the discourse context, in particular the attachment site, is crucial to their interpretation. In this the proposed account differs from most other recent investigations (Portner 2004; Mastop 2005). Directives are only defeasibly a function of mood; imperatives only yield directives in certain contexts. The discourse context contains crucial information about the discourse function and the types of speech act that an imperative may possess. For questions and assertions, we learn the same lesson, but perhaps a little less dramatically. In any case, our semantics must be flexible enough to permit the wide variety of uses to which imperatives, interrogatives, and indicatives are put.

Adding a discourse semantics level to the analysis permits us also to simplify the underlying logic. We can dispense with operators like [ ] for quantifying over actions, and perhaps $+$ as well. So what we have is a uniform set of connectives both for indicatives and for imperatives: sequence ";," negation "$\neg$," and both weak and normal epistemic conditionals "$>$" and "$\rightarrow$," together with various quantifiers. Natural language *or* either gives rise to a discourse relation or in the rare cases where that is blocked to an operator that we can define in terms of "$\neg$" and ";."

In addition to the detailed work on imperatives, I have tried here to integrate work on imperatives with work on interrogatives, principally that of Groenendijk and Stokhof. The resulting semantics allows for all sorts of embedded speech acts. Many sorts of embedded speech acts may be rare or difficult for pragmatic reasons, or ungrammatical for syntactic reasons. In general, however, my contention is that the semantics of various moods and the logical nature of the speech acts they can give rise to do not block embedding, contrary to what many have suggested.

NOTES

1 The question about embeddings for performatives is complex and interesting, but I do not have space to go into this issue here.

2 Some might take the last proposition in the answer set to be presupposed by the question. In that case the direct answer set would only contain the first three propositions.

3 When a formula functions as a test, an element of the input context either satisfies the formula and so passes on into the output context or does not satisfy the formula and so fails to be an element of the output context.

4 As in Asher and Lascarides (2003), I take answers to questions to be non-exhaustive and so satisfied by several elements of the partition given by a question; unlike Asher and Lascarides (2003) or earlier work on questions in SDRT, I now believe that thinking of the meaning of a question as a partition is the best and cleanest approach. By breaking apart the meaning of a question and the set of linguistically acceptable answers, we can have both the elegant dynamic semantics that Groenendijk put forward and the linguistically plausible view of answers argued for by Ginzburg (1995) and adopted in SDRT.

5 See Asher and McCready (2007), Asher and Wang (2003), van den Berg (1996).

6 This is probably an oversimplification; once rhetorical questions are taken into account, it is no longer clear that interrogatives always express questions.

7 Note that this semantics is exactly the same for imperative as for indicative clauses.

8 Thanks to Brian Reese for suggesting this explanation.

9 Alternatively one could leave the quantifier in situ, as Portner (2004) has argued, and stipulate that there is a group of addressees that must function as a restrictor of the quantifier.

10 All the glue logic axioms have this basic form; for a discussion see Asher and Lascarides (2003).

11 I now think that the analysis presented in Asher and Lascarides (2003) is wrong; there we said that it was only the fact that a particular action was undesirable that made it not a directive. But that is not right. Consider:

(39) Play the lottery enough times and you'll win.

(40) You're going to die anyway. So go ahead. Smoke three packs a day.

(39) clearly has a generic reading. Nevertheless, it is not that the end state of winning the lottery is undesirable. On the other hand, smoking three packs a day is directed in (40), even though it has consequences that are undesirable. So such examples seem to be counterexamples to the analysis proposed in Asher and Lascarides (2003).

12 As Asher and Bonevac (2005) argue, however, this inference to Alternation from the presence of a disjunction is defeasible.

13 A possible exception might be the very colloquial and recently added English construction, *John went to school and then he studied. Not!* If such discourses are acceptable, we might hypothesize that so is *close the door! Not!*

Chapter 11

Yes–no questions and the myth
of content invariance

SAVAS L. TSOHATZIDIS

1 TWO KINDS OF FORCE-CONTENT DISTINCTION

No theory of sentence meaning would be adequate if it failed to entail that a nondeclarative sentence like *Is water odourless?* and a declarative sentence like *Water is odourless*, though both meaningful, do not have the same meaning, and only theories of meaning that, like Searle's, aim to systematically relate differences in sentence meaning to differences in illocutionary act potential would have any chance of engendering such entailments. Still, not all ways of relating sentence meanings to illocutionary acts are adequate, and in this chapter I want to argue that a fundamental assumption that Searle uses in analyzing sentence meaning in terms of illocutionary acts is mistaken. The assumption (which is very widely shared among those who, along with Searle, duly acknowledge that no account of sentence meaning can dispense with an account of sentence mood) has to do with the particular way in which Searle interprets the distinction between the *force* and the *content* of illocutionary acts and applies it to the analysis of sentence meaning.

There is an innocuous way of interpreting the force-content distinction against which there can be no objection, and which I would be perfectly happy to accept. On that innocuous interpretation, saying that illocutionary acts (and the sentence meanings that one aims to characterize in their terms) should be thought of as consisting in the attachment of a *force* to a *content* simply means that, in order to fully specify an illocutionary act in a semantically relevant way, it is not enough to merely specify the *kind* of illocutionary act it is (whether, for example, it is a yes–no question, or an assertion, or a command, etc.), but it is also necessary to specify what it is about its meaning that distinguishes it from all other illocutionary acts of the *same* kind (for example, what it is about the meaning of a yes–no question that makes it different from

244

another yes–no question, what it is about the meaning of an assertion that makes it different from another assertion, what it is about the meaning of a command that make it different from another command, and so on). That both of these kinds of specification are required is obvious, but merely registering that requirement in the way the innocuous interpretation does is not tantamount to adopting any *particular* way in which one might propose to fulfill it. As far as the innocuous interpretation is concerned, the force of an illocutionary act is *whatever* turns out to properly distinguish that act, in semantically relevant terms, from all illocutionary acts of *other* kinds, and the content of an illocutionary act is *whatever* turns out to properly distinguish that act, in semantically relevant terms, from all illocutionary acts of the *same* kind. But accepting the force-content distinction in that innocuous sense involves no strong commitments as to what sorts of things forces or contents will turn out to be, and is, in particular, perfectly consistent with the possibility that there may not be a single *kind* of content uniformly attributable *across* illocutionary act kinds – it is perfectly consistent, for example, with the possibility that what makes a yes–no question semantically distinct from another yes–no question is a different *sort* of thing from what makes an assertion semantically distinct from another assertion, which in turn is a different *sort* of thing from what makes a command semantically distinct from another command, and so on.

In contrast to the innocuous interpretation, however, the standard interpretation of the force-content distinction, of which Searle is a paradigmatic representative, involves quite strong commitments both as to what forces are and as to what contents are. And it is an implication of its commitments in the latter area that there does exist a single *kind* of content that is uniformly attributable across illocutionary act types in all theoretically fundamental cases (i.e. in all cases in which the content in question is representable by means of a complete sentence), and that ensures, among other things, that the *sort* of thing that makes a yes–no question semantically distinct from another yes–no question is the same as the *sort* of thing that makes an assertion semantically distinct from another assertion, which in turn is the same as the *sort* of thing that makes a command semantically distinct from a another command, and so on. In Searle's case (which, in this respect too, is fully representative of standard assumptions) the unique sort of thing that plays the role of illocutionary act *content* in all theoretically central cases is a *proposition*, and it is the differences between the *propositions* to which they associate the same force that accounts for differences in meaning between illocutionary acts of the same kind. Furthermore, just as there are differences in meaning between illocutionary acts that are due exclusively to the fact that different *propositions* get attached to the same force, there are also, in Searle's view, differences in meaning between illocutionary acts that are due exclusively to the fact that different forces get attached to *the same proposition*. And it is differences of that last kind that, according to Searle and many others, account for the distinctive semantic contribution of sentence mood: semantically distinct sentences that differ only in mood are sentences whose semantic nonidentity is uniquely attributable to the fact that each of them associates a different kind of force to the very same *proposition*.

I will argue that these views cannot be maintained if some familiar and fundamental facts regarding the interpretation of yes–no questions are to be respected. And since a theory of sentence mood – and so, of sentence meaning – that cannot deliver a satisfactory analysis of as simple and basic a sentence type as a yes–no question cannot be accepted, I will conclude that no theory of sentence meaning will be adequate if it incorporates the standard interpretation of the force-content distinction, and in particular its assumption that the contents to which illocutionary forces are attached are propositional. Along the way, I will be gesturing towards the sort of analysis of yes–no questions that I would regard as appropriate; my primary purpose, however, is not to fully work out such an analysis, but rather to argue that certain features of yes–no questions that *any* analysis should accommodate are not consistent with certain basic assumptions that many theories of meaning routinely endorse.

2 YES–NO QUESTIONS AND THE ANALYSIS OF ILLOCUTIONARY ACTS

According to Searle, the literal meaning of a sentence derives from (in the sense, presumably, of being a logical construction out of) the illocutionary acts that linguistic conventions allow its speakers to perform in uttering it, and a typical illocutionary act, noted $F(p)$, consists of an illocutionary force F attached to a proposition p, which represents the act's content: "throughout the analysis of speech acts," Searle explains, he is observing a distinction between "what might be called *content* and *function*," where "the content is the proposition" and "the function is the illocutionary force with which the proposition is presented" (1969: 125).

The principal virtue of the distinction between illocutionary force and propositional content as the two semantically relevant components of an illocutionary act is, Searle suggests, that it enables us to appreciate that differences in meaning between illocutionary acts can result either from keeping an illocutionary force constant and varying the propositions to which that force is attached or from keeping a propositional content constant and varying the illocutionary forces attached to it (and it is, as already mentioned, the latter possibility that is the key to Searle's – and to many others' – account of sentence mood). Thus, the sentences *Water is odourless* and *Blood is colourless* differ in meaning because the illocutionary acts that linguistic conventions allow their speakers to perform are different by virtue of attaching the same force (the force of assertion) to two *different* propositions (the proposition <u>that water is odourless</u> and the proposition <u>that blood is colourless</u>, respectively). On the other hand, the sentences *Water is odourless* and *Is water odourless?* differ in meaning because the illocutionary acts that linguistic conventions allow their speakers to perform are different by virtue of attaching two *different* forces (the force of assertion and the force of question, respectively) to the *same* proposition (the proposition <u>that water is odourless</u>); and similarly, the sentences *Blood is colourless* and *Is blood colourless?* differ in meaning because the illocutionary acts that linguistic conventions allow their speakers to perform are different by virtue of attaching two different forces (the forces of question and assertion, respectively) to a single proposition (the proposition <u>that blood is colourless</u>).

   The relation, illustrated by the last two pairs of examples, between a yes–no question and its grammatically corresponding assertion, has always been presented by Searle as an exceptionally clear case of a relation between sentences that are conventionally dedicated to the performance of acts with *different* illocutionary forces but the *same* propositional content, and this fact fully justifies attributing to him the following thesis, which will be central to the present discussion, and which I will call the Content Invariance Thesis:

Content Invariance Thesis (CIT)
Under uniform interpretations of corresponding sub-sentential constituents, a yes–no question and its grammatically corresponding assertion *express the same proposition*.

Thus, in discussing the examples *Sam smokes habitually* and *Does Sam smoke habitually?*, which are the very first examples by means of which the distinction between illocutionary force and propositional content is introduced in *Speech Acts*, Searle explicitly claims that, in utterances of them where the same individual, Sam, is being referred to, "the same proposition is expressed" (Searle 1969: 29) – the proposition, namely, that Sam smokes habitually. In his discussion of predication later in the same book (Searle 1969: 124), he explicitly assumes that "the man who asserts that Socrates is wise [and] the man who asks whether he is wise" express the same proposition – the proposition, namely, that Socrates is wise. In his discussion of Russell's theory of descriptions toward the end of the same book (Searle 1969: 150–62), he maintains that no theory of descriptions would be adequate if it could not acknowledge the fact that *the same proposition* is expressed by the assertion *The King of France is bald* and by the yes–no question *Is the King of France bald?* In discussing the problem of opacity in *Intentionality* (Searle 1983: 180–96), he remarks that, assuming that their subject terms refer to the same individual, the assertion *Mr. Howard is an honest man* and the yes–no question *Is Mr. Howard an honest man?* have the same propositional content – the content, namely, that Mr. Howard is an honest man – and emphasizes that exactly the same content is expressed by the complement clauses of their respective indirect speech reports (that is, by the complement clauses of such sentences as *X asserted that Mr. Howard is an honest man* and *X asked whether Mr. Howard is an honest man*), notwithstanding the fact that different complementizers – "that" and "whether" respectively – would be grammatically required to introduce the two complement clauses in question. And in a more recent book summarizing some of his main philosophical contributions (Searle 1998), he begins his discussion of language by drawing attention to the significance of the distinction between the force and the content of illocutionary acts, offering as an "obvious example" of cases illustrating that distinction the assertion *You will leave the room* and the yes–no question *Will you leave the room?*, which, he remarks, are clearly different in one respect (namely, in the force that each one carries) but, equally clearly, identical in another respect, namely, in the proposition that each one expresses, which is "the proposition that you will leave the room" (1998: 138; the same examples, reported in indirect speech, are used to make the same point in Searle 2004: 166). There can be no doubt, then, that, according to Searle, *the same proposition* is expressed by a yes–no question and by its grammatically corresponding assertion (as well as by the complement clauses of correct indirect speech

reports of these), under uniform interpretations of their corresponding subsentential constituents. And in holding that Searle is, of
course, far from alone: terminological differences aside, what the
Content Invariance Thesis proposes is accepted as a matter of course
by several other prominent philosophers – perhaps not surprisingly,
since the original formulation of the thesis occurs, in the context of a
general discussion of the force-content distinction, in a late essay by
Frege (1918) that is widely regarded as a founding document of
modern philosophy of language.

I am going to argue that no acceptable account of either propositions
or illocutionary acts is consistent with adherence to the Content
Invariance Thesis, and that that thesis should consequently be rejected.
(Rejecting CIT need not, of course, involve commitment to the thesis that
yes–no questions have *different* propositional contents from their grammatically corresponding assertions: it may rather involve commitment to
the thesis that, unlike their grammatically corresponding assertions,
yes–no questions have no *propositional* contents at all.) The argument
relies on two theses that neither Searle nor anyone else would presumably have the desire to controvert, and consists in showing that, when
taken in conjunction with these uncontroversial theses, CIT has a range
of implications that turn out to be obviously false. The two uncontroversial theses, which I will respectively call the Propositional Distinctness
Thesis and the Illocutionary Distinctness Thesis, are the following:

Propositional Distinctness Thesis (PDT)
Two propositions are not identical if the one is true and the other false with
respect to the same situation.

Illocutionary Distinctness Thesis (IDT)
Two illocutionary acts are not identical if they result from attaching the same
force to two propositions that are not identical.

In the sense relevant to the present discussion, propositions are entities
that, by definition, have truth conditions ("to know the meaning of
a proposition," Searle acknowledges [1969: 125], "is to know under
what conditions it is true or false"); and although not everyone
would admit that it is sufficient for two propositions to have the same
truth conditions in order for them to be identical, absolutely no one
would deny that it *is* sufficient for two propositions *not* to have the same
truth conditions in order for them *not* to be identical. The PDT thesis
simply states that universally accepted condition, and should therefore

be embraced by anyone who cares to speak about propositions at all: if, with respect to the *same* situation, one proposition is true and another false, then they are certainly not *the same* proposition. As for the IDT thesis, it could hardly be denied by anyone who contemplates importing talk of propositions into the analysis of illocutionary acts: *if* attaching its force to a particular proposition is rightly taken to be essential to an illocutionary act's identity, then attachments of nonidentical propositions to a given illocutionary force should be expected to make a crucial difference to the identity of the resulting illocutionary acts, and the IDT thesis simply spells out the expected crucial difference – namely, that if two illocutionary acts consist in attaching the *same* force to two propositions that are *not* identical, then the illocutionary acts *themselves* will not be identical.

We are now going to see that, in conjunction with CIT, the two uncontroversial theses just stated have implications that, though not false in the case of assertions, are clearly false in the case of yes–no questions. The few examples to be discussed will be easy to generalize in obvious ways. Assuming uniform interpretations of subsentential constituents, the assertion in (1) and the yes–no question in (2) express, according to CIT, the *same* proposition – namely, the proposition that Sam is autistic:

(1) Sam is autistic.
(2) Is Sam autistic?

And, assuming again uniform interpretations of subsentential constituents, the assertion in (3) and the yes–no question in (4) express, according to CIT, the *same* proposition – namely, the proposition that Sam is not autistic:

(3) Sam isn't autistic.
(4) Isn't Sam autistic?

Now, the proposition that Sam is autistic and the proposition that Sam is not autistic are certainly not identical propositions, for the kind of reason that PDT states – namely, because their truth conditions are not identical. But then, given IDT, one should expect these nonidentical propositions to give rise to nonidentical illocutionary acts, when the same force attaches to them. And that turns out *not* to be invariably the case: utterances in which the two propositions are associated with the force of *assertion* do indeed instantiate *different assertions*, rather than different *ways* of making the *same* assertion:

clearly, (1) and (3) are not different ways of making the *same* assertion, they are simply different, indeed incompatible, assertions:

(1) Sam is autistic.
(3) Sam isn't autistic.

However, utterances in which the two propositions are putatively associated with the force of *question* do *not* instantiate different questions, but merely different *ways* of posing *the same question*: clearly, (2) and (4) do not pose different questions each, but merely constitute two different *ways* of posing *the same question*:

(2) Is Sam autistic?
(4) Isn't Sam autistic?

That (2) and (4) instantiate the same question even though (1) and (3) instantiate different assertions is evident from the fact that, although the positive and negative claims about identity that (5) and (7) contain are obviously true, there is no interpretation in which the positive or negative claims about identity that (6) and (8) contain are true:

(5) I already asked you whether Sam is autistic, and I am now asking you the same thing again: isn't he autistic?
(6) # I already told you that Sam is autistic, and I am now telling you the same thing again: he isn't autistic.
(7) I did tell you before that Sam is autistic, but what I am now telling you is different: he isn't autistic.
(8) # I did ask you before whether Sam is autistic, but what I am now asking you is different: isn't he autistic?

These contrasts are impossible to explain unless one assumes that, whereas *Sam is autistic* and *Sam isn't autistic* instantiate different assertions (and not different *ways* of making the same assertion), *Is Sam autistic?* and *Isn't Sam autistic?* do *not* instantiate different questions (but merely different ways of posing the *same* question). Furthermore, if *Is Sam autistic?* and *Isn't Sam autistic?* were instantiating *different* questions, it should be possible for one of those questions to be *settled* – that is, to have its correct answer selected among relevant alternatives – *without* the other being thereby settled. But that is simply impossible, as the following contradictory statements illustrate:

(9) The question whether Sam is autistic has now been settled, but it is not yet settled whether he isn't autistic.

(10) The question whether Sam isn't autistic has now been settled, but it is not yet settled whether he is autistic.

And, of course, if (2) and (4) were instantiating different questions, it should be possible for someone to come to know, or to need to know, the answer to the one *without* thereby coming to know, or having the need to know, the answer to the other. But that, again, is simply impossible, as the following incoherent pronouncements indicate:

(11) I know very well whether Sam is autistic, but what I still don't know is this: is he not autistic?
(12) I have no need to know whether Sam is not autistic, but what I do need to know is this: is he autistic?

In short, and contrary to what one should expect given CIT and the undisputed theses PDT and IDT, it is just as clear that (2) and (4) instantiate the *same* question as it is clear that (1) and (3) do *not* instantiate the same assertion. And this, of course, is hardly an isolated fact. Any pair of *declarative* sentences of which the one combines a singular term with a given predicate and the other the same singular term with the negation of that predicate will be a pair of sentences whose members are conventionally dedicated to instantiating *different*, indeed incompatible, assertions. On the other hand, any pair of *interrogative* sentences of which the one combines a singular term with a given predicate and the other the same singular term with the negation of that predicate will be a pair of sentences whose members are conventionally dedicated to instantiating the *same* question. And, just as one would expect, the same kind of contrast can be observed when the relevant declarative and interrogative sentences are of greater logical complexity. For example, the proposition that there is nothing divisible by zero and the proposition that there is something divisible by zero are certainly not identical propositions, for the kind of reason stated in PDT – namely, because their truth conditions are different. In conjunction with IDT, then, the Content Invariance Thesis would entail not only that the result of attaching the force of *assertion* to these nonidentical propositions would be two different assertions, but also that the result of attaching the force of *question* to these nonidentical propositions would be two different questions. But that turns out *not* to be the case. When the force that is being attached is the force of assertion, the resulting illocutionary acts are indeed different – interpreted with respect to the same quantificational domain, the declarative sentences in (13) and (14) instantiate different, indeed incompatible, assertions, and not different *ways* of making the *same* assertion:

(13) There is nothing divisible by zero.
(14) There is something divisible by zero.

When, however, the force that is being attached is the force of question, the resulting illocutionary acts are identical – interpreted with respect to the same quantificational domain, the interrogative sentences in (15) and (16) do *not* instantiate different questions, but merely different *ways* of posing the *same* question:

(15) Is there nothing divisible by zero?
(16) Is there something divisible by zero?

And that, as before, is easy confirmable. Sentences such as those in (17) and (18) are obviously contradictory:

(17) The question whether there is something divisible by zero is not yet settled, but it is already settled whether there is nothing divisible by zero.
(18) The question whether there is nothing divisible by zero is not yet settled, but it is already settled whether there is something divisible by zero.

And although the positive and negative claims about identity that (19) and (21) contain are obviously true, there exists no interpretation of (20) and (22) in which the positive or negative claims about identity that *they* contain are true:

(19) I already asked you whether there is nothing divisible by zero, and I am now asking you the same thing again: is there something divisible by zero?
(20) # I already told you that there is nothing divisible by zero, and I am now telling you the same thing again: there is something divisible by zero.
(21) I did tell you that there is nothing divisible by zero, but what I am now telling you is different: there is something divisible by zero.
(22) # I did ask you whether there is nothing divisible by zero, but what I am now asking you is different: is there something divisible by zero?

It must simply be accepted, therefore, that, given two representations that, construed as propositions, would be inconsistent, the results of attaching to them the force of *assertion* are utterances that cannot be instantiations of the same illocutionary act, whereas the results of attaching to them the force of *question* are utterances that *can* be instantiations of exactly the same illocutionary act.[1]

The implications of that fact on the issue under discussion here are straightforward: in order to make the fact consistent with the Content Invariance Thesis, one would have to abandon either the Propositional Distinctness Thesis or the Illocutionary Distinctness Thesis. Choosing the first option would allow one to preserve CIT along with IDT, but would require maintaining, contra PDT, that two propositions can be identical *even when they have nonidentical truth conditions* – which would mean that, for example, the proposition that Sam is autistic and the proposition that Sam is not autistic, despite their obvious truth conditional difference, can mysteriously become *the same proposition* when they are attached to the force of question, though they enjoy separate identities when they are attached to the force of assertion. Choosing the second option would allow one to preserve CIT along with PDT, but would require maintaining, contra IDT, that, although the attachment of its force to a particular proposition is somehow essential to an illocutionary act's identity, and although two propositions are non-identical whenever they have nonidentical truth conditions, neverthe-less the identity of an illocutionary act does *not* depend on whether the propositions to which its force is attached are or are not identical. Clearly, both options are deeply unsatisfactory, if they are intelligible at all. If, as the first option demands, two propositions are to be supposed to be identical even when the one is true and the other false with respect to the *same* situation, then it is completely unclear what sorts of entities propositions could possibly be, and they are certainly not the sorts of entities that anyone has ever taken them to be. And if, as the second option demands, two illocutionary acts are to be supposed to be identical *whether or not* the propositions to which they attach the same force are identical, then it is completely unclear what justification could possibly be given for insisting that the identity of *every* illocu-tionary act depends on the attachment of its force to a particular proposition.

The solution, I suggest, is to maintain PDT and IDT just with respect to those illocutionary acts (for example, positive and negative *assertions*) whose analysis mandates, or at least tolerates, the hypothesis that their content is propositional, and to deny that yes–no *questions* have con-tents that are propositional, and so to reject the Content Invariance Thesis – for, clearly, if the content of a yes–no question is *not* a proposi-tion, then the yes–no question cannot consist in attaching a force to *the same proposition* as its grammatically corresponding assertion; and the idea that a yes–no question and its grammatically corresponding asser-tion do attach their respective illocutionary forces to *the same proposition* was precisely what the Content Invariance Thesis was all about. Restricting the domain of applicability of PDT and IDT in the indicated way would allow one to recognize the obvious fact that, for example,

Sam is autistic and *Sam isn't autistic* instantiate different assertions rather than different ways of making the *same* assertion. Rejecting, at the same time, the Content Invariance Thesis would allow one to recognize the equally obvious fact that *Is Sam autistic?* and *Isn't Sam autistic?* do *not* instantiate different questions, but merely constitute different *ways* of posing the same question (constitute, as one might put it, different utterance acts dedicated to the performance of the same illocutionary act). Since both facts are central and undeniable, any theory of illocutionary acts that fails to accommodate them would be unsatisfactory. And Searle's theory does fail to accommodate them, because of commitments that, without proper motivation, it undertakes at a fundamental level: if one believes that the sententially representable content of *every* illocutionary act is necessarily a proposition, then, given that yes–no questions are obviously illocutionary acts with sententially representable contents, one is led to assume that their contents *must* be propositions; and if one accepts that the content of a yes–no question must be a proposition, then it is difficult to imagine what that proposition could possibly be unless it was the same as the proposition expressed by its grammatically corresponding assertion; the Content Invariance Thesis becomes then irresistible, with the unacceptable consequences we have noticed. But the unacceptable consequences do not follow if one refuses to grant the initial assumption, and that by itself is a perfectly good reason for refusing to grant it.

Notice that the initial assumption has, in any case, nothing self-recommendable about it, and that, at least as far as yes–no questions are concerned, definitely preferable alternatives to it can be made available. Certainly no *argument* has ever been given for the assumption that the sententially representable content of *every* illocutionary act *must* be a proposition; the assumption seems to have been mainly motivated by the thought that, since the contents of *assertions* can profitably be taken to be propositional (actually, on many traditional accounts, "proposition" just *means* "content of an assertion"), one must *hope* that the sententially representable contents of all other kinds of illocutionary act will turn out to be propositional as well; but the only consideration nurturing that hope appears to have been that, if the sententially representable content of every nonassertoric illocutionary act turned out to be propositional, then the principle of least effort (which is sometimes misidentified as "the principle of compositionality") would have been vindicated as a useful methodological principle in the philosophy of language: one would have nothing more to do in analyzing illocutionary acts than recycling a ready-made account of propositions and appending to it an account of force. As one should expect, however, the principle of least effort is not a reliable guide to truth, and the case of yes–no questions makes that especially clear, since the hypothesis that the content of yes–no questions is propositional leads, as we have seen, to consequences that no account of either propositions or illocutions could credibly endorse.

Besides, virtually no extant account of the content of yes–no questions in formal discussions of meaning (for a survey of such accounts, see Higginbotham 1996) has any use for the view that the content of a yes–no question is a proposition, suggesting instead (to put it in a way that abstracts away from differences among individual proposals, and adds an often neglected but essential condition) that its content is *the set of alternatives* among which some must be eliminated and some others must be selected if the question is to be *settled*. And these accounts, whatever their other limitations might be, can certainly avoid the problems that make the propositional account founder (even though they have not been put forward with these problems in mind), since, combined with the *innocuous* interpretation of the force-content distinction that I distinguished from the standard one, they can easily acknowledge the obvious identities and differences between yes–no questions that the standard interpretation is forced to deny – the fact, for example, that relevant occurrences of the interrogatives *Is Sam autistic?* and *Isn't Sam autistic?* instantiate the very *same* yes–no question, the fact that relevant occurrences of the interrogatives *Is there nothing divisible by zero?* and *Is there something divisible by zero?* instantiate the very *same* yes–no question, and the fact that the question that the first two of these interrogatives co-instantiate is *not* the same as the question that the last two co-instantiate. Assuming the innocuous interpretation of the force-content distinction, and taking the content of a yes–no question to be the set of answers that would be relevant to its settlement, the observed identities and differences would be accounted as follows: *Is Sam autistic?* and *Isn't Sam autistic?* instantiate the *same* yes–no question because, besides having the same illocutionary force, they have the same content; and they have the same content because each determines the same *set* of relevant answers (namely, the set {"Sam is autistic," "Sam isn't autistic"}), and each is settled by selecting the *same* member of that set to the exclusion of the other. Similarly, *Is there nothing divisible by zero?* and *Is there something divisible by zero?* instantiate the *same* question since, besides having the same illocutionary force, they have the same content; and they have the same content because each determines the same *set* of relevant answers (namely, the set {"There is nothing divisible by zero," "There is something divisible by zero"}), and each is settled by selecting the *same* member of that set to the exclusion of the other. Finally, the question co-instantiated by *Is Sam autistic?* and *Isn't Sam autistic?* is *not* the same as the question co-instantiated by *Is there nothing divisible by zero?* and *Is there something divisible by zero?* because, although the illocutionary force of all four of these interrogatives is the same, the common content of the first two is different from the common content of the last two; and the common content of the first two is different from the common content of the last two because the answer set determined by each of the first two is disjoint from the answer set determined by each of the last two, with the consequence that no settlement of either of the first two can amount to a settlement of either of the last two, or conversely. Notice that what makes an account of this sort capable of acknowledging these obvious identities and differences between yes–no questions is precisely the fact that it takes the content of a yes–no question *not* to be a proposition: although an answer may have a truth condition, and although a proposition (supposing that answers regularly express propositions) must have a truth condition, a *set* of answers, or a *set* of propositions, *cannot*, as such, have a truth condition (just as a *set* of people cannot, as such, have a sex, even though each member of the set may well have a sex); and since an object that is incapable of having a truth condition cannot be a proposition, it follows that the object that, on such an account, provides the content of a yes–no question (namely, the answer *set* relative to which the question could be settled) cannot be a proposition.

There are, of course, significant issues that should be addressed before an account of this sort could be taken to constitute a full account of the content of yes–no questions. For example, it is usually taken for granted in formal discussions of yes–no questions that, although a question's answer set, and so a question's content, cannot be a proposition, the individual members of that set might well be taken to be propositions. But I think that this is a far from obviously correct assumption, and that a far better way of conceiving of a question's possible answers (and a way that Searle would surely welcome) would be to conceive of them as possible *illocutionary acts* of certain types (a given yes–no question's answer set may consist of a possible assertion and a possible denial, a different yes–no question's answer set may consist of a possible permission and a possible prohibition, a still different yes–no question's answer set may consist of a possible approval and a possible disapproval; and so on). What is of primary importance in the present context, however, is the idea that, no matter how a yes–no question's possible answers are to be best characterized, it is the *set* of those answers, which *cannot* be a proposition, that provides the question's content. Since we already know that the assumption that the content of a yes–no question is a proposition has clearly unacceptable consequences, and since the alternative idea just rehearsed can be easily put to work to account for at least those differences and identities between yes–no questions that a propositional conception of their content cannot coherently account for, the conclusion must be that there is no good reason to uphold either Searle's Content Invariance Thesis or the even more fundamental thesis that motivates it, namely, the thesis that *every* sententially representable illocutionary act content is a proposition. My purpose in the next section will be to reinforce that conclusion by providing independent evidence in its favor that derives from considering how Searle's propositional conception of the content of yes–no questions creates insuperable problems for his well-known and widely influential classification of illocutionary acts.

3 YES–NO QUESTIONS AND THE CLASSIFICATION OF ILLOCUTIONARY ACTS

Searle's classification (Searle 1975a, reprinted as ch. 1 of Searle 1979) explicitly assumes that all contentful illocutionary acts have the general form $F(p)$ where F is a variable for forces and p a variable for *propositions* to which forces are attached, and, taking types of act to be determined by types of force, aims at arriving at a system of categories within which all possible types of force (and so, all possible types of illocutionary act) can be accommodated. The proposed fundamental principle of classification is the intrinsic point or purpose of an illocutionary act with a given force – in other words, the purpose that a speaker cannot fail to have if he is to perform an illocutionary act with that force – and, on its basis, Searle arrives at his five major categories of illocutionary acts (assertives, directives, commissives, expressives, and declarations) whose respective intrinsic points correspond to the five major types of purpose that, according to Searle, the expression of a proposition could possibly have. A speaker performs an assertive illocutionary act iff his point is to present as actual, without thereby making actual, the state of affairs represented by the proposition he expresses. A speaker performs a directive illocutionary act iff his point is to attempt to make his hearer make actual the state of affairs represented by the proposition he expresses. A speaker performs a commissive illocutionary act iff his point is to commit himself to making actual the state of affairs represented in the proposition he expresses. A speaker performs an expressive illocutionary act iff his point is to express his feelings and attitudes toward an already existing state of affairs represented by the proposition he expresses. And finally, a speaker performs a declarational illocutionary act iff his purpose is to make actual, simply by presenting it as actual, the state of affairs represented by the proposition he expresses. "If we take the illocutionary act (that is, the full blown illocutionary act with its illocutionary force and propositional content) as the unit of analysis," Searle says in a later summary of his classification, "then we find there are five general ways of using language, five general categories of illocutionary acts. We tell people how things are (Assertives), we try to get them to do things (Directives), we commit ourselves to doing things (Commissives), we express our feelings and attitudes (Expressives), and we bring about changes in the world through our utterances (Declarations)" (Searle 1979: vii–viii); it may be worth noting that Searle's fundamental assumption that this classification is exhaustive is the basis of the later formalization of his theory of speech acts in Searle and Vanderveken (1985).

Now, if, as Searle insists, these are the "five and only five" (1998: 148) categories of illocutionary acts that exist, one should expect that yes–no questions, which are undoubtedly central illocutionary acts, could be easily seen to belong to one or another of these five categories. However, it can easily be seen (though, to my knowledge, it has never been pointed out) that yes–no questions cannot belong to *any* of these categories, *if* their content is taken to be, as Searle's Content Invariance Thesis demands, the same as the content of their grammatically corresponding assertions. Take any yes–no question, for example the question *Does Sam smoke habitually?*, which, according to Searle, expresses the same proposition as its grammatically corresponding assertion – namely, the proposition that Sam smokes habitually. Clearly, a speaker who poses the question, *Does Sam smoke habitually?* does not aim to "present it as actual" that Sam smokes habitually, so he is not performing an assertive illocutionary act; but neither does he aim to "try to get his hearer to make it actual" that Sam smokes habitually, so he is not performing a directive illocutionary act; nor does he aim to "commit himself to making it actual" that Sam smokes habitually, so he is not performing a commissive illocutionary act; nor does he aim to "express his feelings and attitudes towards the antecedently obtaining fact" that Sam smokes habitually, so he is not performing an expressive illocutionary act; nor does he aim to "make it actual just by virtue of presenting it as actual" that Sam smokes habitually, so he is not performing a declarational illocutionary act. But if a speaker who, in posing the question, *Does Sam smoke habitually?*, does not attach to the proposition that, allegedly, he thereby expresses – that is, to the proposition <u>that Sam smokes habitually</u> – neither an assertive, nor a directive, nor a commissive, nor an expressive, nor a declarational illocutionary force, it follows that yes–no questions cannot belong to *any* of the "five and only five" categories of illocutionary acts that, according to Searle, exist. And since a classification of illocutionary acts that provides no place at all for yes–no questions is obviously unacceptable, it must be concluded that Searle's Content Invariance Thesis has the significant added disadvantage of making it impossible for him to construct an acceptable classification of illocutionary acts.

As far as I can tell, Searle has never clearly recognized either this problem or the fact that, in order to properly respond to it, he should reconsider either his method of classifying illocutionary acts or his views about the content of yes–no questions (or, possibly, both). On the contrary, his position appears to be that his classification is perfectly satisfactory as it stands and that yes–no questions, with exactly the content prescribed for them by the Content Invariance Thesis, can be easily accommodated within one of the categories that the classification provides. When, however, one turns to the actual analysis of yes–no questions that Searle sketches in the course of arguing that they can be accommodated within his classification, what one finds is, first, that the proposed analysis, whether viable or not, ascribes to yes–no questions a content that is *not* the content prescribed by Content Invariance Thesis, and second, that the proposed analysis is, in any case, not viable. I will now argue for these points in turn, and will conclude that there is no way of either properly analyzing or properly classifying yes–no questions within Searle's system without rejecting the Content Invariance Thesis and the standard interpretation of the force-content distinction that underlies it.

Searle's view as to how questions in general, and yes–no questions in particular, could be accommodated within his proposed classification of illocutionary acts is stated very simply: "Questions," he says, "are a subclass of directives since they are attempts by S [that is, by the speaker] to get H [that is, the hearer] to answer, i.e. to perform a speech act" (1979: 14; interestingly, the same sort of account is suggested in Frege 1918). What Searle appears to be forgetting in putting forward this classificatory proposal, however, is that *if* yes–no questions are indeed directives by means of which speakers try to elicit answers from hearers (a claim that, just for the time being, we shall leave undisputed), then their propositional contents *cannot* be the same as the contents of their grammatically corresponding assertions, contrary to what the Content Invariance Thesis demands. For, by Searle's own definitions, each directive is an illocutionary act whose propositional content specifies *the action that the speaker is attempting to make the hearer perform* (if, for example, a speaker requests of his hearer to climb Mount Everest, then the propositional content of the request is <u>that the hearer climb Mount Everest</u>; if a speaker requests of his hearer to kill the discoverer of penicillin, then the propositional content of the request is <u>that the hearer kill the discoverer of penicillin</u>; and so on). Consequently, if yes–no questions are, as Searle contends, a particular subclass of directives where the action that the speaker is attempting to make the hearer perform is the action of supplying an answer, then *that action itself* must be represented in the propositional content of those directives. And if it *is* represented there, then it is logically impossible for the propositional contents of those directives to ever be the same as the propositional contents that, according to Searle, yes–no questions allegedly *share* with their grammatically corresponding *assertions*. If, for example, the yes–no question *Is water odourless?* really is a request to the effect that its hearer tell its speaker whether water is odourless, then, obviously, its propositional content (whether explicitly given or not) is <u>that the hearer tell the speaker whether water is odourless</u> – in other words, it is the same as the propositional content that would be expressed by the same speaker if he was to address to the same hearer the imperative *Tell me whether water is odourless!*; but the propositional content <u>that the hearer tell the speaker whether water is odourless</u> is certainly not identical to the propositional content <u>that water is odourless</u>, which Searle was taking to be the propositional content of the question *Is water odourless?*, when he was claiming that that question has *the same propositional content* as the assertion *Water is odourless*; for, the proposition <u>that water is odourless</u> (which, of course, *is* the proposition expressed by the assertion *Water is odourless*) concerns only water and odourlessness, and not any speakers, any hearers, or any speech acts (of telling, answering, replying, or whatnot) that speakers may be attempting to get hearers to perform. Clearly, then, no analysis of yes–no questions could consistently maintain both that yes–no questions are directives aimed at eliciting answers *and* that their propositional contents are the same as the contents of their grammatically corresponding assertions. (Note that Frege [1918] gets himself involved in the same inconsistency as Searle in this connection.) And that, of course, means that, even if the analysis of yes–no questions implied by Searle's classificatory proposal were viable, it would still require him to fully reject the Content Invariance Thesis, according to which the propositional content of a yes–no question simply *is* the same as the propositional content of its grammatically corresponding assertion.

Let me finally turn to the analysis of yes–no questions implied by Searle's classificatory proposal and briefly examine its central claim that the question as to whether something is the case is equivalent to a speaker's request that his hearer tell him whether that thing is the case. Notice first of all that even if the indicated equivalence did hold, it is quite unclear that it could be taken to provide an adequate *analysis* of yes–no questions, since, understood as an analysis, the proposed equivalence would seem not to satisfy the requirement on noncircularity that an adequate analysis should satisfy. For, arguably, a person tells *whether* something is the case (as opposed to merely telling *that* something is the case) if and only if that person says something that settles the actual or potential *question* as to whether that thing is the case. And if this is so, the claim that the *question* whether something is the case is equivalent to the request that someone tell *whether* that thing is the case would not constitute, even if it were otherwise acceptable, a noncircular analysis of questioning. In any event, the claim is not acceptable on several independent grounds. A first (and widely neglected) type of evidence against it comes from the fact that a question whether something is the case and a request for telling whether that thing is the case are two types of speech act that, on the one hand, may sometimes not even be grammatically interchangeable and, on the other hand, are often constrained to receive markedly divergent interpretations even when they are grammatically inter-changeable. Thus, although there is nothing wrong about the request in (23), there is nothing right about the purported question in (24), even though the latter should be, if the proposal under discussion were correct, in all relevant respects indistinguishable from the former:

(23) If you are interested in my offer, please tell me whether that is so.
(24) * If you are interested in my offer, is that so?

What is more, even when both a yes–no question and its allegedly equivalent request are grammatical and interpretable, the interpretation of the one may be *required* to be different from the interpretation of the other. For example, (25) has obviously not the same meaning as (26), but that fact could hardly be explained if one accepted the idea that a speaker's question as to whether something is the case is the very same thing as a speaker's request that his hearer tell him whether that thing is the case:

(25) If you are not busy, will you come to my party?
(26) If you are not busy, tell me whether you will come to my party.

But the most direct evidence against the proposed analysis comes from two other facts. The first is that a speaker can without semantic oddity pose a question and explicitly deny that he is requesting of his hearer to provide its answer. For example, there is nothing semantically incongruous about utterances such as those in (27) and (28), but something should be radically incongruous about each one of them if, as Searle supposes, questions were *necessarily* requests aimed at eliciting hearer responses:

(27) Will my lottery ticket win? – I am not, of course, asking you to tell me whether it will, I simply wonder whether it will.
(28) Do I really want to marry her? – I am not, of course, asking *you* to tell me whether I do, I am just trying to make up my mind.

And the second fact is that questions in general, and yes–no questions in particular, can have perfectly meaningful occurrences in contexts where their speakers neither have nor can presume to have any hearers, and therefore cannot coherently be supposed to be requesting verbal actions on the part of their nonexistent hearers. For example, several minutes after leaving his house alone, a speaker might interrupt his solitary walk and utter the sentence in (29):

(29) Have I locked the front door?

Since such a speaker could very well know that he does not have a hearer, he could hardly be supposed to be "requesting of his hearer to provide an answer." But he would have certainly *posed the question* whether he has locked his front door, and anyone knowing the language would know exactly what the *possible* answers would be, relative to which his question could be settled.

Indeed, given the absence of a *necessary* connection between posing a question and requesting of a hearer to provide an answer, it could be suggested that the fact that, when one poses a question, one is *usually*, but not invariably, interpreted as requesting of a hearer to provide an answer, should be analyzed by Searle along the same Gricean lines that he had followed (Searle 1975b, reprinted as ch. 2 of Searle 1979) when discussing the familiar fact that, in uttering *any* sentence, one may often be interpreted as performing, apart from the *direct* illocutionary act that is part of the sentence's conventional meaning, various *indirect* illocutionary acts that are in no way part of the sentence's conventional meaning, but can reasonably be attributed to the speaker *if* there are no contextual indications disallowing the attribution. That these latter acts are *not* part of the sentence's conventional meaning, Searle was then claiming, is shown by the fact that they are *cancelable* – either in the sense that there exist contexts where the tendency to attribute them would not even arise, or in the sense that, even in contexts where the tendency to attribute them might arise, the speaker could effectively block their attribution by denying without semantic oddity the intention to perform them. What we have just seen is precisely that the interpretation of a question as a request for a hearer's answer is cancelable in both of these senses and should not, therefore, be taken by Searle to be part of the question's conventional meaning. And since Searle's intention in analyzing questions as requests for answers was, evidently, to elucidate their conventional meaning (to elucidate, in other words, the illocutionary acts that their speakers *directly* perform, and not any illocutionary acts that they might on occasion *indirectly* perform), it would seem that, if nothing else, Searle's own doctrine of direct and indirect illocutionary acts should have discouraged him from adopting the analysis under discussion.

I take it to be evident that, if there is no significant chance of accommodating yes–no questions (conceived of as a semantically homogeneous class) within Searle's category of directives, there is even less chance of accommodating them within any of his remaining categories of illocutionary acts. It seems, then, that there is no way, consistent with Searle's independent commitments, of making room for yes–no questions within his classification of illocutionary acts, and that the only basis on which he could maintain, together with those commitments, his fundamental claim that the classification is exhaustive would be the clearly untenable thesis that yes–no questions are not illocutionary acts at all. This result should not be surprising. If, as I have been arguing, yes–no questions have contents that are *not* propositional, then one should expect that a classification of illocutionary acts that, like Searle's, assumes that all such acts have contents that *are* propositional will not be able to accommodate yes–no questions. And the proper response to that situation is not, of course, to deny that yes–no questions are illocutionary acts, but rather to reject the standard interpretation of the force-content distinction that is uncritically applied to the analysis of all illocutionary acts, and to exploit the classificatory options that that rejection makes available. Assuming the innocuous interpretation of the force-content distinction that I distinguished from the standard one, a proper classification of illocutionary acts should, I suggest, accept as its fundamental distinction the distinction between *first-order* illocutionary acts, whose defining feature is that they attach their forces to contents that *are* propositions, and *higher-order* illocutionary acts, whose defining feature is that they attach their forces to contents that are *not* propositions but are, rather, sets of possible *first-order illocutionary acts*. Assertions and denials, acceptances and refusals, permissions and prohibitions, approvals and disapprovals are plausible examples of first-order illocutionary acts, since there is no obvious obstacle to assuming that the contents to which their respective forces are attached are propositions. However, questions of all sorts, and so yes–no questions, are higher-order illocutionary acts, since the contents to which their forces are attached are not propositions but rather sets of possible first-order illocutionary acts. A yes–no question, in particular, attaches its force to a set whose members are two possible first-order illocutionary acts (in many cases, a possible assertion and a possible denial, but in other cases, a possible acceptance and a possible refusal, or a possible permission and a possible prohibition, or a possible approval and a possible disapproval, etc.) which are such that, *if* one of them were to be felicitously performed to the exclusion of the other, the question would have been settled.

This, of course, could only be the beginning of an adequate account of yes–no questions. For it is only by specifying exactly what is involved in a question's being *settled* by an appropriate choice from its answer set, and exactly what determines the appropriateness of such choices, that one would be in position to say exactly what the illocutionary *force* of questioning is; and it is only by analyzing a question's illocutionary *force*, and not merely by describing the answer set that provides its content, that a full account of its meaning would be possible. Nevertheless, a proper conception of a question's content is an essential prerequisite to addressing the issue of its force, and my primary purpose in this chapter has been to argue that that essential prerequisite is impossible to fulfill unless certain widely held assumptions about content in the theory of meaning are rejected. The most important of these assumptions is the assumption that the content (as distinct from the force) of every theoretically significant instance of meaningful speech consists in the expression of a proposition. If I am right, Searle has been too quick to concede to "the older philosophers" that propositions can be accorded that role, and to complain only that "their account was incomplete, for they did not discuss the different illocutionary acts in which a proposition could occur" (Searle 1969: 125). For if illocutionary acts as central as yes–no questions do *not* consist in the attachment of a force to a content that *is* propositional, then it seems that "the older philosophers," and their many contemporary followers, have made an even more limited contribution to the study of meaning than Searle was claiming they did when he made his own outstanding contributions to that subject.

NOTE

1 The correct claim that relevant occurrences of *Is Sam autistic?* and *Isn't Sam autistic?* (or of *Is there nothing divisible by zero?* and *Is there something divisible by zero?*) can instantiate exactly the same *illocutionary* act is not, of course, to be confused with the incorrect claim that such occurrences are identical in all their *pre*-illocutionary or *post*-illocutionary properties. They are obviously different in their pre-illocutionary properties, since they constitute different *utterance* acts (in the sense of Searle 1969: 24); that difference, however, is not relevant to the present discussion, since, as Searle would be the first to acknowledge, utterance act identity is neither necessary nor sufficient for illocutionary act identity. And they may also be different in their post-illocutionary and in particular in their perlocutionary properties (in the sense of Searle 1969: 24), since their perlocutionary effects (including their "preferred" conversational sequels) may be different; that difference, however, is not relevant either, since, as Searle would again acknowledge, perlocutionary effect identity is neither necessary nor sufficient for illocutionary act identity. The only fact relevant to the present discussion is that the same *illocutionary* act can be instantiated by the occurrences under discussion, even though the pre-illocutionary or post-illocutionary properties of those occurrences may be different.

Chapter 12

How do speech acts express psychological states?

MITCHELL GREEN

1 INTRODUCTION[1]

In *Speech Acts* (1969), John Searle lists a number of general hypotheses concerning illocutionary acts, the first of which relates those acts to the activity of expression:

Whenever there is a psychological state specified in the sincerity condition, the performance of the act counts as an *expression* of that psychological state.

(1969: 65, italics in original)

Searle goes on to tell us that this is the case whether or not the speech act is sincere, so that even if I do not believe what I assert, that assertion is still an expression of belief. Further,

to assert, affirm, or state that p counts as an expression of belief (that *p*). To request, ask, order, entreat, enjoin, pray, or command (that *A* be done) counts as *an expression of a wish or desire* (that *A* be done). To promise, vow, threaten, or pledge (that *A*) counts as *an expression of intention* (to do *A*). To thank, welcome or congratulate counts as *an expression of gratitude, pleasure* (at H's arrival), or *pleasure* (at H's good fortune).[2]

In his published discussions of speech acts in subsequent years, Searle, together with his collaborator Vanderveken, take the notion of expression as an unexplained explainer with respect to the properties of speech acts. That by itself is not objectionable. However, this notion of expression raises questions that a deeper insight into the possibilities and limits of communication would hope to answer. First of all, as I show in section 2, Searle's purported explanation of Moore's Paradox is incomplete at best, and this incompleteness is due to insufficient elucidation of the notion of expression. Second (section 3), expression of the sort germane to speech acts *shows* – or at least purports to show – the agent's psychological state in such a way as to enable knowledge of it in appropriate observers. As a result, a sincere speech act shows the state that is its sincerity condition. This form of showing I term *showing that*, which is (not necessarily conclusive) demonstration. Yet this in turn raises the question of how it is possible for a speech act to demonstrate what is within. Could my assertion of *p* really be a demonstration of my belief? The problem is not that for few if any of my beliefs am I in a position to give a formal derivation whose conclusion is that I harbor the belief in question; demonstration does not require deductive proof. Rather, the problem is that it is difficult to see how the illocutionary force, even of a sincere speech act, could demonstrate the presence of a thought or feeling even on a sufficiently expansive understanding of demonstration: the force would seem to have to create evidence *ex nihilo* for an agent's state of thought or feeling. After explaining (section 4) some concepts from the evolutionary biology of communication, I suggest (section 5) an account of how force shows psychological states that emphasizes the way in which, in performing certain speech acts, we make ourselves vulnerable to a loss of credibility.

2 EXPRESSION AND MOOREAN ABSURDITY

Expression of the sort found in speech acts is tightly bound up with the distinctive absurdity exemplified in such utterances as "It's raining but I don't believe it is." The content here expressed is one that could be true, and yet a speaker who utters such a sentence seriously – that is, in such a way as to speaker-mean it - is being absurd.[3] Similar remarks apply to those who judge true some such sentence as that just quoted.[4] Searle attempts to explain the source of Moorean absurdity in the following way:

> The explanation in every case is that one cannot, in consistency, express a psychological state, and simultaneously deny the existence of the psychological state expressed. (1991a: 187)

The suggestion evidently has the following shape: One who asserts "*p* but I don't believe it," asserts both *p* and that she does not believe that *p*. (This assumes assertion-distribution: one who asserts *p* and *q* asserts *p* and asserts *q*.) Further, one who asserts *p* expresses the belief that *p*. However, one who expresses the belief that *p* is inconsistent if she simultaneously denies that she is in that belief state.

But why should that be? Just bearing relation R to something while denying that one bears that relation does not make one inconsistent: if

I *touch* an object while denying that I am touching it, I am wrong but not inconsistent. So what is distinctive about the expressing relation that makes one inconsistent here? Could it instead be that expression of a psychological state is evidence for that state? Again apparently not: the bulging vein on my temple is evidence of my anger, but if I deny that I am angry while my vein bulges, I may once again be in error but am not inconsistent.

This is not to deny Searle's claim that one who expresses a psychological state while denying the existence of that state is being inconsistent or in some other way in violation of a norm of rationality. It does, however, make clear that we need a further elucidation of the notion of expression if we are to find that claim both plausible and illuminating. Further, it is now widely acknowledged that Moorean absurdity is exemplified not just in an "omissive" form such as that above, but also in a "comissive" form such as "I believe that *p*, but not-*p*." It is not clear how Searle's explanation schema applies to such cases: whereas the latter conjunct may be an expression of belief that not-*p*, the former asserts, rather than expresses, belief that *p*. Since these two beliefs with contradictory contents are "distinct existences," whence the inconsistency? Here too I do not claim that Searle is unable to account for such a case; rather we need a deeper account of the notion of expression if we are to be convinced that he is able to do so.[5]

3   EXPRESSION AS DESIGNED SHOWING

Consider the difference between my scowling and my saying coolly, "I'm angry." The scowl, at least if it is caused in the right way by a felt anger, shows my anger. It also expresses that anger. By contrast, the cool assertion, "I'm angry," reports my anger, but it is not plausible to describe it as either showing or expressing anger (Stampe 1975). Showing and expressing can be jointly instantiated, and some speech acts might exemplify neither. However, I wish here to argue for a stronger claim, namely that all cases of expression are also cases of showing.[6]

As the example of scowling suggests, expression differs from representation at least in that the former involves making a state of the self palpable. This is reinforced by the Latin origin of the word "exprimere," meaning "to press out."[7] It is also reinforced by some paradigm usages. As Frederick Douglass recalls the songs he and his fellow slaves would sing while not working for their masters, he notices that, "an expression

269

of feeling has already found its way down my cheek" (*Narrative of the Life of Frederick Douglass, an American Slave*, 1845). This tear is an expression of feeling because it is a direct manifestation thereof. Likewise, in his *The Expression of Emotions in Man and Animals*, Charles Darwin speaks of expressive movements as revealing our thoughts and impressions more reliably than do our words (Darwin [1872] 1998: 359). This comports with the fact that an expression of emotion or thought is more than an indication of that thought or emotion. Assume indication is an evidential relation such that if A indicates B, A's presence increases the probability of B's occurrence. When I am angry my respiration increases, as a result of which I produce more CO_2. An increase in CO_2 around my body is thus an indication of the present sense of my anger. It is not, however, an expression of anger because its presence is compatible, even under normal circumstances, with many other etiologies. By contrast, in lieu of reasons to think that onions were being sliced near where Douglass was writing his memoirs, etc., the tear running down his cheek provides a good deal more evidence than mere indication.

Again, to express my love I need to put the strength and depth of my feelings on the table – if at all possible in the form of a self-sacrificing act or pricey artifact. This, however, is just to say that to express my psychological state I must make it knowable to an appropriate observer. Although the relation between expression and what is expressed is not always so straightforward as the relation between tears and grief, I suggest that one theme binding together different forms of expression is the ability of the expressive behavior or artifact to convey, or at least enable in an appropriate observer, knowledge of what it expresses. We have seen that this is in contrast to indication. It is also in contrast to representation. Although some representations are produced by sufficiently reliable causal chains to enable knowledge of what they represent, a representation of a state of affairs is not, per se, enough to enable knowledge of that state of affairs. An expression is.[8]

Expression makes something knowable to appropriate observers; making something knowable to appropriate observers is, in turn, to show it; hence expression is a species of showing. As we saw in the last section, showing can occur whether or not anyone cottons on. Since expression is a species of showing, the same goes for it: although I express my love, trepidation, regret, you might be too distracted, obtuse, or self-absorbed to get my drift.

I express a psychological state, then, by showing it in such a way as to enable propositional knowledge of it in appropriate observers. Yet expression is more than showing such a state: it is also a form of showing that is the product of design. Suppose a certain vein in my forehead bulges when and only when I am angry, and that its doing so is not under my direct voluntary control. Then the bulging of that vein shows my anger. It does not, however, express that anger. What, then, is the difference between my bulging vein and Douglass's tear? I suggest that the difference is that the latter, but not the former, is *designed* to show a state of the agent. The vein's tendency to bulge is not designed to convey information, but rather it is designed to convey blood in situations of agitation. By contrast, it is a plausible empirical hypothesis that tears are designed to show grief, sadness, and related emotions.[9]

The design lying back of expression might – as is most likely the case in Douglass's scenario – be the product of natural selection. Instead it might be the product of artificial selection. Alternatively it may be the work of an intelligent, sentient agent. (Even if evolution by natural selection is an intelligent process, it is not a sentient process.) How precisely to conceptualize the contributions of culture according to this partition is an open question, but not one we need to settle here. What is clear is that culture does create expressive institutions. A gesture, for instance, could begin life in a one-off case of speaker meaning, and then grow into a conventional expression of contempt. Perhaps an extended middle finger is an iconic sign of sexual violation, and its first use was intelligible as such in the absence of any convention governing it. Whether the gesture's iconicity helps to account for its role in Western culture is a question for an anthropology of gestures; by now, however, culture has endowed that gesture with an expressive significance. That means, in our terms, that the extended middle finger shows, and has been designed to show, contempt. (I have not yet explained how it does this; I turn to that task in section 4.)

Speech acts, then, are devices we use to provide knowledge-enabling evidence of psychological states. When I make an assertion that it is raining, I do not state that I believe that it is raining. I do nevertheless express that belief so long as I am sincere. Given what we have suggested so far, this also means that assertion is a device we use to show our belief, and (so long as we are sincere) in fact show it by providing sufficient evidence for it.[10] A speaker who is not sincere provides good evidence for a belief that she lacks, and thus only appears to show her belief.

271

4 CONVENTIONS, NORMS, AND HANDICAPS

What we have established so far allows us to focus our central question: how can the use of an illocutionary force constitute strong enough evidence of a psychological state to enable knowledge in an appropriate observer? One answer is suggested by Searle's use of the "counts as" locution in the quotation with which we began. In saying that the performance of an illocutionary act counts as the expression of a psychological state, Searle is being consistent with the *force conventionalism* that runs throughout *Speech Acts*. According to a strong version of this view, for every speech act that is performed, there is an extra-semantic convention that will have been invoked in order to make that speech act occur. Austin (1961) espoused this view, and Searle largely follows him.[11]

In the quotation with which we began, Searle seems to hold that it is also an aspect of the conventional nature of speech acts that they conventionally express what they do. Given our account of expression as a species of showing, that commits him to the view that speech acts conventionally show what they do.[12] However, it is doubtful that an entity could be conventionally imbued with the capacity to provide evidence for something distinct from itself. What implies what is a matter beyond our control, conventional or otherwise; as Geach once put it (1976), no power in Heaven or Earth could make one proposition imply another if it does not already do so. I take the same point to carry over to the issue of what is evidence for what: whether a proposition or state of affairs is evidence for another is not something we can decide, even by unanimous referendum. If we are to understand how illocutionary force provides evidence of what is within, we need to look somewhere else. For help I shall consider some concepts from the evolutionary biology of communication.

Here is some terminology that is fairly standard in that literature. A *cue* is any feature of an entity that conveys information (including misinformation). That information might pertain to how things were, how things are, how things will be, or how things ought to be. A *signal* is a cue that was designed for its ability to convey the information it does. The design in question may be the result of natural selection, artificial selection, or conscious intention.[13]

A signal may be inaccurate, and animals exploit this fact to their advantage. To escape predation some anurans bear bright colors even when they are neither poisonous nor noxious. Although in any given case a signal can misrepresent, the stability over time of any signaling system mandates that it be on the whole reliable. Natural selection thus tends to find ways of vouchsafing the veracity of signals. Funnel-web spiders, *Agelenopsis aperta*, find themselves in contests over webs. Two spiders will vibrate on a disputed web. If two contesting spiders differ in weight by 10 percent or more, the lighter spider retreats 90 percent of the time rather than fighting. Furthermore, a losing spider can be made into a winner by placing a weight on its back (Reichert 1984). This strongly suggests that vibrating on a web is a spider's signal of its size. Further, in the absence of scientists placing weights on their backs, funnel-web spiders cannot fake these signals. Signals that can only be faked with great difficulty as a result of physical limitations on the organism are *indices*. The "vibrating game" thus exploits not just a signal, but also an index of spider size.

Another way of ensuring the difficulty of faking a signal is by making it more costly than is required just to produce a signal of that type. Male peacocks have flamboyant trains making them less agile and easier for predators to spot; growing such feathers also costs extra calories (Zahavi and Zahavi 1997). They nevertheless give males an advantage in sexual selection (Petrie, Halliday, and Sanders 1991). An ostentatious display is like saying, "Just think of how fit I must be if I can survive with this baggage!" Signals such as these, that can only be faked with great difficulty as a result of being very costly to produce, are *handicaps*. A signal's being costly to produce is thus one way of being difficult to fake because of limitations on an organism. A handicap is, accordingly, a special type of index.

An index not only signals some property of the organism; it also shows that property: the extent of the spider's vibration shows its size; the size of the peacock's train shows his viability. Further, it is its ability to show, rather than merely signal, a property that vouchsafes the stability of a signaling strategy. Yet the examples of handicaps I have given thus far are pretty rigid: the magnitude of the spider's vibration and the peacock's train cannot be modified, either intentionally or in response to environmental changes. Some handicaps can be produced in response to environmental stimuli – for instance musth in male African elephants (Poole 1989; Maynard Smith and Harper 2004: 35). Musth is thus a signal that is more flexible than either tail feathers or vibration magnitude. Nevertheless it still seems a far cry from the signaling possibilities available to primates, to say nothing of our own species.

As a first step in bridging this gap let us notice that one kind of cost social mammals can incur is a loss of status. In our own species that cost often takes the form of a loss of credibility. Finding someone credible is a matter of believing what they say to be reliable; it is also a matter of believing them to be sincere if their utterance admits of sincerity. A credible assertor can be trusted to be right and sincere; a credible promissor can be depended upon both to intend to keep her promise and keep it; and so on. The more credible a person, the more likely we are to take their utterances at face value. Appreciating this permits a natural refinement of the well-known "scorekeeping" model of conversational dynamics pioneered by Stalnaker (1972, 1973, 1974, 1984), Lewis (1979, 1980), and Thomason (1990). On that model, interlocutors perform speech acts whose content is accepted into "common ground" so long as no one demurs from the proffered contribution. Conversational "score" can be tracked by the contents of common ground (along, optionally, with other factors such as relations of salience, standards of precision, domain of discourse, and so on), which in turn determines what interlocutors may presuppose in subsequent speech acts; it can also determine the very content of those speech acts via the process of impliciture (Bach 1994b). A natural refinement of this picture would keep tabs on which interlocutors are credible and to what extent; that will in turn determine the *weight* – as one might call it – of their conversational contributions. An expert's pronouncements on her field of interest have more weight than do those of a dabbler; likewise for the *London Times* as compared with a supermarket-checkout magazine. It is, likewise, precisely the gravamen of *ad hominem* arguments to undermine the weight of a person's remarks.

One's credibility, then, determines the weight of one's pronouncements, and for this reason many of us jealously guard that credibility. A speaker whose remarks are weighty enjoys a presumption in her favor: a proffered assertoric contribution to common ground puts the onus on one who would challenge her to give good reasons for that challenge ("I know the expert consensus is that *p*, but I submit that a superior alternative explanation is the following . . ."). By contrast, one whose remarks are, in the appropriate sense, light, creates no such burden, and may even be disallowed all contributions save those that are either self-evident or that can be substantiated by immediately available evidence.

A signal *S*'s being a handicap may appear incompatible with a signaler *O*'s being able to choose whether or not to produce *S*. After all, *O*'s having a choice in the matter seems precisely to show that *S* is not an index (save perhaps of *S*'s choice), and thus not a handicap. This, I suggest, is where norms come in. A norm can make a signal costly to produce, not by exacting calories or territory, but rather by making an agent *subject to a loss of credibility*. For a norm might have the following schematic content:

One who produces *S* is to be in condition *C*; otherwise she is subject to a loss of credibility.

A loss of credibility will, as we have suggested, reduce the weight of a speaker's speech acts, thereby hobbling her ability to serve as a conversational "player." As the likelihood and severity of a loss of credibility increase, so does the exposure to risk for those who produce *S* without being in condition *C*. Exposure to risk does not, of course, guarantee harm: I could go all my life without a seatbelt or a scratch. However, even in such a case I have paid a price in the sense of having closed off a possibility. As Adams (2001) points out, a creature can "burn its bridges" by performing an action that closes off options that would otherwise have been open. Transposed to the norm schema displayed above, we may say that this norm guarantees that one who produces *S* forfeits the option of failing to be in condition *C* without exposure to censure. The more specific norms that we formulate below will conform to this pattern.[14]

   If, then, a norm conforming to the above schema is in force, and it is common knowledge that it is, a signal *S* of condition *C* will be difficult to fake precisely because of the cost involved. For this reason producing *S* will be an index of *C* by being a handicap. Further, when such a norm is in force the production of *S* will be a handicap even when producing *S* is subject to an agent's choice. In addition, the condition of which *S* is an index need not be the organism's overall fitness. Instead it could be any feature of the organism that it has reason to signal. For instance, it could be something on which *O* can introspect if she is possessed of a capacity for introspection. As a result, if *O* can signal one of her introspectible states by incurring a handicap, then *O* may be able to express that state as well. Thus consider the one-word expression of gratitude, "Thanks!" Its use is governed by the norm

One who utters and speaker-means "Thanks!" is to be feeling gratitude toward her addressee; otherwise she is subject to a loss of credibility.[15]

No test, of course, is going decisively to settle whether a speaker has respected this norm. However, we have many ways of justifying conclusions about a person's sincerity: my thanking a person and then sniggering behind their back; my failure to show any inclination to return the kindness for which I purport to show gratitude; my scoffing at others who show similar kindness, are all evidence that my ostensible gratitude is hollow.

The hypothesis that some such norm as the above governs the use of "Thanks!" explains how one's sincere use of that word can express one's gratitude: it does so by enabling the speaker to incur the risk of a loss of credibility if she is not feeling gratitude. As such it justifies the thought, whether consciously entertained or not, in the addressee: she would not say it if she did not feel that way. (Compare: that peacock must be awfully fit to sport such an elaborate train!) The speaker thus expresses gratitude by performing an act that shows, and was designed to show, this introspectible state.

Our hypothesis does not imbue linguistic communities with the power conventionally to stipulate that one thing is evidence for another. What linguistic communities do is stipulate that one action type (saying "Thanks!" without feeling gratitude, etc.) is to merit an agent's censure through her loss of credibility. Such norms, when promulgated in the form of common knowledge, enable agents to show their psychological states.[16]

5 EXPRESSIVE SPEECH ACTS AS HANDICAPS[17]

It may seem that in producing this account of how speech acts express what is within we have painted ourselves into a corner. For each indicative sentence, there are many psychological states that it can express – one for each speech act whose content it is, and for which Moorean absurdity is possible. Surely, however, we do not have as many distinct norms as this?

Such a proliferation of norms is not, however, needed. The reason is that each type of illocutionary force for which Moorean absurdity is possible is characterized at least in part by a norm determining what psychological state the user of that force is to be in; in some cases, furthermore, the norm also mandates some feature of that state – as justified or not, for instance. In *Speech Acts* Searle characterizes assertion of p as, "an undertaking to the effect that p represents an actual state of affairs" (1969: 66). Such an undertaking puts the assertor in a position such that she is correct on the issue of p if p, and incorrect on that issue otherwise. But assertion does more than this: one who guesses that p is also correct or not depending on how things are with p. When a speaker asserts p, it is sometimes within the rights of an addressee to reply with the challenge, "How do you know?"; in other cases, as we have just seen, the onus is on the addressee to give reasons for challenging the claim. In either case, in response to a proper challenge the assertor should either offer reasons of her own, or defer to another's authority; otherwise she should retract the challenged assertion. A norm governing assertion might, accordingly, go somewhat as follows:

One who asserts p is to believe p with justification adequate for knowledge; otherwise she is subject to a loss of credibility.

I hasten to add, however, that for present purposes we need not settle current controversies surrounding the alleged norms governing assertion. Perhaps Williamson (1996, 2000) is correct that one is only to assert what one knows; perhaps, on the other hand, weaker norms are more appropriate. What matters for our purposes is that assertion is governed by a norm of sincerity, that the sincerity condition be a belief, and that the belief be justified.

Compare assertion with conjecture: If I offer p as a conjecture, it is inappropriate to reply with, "How do you know that?" A legitimate challenge would instead involve showing that what I say is demonstrably wrong or very unlikely. Likewise, a conjecture should be backed with some justification or other; otherwise, it should be put forth as a guess. However, if you do put it forth as a conjecture, the required justification need not be as powerful as that for assertion (Green 1999b).

Assertions, conjectures, suggestions, guesses, presumptions, and the like are cousins sharing the property of commitment to a propositional content. They differ from one another in the norms by which they are governed, and thereby in the nature of that commitment. Consequently, the speaker incurs a distinctive vulnerability for each such speech act – including a liability to being in error, the danger of being shown to be insincere, and, in some cases, a mandate to defend what she has said if appropriately challenged. These liabilities to error, exposed insincerity, and injunctions to defend put the speaker at risk of losing credibility in the community in which she has a reputation (Brandom 1983; Green 2000a and Green 2000b). That is precisely what it is to stick out one's neck.

For many speech acts, then, in performing them I incur a liability – a handicap in our technical sense. The nature of that liability determines not just what intentional state is shown, but also in what light it is shown: just as different pictures of one and the same sitter might show him as brave, as menacing, as a fop, etc., different speech acts can show a single psychological state in different lights. The liability that an assertor undertakes by incurring the commitments characteristic of that speech act give strong (not conclusive) evidence that the assertion is both sincere and justified. That liability is less stringent for the case of conjecture, with the result that a conjecture does not show one's belief as justified in a way appropriate for knowledge; instead it merely requires showing one's belief as having some justification or other. Standards are even less stringent for a so-called educated guess. Further, for a guess these standards only put the speaker in danger of being wrong if her guess turns out to be incorrect. Table 12.1 may help to clarify these points. The second and third columns describe what felicitous speech acts show, and in what way they show this. While all four speech acts considered here involve commitment to a propositional content, only two require belief for their sincerity condition. Guesses and educated guesses require only acceptance for their sincerity condition *sensu* Stalnaker (1984).[18]

Can the current proposal be generalized to other types of speech act for which Moorean absurdity is possible? I will try partially to justify the claim that it can by considering the case of promising. Assuming once again that a promise expresses an intention, it will follow that a promise shows, or purports to show, an intention to carry out the promised act. It does that precisely by virtue of the fact that one who promises incurs the liability of a loss of credibility if she fails to perform

Table 12.1

Speech act	Shows	as
Assertion that p	Belief that p	Justified appropriate for knowledge
Conjecture that p	Belief that p	Justified
Educated guess that p	Acceptance or belief that p	Justified
Guess that p	Acceptance of p	n/a
Presumption of p	Acceptance of p	Justified for current conversational purposes
Supposition of p (for argument)	Acceptance of p	Aimed at the production of justification for some related content r

the promised act. (We tend to cut slack for those who fail to keep their promises for reasons beyond their control.) A promise is, accordingly, like earnest money put down in lieu of full payment for a car: whereas the latter, if the sum is sufficiently large, shows your intention of coming back to purchase the vehicle, the former, because of the stringent norms to which promissors are held, shows your intention of fulfilling the promise. In contrast with assertion and its cousins, however, a promise does not appear to show the relevant intention as justified or not. Although our intentions are sometimes justified, and sometimes not, our linguistic institutions appear not to have developed ways of indicating the justificatory status of the intentions we show in promising.

In some situations talk is cheap. Asked for directions to the train station in a crowded place by a person I am sure I shall never encounter again, in no very strong sense am I sticking my neck out in answering as I do. As a result I am not, or at least barely, incurring a handicap in answering in whatever way I happen to. This will imply that even if I speak sincerely, it will be difficult for me to express my belief that the station is three blocks east on the left side of the road when I say, "It's three blocks east on the left side of the road."[19] I take this to be an appealing consequence of the present approach: outside their typical "ecological niche," speech acts might not have the epistemic powers that make them so special in human culture.

In a passage similar to the one with which we began, Searle and Vanderveken claim that in every performance of a speech act one expresses a psychological state with that same content (1985: 18). This claim is dubious, and nothing in the hypothesis I have formulated above requires it. Consider appointing: if appropriately empowered, I can appoint someone to a certain administrative post by saying – more precisely by speaker-meaning – that I am doing so. The propositional content is that the addressee of the speech act is appointed to the post in question. However, it is doubtful that a psychological state is being expressed by a speech act such as this. Such a state would not be a belief: even if I speaker-mean, "I hereby appoint you, but don't believe that I am doing so," I can be understood as expressing doubts about the ability of my words to effect an appointment. Such an utterance need not be absurd. An appointment also does not express an intention: whereas the disavowal of an intention to perform a promised act may make a putative promise absurd ("I promise to meet you but have no intention of doing so"), what you intend seems irrelevant to the question whether the concurrent utterance of "I hereby appoint you" succeeds as an appointment. Similarly for excommunicating, declaring open (closed, etc.), demoting, resigning, vetoing.

It is also unclear that directives express psychological states. I can speaker-mean all of an order, for instance, without hoping or intending that the addressee follow it. I can also report the absence of such a psychological state, as in "I order you to attack that enemy entrenchment, though I don't want you to do so." Why should doing so be absurd? After all, as a military authority I must pass down orders through the chain of command, and must sometimes direct my troops regardless of my feelings or wants.[20]

So-called directives and declarations do not, in general, commit the speaker to a future course of action (as do commissives such as promises), or even to a disposition to a future course of action (as do many assertives such as assertions). Instead, appointing, excommunicating, declaring open, commanding, and the like are done once they are (felicitously) said. While many, and perhaps the most important, speech acts characteristically express psychological states, it is doubtful that all do, and we do not assume it here.[21]

Why, finally, should some speech acts have an expressive dimension while others do not? While I cannot do justice to that large question here, I will offer a suggestion that applies to the "assertive" family of speech acts that have been our focus – assertion, conjecture, supposition, and the like. As contributors to inquiries it behooves us not only to offer up contents to common ground, but also to indicate the status of those contents – as known, as conjectured, as guessed, etc. Holding fixed what is said, expressive norms enable us to indicate how what is said is to be taken and what would count as an appropriate reply. Such norms enable us to do that by enabling us to show the psychological state (belief, acceptance, belief as justified, etc.) from which the conversational contribution flows. One could also report the psychological state from which the contribution flows ("I believe that p," etc.), but for most purposes such explicitness is otiose as compared to the stunning power of speech acts to telegraph our states of mind.[22]

NOTES

1 One of my first philosophy teachers, John Searle inspired in me while I was an undergraduate at Berkeley an enthusiasm for philosophy, and for philosophy of language in particular, that has remained for over two decades. This chapter is dedicated to him.

2 Searle (1969: 65); see also Searle (1979: 4) and Searle and Vanderveken (1985: 18).

3 Although this phenomenon is often referred to as "Moore's Paradox", I follow Moore in distinguishing absurdity from paradox: absurdity is exemplified in utterances such as "It's raining but I don't believe it"; what is paradoxical is that there should be such absurdity in spite of the fact that this is no semantic contradiction. See Green (2007) for a fuller discussion of this distinction. Also, I take speaker-meaning to consist in intentionally and overtly committing oneself to a content: it does not require intentions to produce effects in an audience, to say nothing of intentions to produce effects by means of recognition of those intentions – see Green (2003).

4 Discussions of Moorean absurdity routinely acknowledge Wittgenstein's example of a railway announcer who is convinced that the train whose scheduled arrival he is obliged to report will not arrive. He announces its impending arrival and adds, "Personally I don't believe it." Here the announcer does not fully speaker-mean all of what he says when announcing the arrival time. Our claim in the text is only that one who fully speaker-means in its entirety some such sentence as "It's raining but I don't believe it" is being absurd. For further details see Green (2007).

5 See Green (2007) for a more comprehensive discussion of the desiderata that an account of Moorean absurdity must meet.

6 In Green (forthcoming a), I distinguish among *showing-that* (which enables, but does not guarantee propositional knowledge), *showing-α* (which makes an object perceptible), and *showing-how* (which enables one to know how an emotion, mood or experience feels). Speech acts, if they show anything, enable propositional knowledge, and in what follows, by "show" and its cognates I will refer only to showing-that.

7 *Oxford English Dictionary*, Compact edn.

8 As we have seen, Searle says that an assertion, for instance, is an expression of belief even when the speaker lies. How we treat such a case is largely a matter of nomenclature: I prefer to say that in such a case the assertion is *expressive* of belief but does not express the speaker's belief (for he has none). (This is analogous to a usage in esthetics in which a composer might write music that is expressive of grief without expressing her grief at all – she might be in the highest spirits.) In adopting this usage I am begging no questions against Searle, since there remains the substantial issue of how a sincere speech act shows what it expresses. Likewise, we could readily transpose the claim of the text to say that while representation does not, as such, enable knowledge of what is represented, expression of one's cognitive, affective or experiential state does enable knowledge of what is expressed. In the interests of brevity I shall refrain from such a transposition.

9 I am suggesting that it is implicit in our commonsense view of the nature of tears that they have the job of showing emotion. That commonsense view

might of course be false, and if it is, our commonsense is incorrect in ascribing to tears an expressive role. Yet even if that is so, we will have an explanation of why there intuitively seems to be a difference between tears and the bulging vein.

10 This does not imply that speakers make assertions with the, or an, intention of showing their belief, any more than does the fact that scowling is designed to show anger imply that those who scowl intend to show their anger.

11 Searle adopts a weaker form of force conventionalism than does Austin in leaving open the possibility that some speech acts can be performed without constitutive rules: a dog requesting to be let outside (1969: 39), pronouncements by God, and verbal stipulations (1979: 18) do not in his view require extra-semantic conventions. For further discussion see Green (forthcoming b).

12 I assume that "It is a convention that ..." is an extensional context: if it is a convention that Hesperus is venerated at midnight, then it is also a convention that Phosphorus is whether or not all parties to this convention are aware of this fact.

13 When the process of natural selection accounts for a trait as an adaptation, that shows it to be designed without justifying the inference that there must have been an intelligent designer. Also, this definition of a signal is close to the notion of communication found in Johnson-Laird (1991), and may be seen as a generalization of a notion offered in recent evolutionary biology. Maynard Smith and Harper offer the following definition: "We define a 'signal' as any act or structure which alters the behaviour of other organisms, which evolved because of that effect, and which is effective because the receiver's response has also evolved" (Maynard Smith and Harper 2004: 3). I shall instead use a more general notion that applies to things other than organisms and to processes other than evolution.

14 Stalnaker (2006) explores the notion of credibility in relating game theory to communication.

15 It may be possible to speaker-mean one's thanks without uttering any words, perhaps with a gesture. One can also utter the expression without speaker-meaning it, for instance on stage. That is why neither of the two conditions is redundant.

16 Similar points apply to the single-digit salute we discussed in the last section: it is governed by the norm that one overtly extending this finger is feeling contempt toward the "addressee." Also, it should be clear that this norm and the one for thanking are not the only norms governing these acts. The latter, for instance, is to be used to *acknowledge* one's gratitude.

17 "Expressive" in the title of this section is meant to restrict discussion to those speech acts having an expressive role; it is not meant to align with Searle's category of expressives.

18 While a conception of certain speech acts as handicaps and, in that light, as showing psychological states, is to the best of my knowledge novel, relating speech acts to one another in terms of "degrees of strength" may seem well-worn territory in the light of Searle's and Vanderveken's writings. However, their notion of "illocutionary implication" is of no use to us here. For them, that notion comes in two forms: Speech act F(p) *strongly illocutionarily implies* speech act G(q) iff any performance of the former is also a performance of the latter (1985: 23). Surely, however, it is not plausible that when I assert that p I have also guessed and conjectured that p – strong illocutionary implication does not seem relevant to such cases. Searle and Vanderveken also define a weaker notion: speech act F(p) *weakly illocutionarily implies* speech act G(q) iff any performance of the former commits the speaker to the performance of the latter although he does not perform the latter and is not committed to its performance (1985: 24). I have been unable to find any sense in this definition, and as a result have been unable to discern whether it is applicable to the cases that concern us here. To better conceptualize relations among the speech acts that are our subject here, I develop a third notion, illocutionary validity, in Green (2000b).

19 I might, on the other hand, have internalized norms of speech acts well enough to feel remorse if I am not sincere. In that case my assertion to the stranger may still express my belief if I am in fact sincere, for it still makes me vulnerable to censure (my own).

20 For further discussion see Heal (1977) and Green (1999a). Returning to the theme of note 4 above, observe that in response to the question, "Do you mean that?," the railway announcer could not truly answer, "Yes." The commander could.

21 This observation also undercuts Searle's account of speaker meaning in terms of an "imposition" of the conditions of satisfaction of an intentional state on that of an utterance. In elucidating this account Searle writes,

> [N]otice that the structure of the speech act, F(p), and the structure of the corresponding Intentional state, S(p), are exactly parallel. Furthermore, they have exactly the same conditions of satisfaction: e.g. my statement that it is raining will be true iff my belief that it is raining is true. Also, the Intentional state is the sincerity condition on the assertion: When I say it is raining I express the belief that it is raining; and if I say it is raining but do not believe it is raining, I am lying.
>
> These very tight connections are not accidental and they suggest the following explanation: To say something and mean it is to impose the conditions of satisfaction of the belief onto the utterance. Since the utterance is itself the condition of satisfaction of the intention to make it, the essence of meaning is the intentional imposition of conditions of satisfaction onto conditions of satisfaction. (1991a: 86)

I take it that, in the second quoted paragraph, Searle is only giving an account of speaker meaning for indicatives. For imperatives, the position would evidently be that to say something and mean it is to impose the conditions of satisfaction of the desire that is the sincerity condition of that speech act onto the utterance; likewise for the other main types of speech act on the Searlian taxonomy. However, this pattern of analysis cannot give us a necessary condition for speaker meaning because, as we have seen, many speech acts, such as appointing and excommunicating, have no sincerity condition at all.

22 My thanks to Savas Tsohatzidis for detailed and insightful comments on an earlier draft of this paper. Research for the paper was supported in part by a Summer Grant from the University of Virginia.

References

Abel, G. (ed.) (2006). *Kreativität*. Hamburg: Felix Meiner Verlag.

Adams, E. (2001). Threat displays in animal communication: handicaps, reputations, and commitments. In R. Nesse (ed.), *Evolution and the Capacity for Commitment*, pp. 99–119. New York: Russell Sage Foundation.

Alston, W. P. (1997). Searle on perception. Read at the mini-conference on the philosophy of John Searle held at the University of Notre Dame in April 1997.

(2000). *Illocutionary Acts and Sentence Meaning*. Ithaca, NY: Cornell University Press.

Armstrong, D. M. (1991). Intentionality, perception and causality: reflections on John Searle's *Intentionality*. In E. Lepore and R. Van Gulick (eds.), *John Searle and his Critics*, pp. 149–58. Oxford: Blackwell.

Asher, N. (1993). *Reference to Abstract Objects in Discourse*. Dordrecht: Kluwer Academic Publishers.

Asher, N. and Bonevac, D. (2005). Free choice permission is strong permission. *Synthese*, 145, 303–23.

Asher, N. and Lascarides, A. (2003). *Logics of Conversation*. Cambridge: Cambridge University Press.

Asher, N. and McCready, E. (2007). "Might", "would" and a compositional account of counterfactuals. *Journal of Semantics*, 24, 93–129.

Asher, N. and Reese, B. (2005). Negative bias in polar questions. In E. Maier, C. Bary, and J. Huitink (eds.), *Proceedings of Sinn und Bedeutung 9*, pp. 30–43. Nijmegen: Nijmegen Centre of Semantics.

Asher, N. and Wang, L. (2003). Ambiguity and anaphora with plurals in discourse. In R. B. Young and Y. Zhou (eds.), *Proceedings of Semantics and Linguistic Theory 13*. Ithaca, NY: Cornell Linguistics Circle Publications.

Austin, J. L. (1961). *How to Do Things with Words*. Oxford: Oxford University Press.

Bach, K. (1978). A representational theory of action. *Philosophical Studies*, 34, 361–79.

(1981). What's in a name. *Australasian Journal of Philosophy*, 59, 371–86.

(1982). *De re* belief and methodological solipsism. In A. Woodfield (ed.), *Thought and Object*, pp. 121–51. Oxford: Oxford University Press.

(1994a). *Thought and Reference*, pbk edn. Oxford: Oxford University Press.

(1994b). Semantic slack: what is said and more. In S. L. Tsohatzidis (ed.), *Foundations of Speech Act Theory: Philosophical and Linguistic Perspectives*, pp. 267–91. London: Routledge.

Barker, S. J. (2004). *Renewing Meaning: A Speech-Act Theoretic Approach*. Oxford: Oxford University Press.

Barwise, J. and Perry, J. (1983). *Situations and Attitudes*. Cambridge, MA: MIT Press.

Belnap, N., Horty, J., and Xu, M. (1995). The deliberative Stit: a study of action, omission, ability and obligation. *Journal of Philosophical Logic*, 24, 583–644.

Blackburn, S. (1990). Wittgenstein's irrealism. In L. Brandl and R. Haller (eds.), *Wittgenstein: Eine Neubewertung*, pp. 13–26. Vienna: Hoelder-Pickler Tempsky.

Bloom, P. (2002). *How Children Learn the Meanings of Words*. Cambridge, MA: MIT Press.

Brandom, R. B. (1983). Asserting. *Noûs*, 17, 637–50.

(1994). *Making It Explicit: Reasoning, Representing and Discursive Commitment*. Cambridge, MA: Harvard University Press.

Brentano, F. ([1874] 1973). *Psychology from an Empirical Standpoint*, trans. A. C. Rancurello, D. B. Terrell, and L. L. McAlister, ed. L. L. McAlister. New York: Humanities Press.

Burge, T. (1977). *De re* belief. *Journal of Philosophy*, 74, 338–62.

(1991). Vision and intentional content. In E. Lepore and R. Van Gulick (eds.), *John Searle and his Critics*, pp. 195–213. Oxford: Blackwell.

Cavell, S. (1990). *Conditions Handsome and Unhandsome: The Constitution of Emersonian Perfectionism*. Chicago, IL: University of Chicago Press.

Clark, H. and Gerrig, R. (1984). On the pretense theory of irony. *Journal of Experimental Psychology: General*, 113, 121–6.

Cocchiarella, N. B. (1984). Philosophical perspectives on quantification in tense and modal logic. In D. Gabbay and F. Guenthner (eds.), *Handbook of Philosophical Logic*, vol. II, pp. 309–53. Dordrecht: Reidel.

Darwin, C. ([1872] 1998). *The Expression of the Emotions in Man and Animals*, ed. P. Ekman. Oxford: Oxford University Press.

Davidson, D. (1975). Thought and talk. In S. Guttenplan (ed.), *Mind and Language*, pp. 7–23. Oxford: Clarendon Press.

(1984). *Inquiries into Truth and Interpretation*. Oxford: Clarendon Press.

Davis, W. A. (2003). *Meaning, Expression, and Thought*. Cambridge: Cambridge University Press.

(2005). *Nondescriptive Meaning and Reference*. Oxford: Oxford University Press.

Devitt, M. (1974). Singular terms. *Journal of Philosophy*, 71, 183–205.

(1981). *Designation*. New York: Columbia University Press.

(1990). Meanings just ain't in the head. In G. Boolos (ed.), *Meaning and Method: Essays in Honour of Hilary Putnam*, pp. 79–104. Cambridge: Cambridge University Press.

Devitt, M. and Sterelny, K. (1987). *Language and Reality: An Introduction to the Philosophy of Language*. Cambridge, MA: MIT Press.

Donnellan, K. (1972). Proper names and identifying descriptions. In G. Harman and D. Davidson (eds.), *Semantics of Natural Language*, pp. 356–79. Dordrecht: Reidel.

Dummett, M. (1963). Realism. Read at Oxford University Philosophical Society in March 1963. First published in M. Dummett, *Truth and Other Enigmas*, London: Duckworth, 1978, pp. 145–65.

(1976). What is a theory of meaning? (II). In G. Evans and J. McDowell (eds.), *Truth and Meaning: Essays in Semantics*, pp. 67–137. Oxford: Clarendon Press.

Evans, G. (1973). The causal theory of names. *Proceedings of the Aristotelian Society, Supplementary Volume*, 47, 187–208.

(1982). *The Varieties of Reference*, ed. J. McDowell. Oxford: Clarendon Press.

Fernandez, J. (2006). The intentionality of memory. *Australasian Journal of Philosophy*, 84, 39–57.

Fitch, W. T. (2005). The evolution of language: a comparative review. *Biology and Philosophy*, 20, 193–230.

Fodor, J. A. (1975). *The Language of Thought*. New York: Thomas Y. Crowell.

(1981). *Representations*. Cambridge, MA: MIT Press.

(1994). *The Elm and the Expert: Mentalese and its Semantics*. Cambridge, MA: MIT Press.

Forguson, L. W. (1973). Locutionary and illocutionary acts. In I. Berlin *et al.*, *Essays on J. L. Austin*, pp. 160–85. Oxford: Clarendon Press.

Frege, G. (1879). *Begriffsschrift, eine der arithmetischen nachgebildete Formelsprache des reinen Denkens*. Halle: L. Nebert.

(1918). Der Gedanke, eine logische Untersuchung. *Beiträge zur Philosophie des deutschen Idealismus* 1, 58–77.

Gärdenfors, P. (2000). *Conceptual Spaces: The Geometry of Thought*. Cambridge, MA: MIT Press.

Gauker, C. (1990). How to learn a language like a chimpanzee. *Philosophical Psychology*, 3, 31–53.

(1991). If children thought like adults. *Philosophical Psychology*, 4, 139–46.

(1994a). Review of C. R. Gallistel (ed.), *Animal Cognition. Philosophical Psychology*, 7, 515–19.

(1994b). *Thinking Out Loud: An Essay on the Relation between Thought and Language*. Princeton, NJ: Princeton University Press.

(2003). *Words without Meaning*. Cambridge, MA: MIT Press.

(2005a). On the evidence for prelinguistic concepts. *Theoria* (Spain), 54, 287–97.

(2005b). *Conditionals in Context*. Cambridge, MA: MIT Press.

Geach, P. T. (1965). Assertion. *Philosophical Review*, 74, 449–65.

(1976). Saying and showing in Frege and Wittgenstein. *Acta Philosophica Fennica*, 28, 54–70.

(1980). Some problems about the sense and reference of proper names. *Canadian Journal of Philosophy Supplement*, 6, 83–96.

Gillies, A. (2004). Epistemic conditionals and conditional epistemics. *Noûs*, 38, 585–616.

Ginzburg, J. (1995). Resolving questions, I. *Linguistics and Philosophy*, 18, 459–527.

References

Goldman, A. I. (1970). *A Theory of Human Action*. Princeton, NJ: Princeton University Press.

Goodale, M. and Milner, D. (1995). *The Visual Brain in Action*. Oxford: Oxford University Press.

(2004). *Sight Unseen: An Exploration of Conscious and Unconscious Vision*. Oxford: Oxford University Press.

Green, M. (1999a). Moore's many paradoxes. *Philosophical Papers*, 28, 97–109.

(1999b). Illocutions, implicata, and what a conversation requires. *Pragmatics and Cognition*, 7, 65–92.

(2000a). The status of supposition. *Noûs*, 34, 376–99.

(2000b). Illocutionary force and semantic content. *Linguistics and Philosophy*, 23, 435–73.

(2003). Grice's frown: on meaning and expression. In G. Meggle and C. Plunze (eds.), *Saying, Meaning, Implicating*, pp. 200–19. Leipzig: University of Leipzig Press.

(2007). Moorean absurdity and showing what's within. In M. Green and J. Williams (eds.), *Moore's Paradox: New Essays on Belief, Rationality and the First Person*, pp. 189–214. Oxford: Oxford University Press.

(forthcoming a). *Self-Expression*. Oxford: Oxford University Press.

(forthcoming b). Speech acts. *Stanford Encyclopedia of Philosophy*.

Grice, H. P. (1957). Meaning. *Philosophical Review*, 66, 377–88.

(1968). Utterer's meaning, sentence-meaning and word-meaning. *Foundations of Language*, 4, 225–42.

Grice, H. P. (1975). Logic and conversation. In P. Cole and J. L. Morgan (eds.), *Syntax and Semantics, 3: Speech Acts*, pp. 41–58. New York: Academic Press.

Groenendijk, J. (1999). The logic of interrogation: classical version. In T. Matthews and D. Strolovitch (eds.), *Proceedings of Semantics and Linguistic Theory 9*, pp. 109–26. Ithaca, NY: Cornell Linguistics Circle Publications.

Groenendijk, J. and Stokhof, M. (1991). Dynamic predicate logic. *Linguistics and Philosophy*, 14, 39–100.

Hamblin, C. (1973). Questions in Montague English. *Foundations of Language*, 10, 41–53.

(1987). *Imperatives*. Oxford: Blackwell.

Han, C. (2000). *The Structure and Interpretation of Imperatives: Mood and Force in Universal Grammar*. New York: Garland.

Harel, D. (1984). Dynamic logic. In D. Gabbay and F. Guenthner (eds.), *Handbook of Philosophical Logic*, vol. II, pp. 497–604. Dordrecht: Reidel.

Heal, J. (1977). Insincerity and commands. *Proceedings of the Aristotelian Society*, 77, 183–202.

Higginbotham, J. (1995). Tensed thoughts. *Mind and Language*, 10, 226–49.

(1996). The semantics of questions. In S. Lappin (ed.), *The Handbook of Contemporary Semantic Theory*, pp. 361–84. Oxford: Blackwell.

(2003). Remembering, imagining, and the first person. In A. Barber (ed.), *Epistemology of Language*, pp. 496–533. Oxford: Oxford University Press.

Hoerl, C. (2001). The phenomenology of episodic recall. In C. Hoerl and T. McCormack (eds.), *Time and Memory*, pp. 315–35. Oxford: Oxford University Press.

References

Horwich, P. (1998). *Meaning*. Oxford: Oxford University Press.

James, W. (1890). *Principles of Psychology*, vol. I. London: Macmillan.

Johnson-Laird, P. (1991). What is communication? In D. H. Mellor (ed.), *Ways of Communicating*, pp. 1–13. Cambridge: Cambridge University Press.

Kaplan, D. (1978). Dthat. In P. Cole (ed.), *Syntax and Semantics, 9: Pragmatics*, pp. 221–53. New York: Academic Press.

(1989). Demonstratives: an essay on the semantics, logic, metaphysics and epistemology of demonstratives and other indexicals. In J. Almog, J. Perry, and H. Wettstein (eds.), *Themes from Kaplan*, pp. 481–563. Oxford: Oxford University Press.

Kölbel, M. (ms). Literal force: a defense of conventional assertion. University of Birmingham.

Korta, K. and Perry, J. (2006). Three demonstrations and a funeral. *Mind and Language*, 21, 166–86.

Krifka, M. (2001). Quantifying into question acts. *Natural Language Semantics*, 9, 1–40.

(2002). Embedded speech acts. Paper read at *In the Mood*, a conference on mood and modality, Wolfgang Goethe University, Frankfurt.

Kripke, S. (1972). Naming and necessity. In G. Harman and D. Davidson (eds.), *Semantics of Natural Language*, pp. 253–355, 763–9. Dordrecht: Reidel.

(1977). Speaker reference and semantic reference. *Midwest Studies in Philosophy*, 2, 255–78.

(1982). *Wittgenstein on Rules and Private Language*. Cambridge, MA: Harvard University Press.

Kusch, M. (2006). *A Sceptical Guide to Meaning and Rules: Defending Kripke's Wittgenstein*. Chesham: Acumen.

Levinson, S. C. (1997). From outer to inner space: linguistic categories and non-linguistic thinking. In J. Nuyts and E. Pederson (eds.), *Language and Conceptualization*, pp. 13–45. Cambridge: Cambridge University Press.

Lewis, D. (1972). General semantics. In G. Harman and D. Davidson (eds.), *Semantics of Natural Language*, pp. 169–218. Dordrecht: Reidel.

(1979). Scorekeeping in a language game. *Journal of Philosophical Logic*, 8, 339–59.

(1980). Index, context, and content. In S. Kanger and S. Öhman (eds.), *Philosophy and Grammar*, pp. 79–100. Dordrecht: Reidel.

Loar, B. (1985). Review of S. Kripke, *Wittgenstein on Rules and Private Language*. *Noûs*, 19, 273–80.

Malcolm, N. (1942). Moore and ordinary language. In P. A. Schilpp (ed.), *The Philosophy of G. E. Moore*, pp. 345–68. Evanston and Chicago, IL: Northwestern University Press.

Margolis, E. and Laurence, S. (1999). Concepts and cognitive science. In E. Margolis and S. Laurence (eds.), *Concepts: Core Readings*, pp. 3–81. Cambridge, MA: MIT Press.

Martin, M. (2001). Out of the past: episodic recall as retained acquaintance. In C. Hoerl and T. McCormack (eds.), *Time and Memory*, pp. 257–84. Oxford: Oxford University Press.

Mastop, R. (2005). What Can You Do? PhD Dissertation, University of Amsterdam.

References

Maynard Smith, J. and Harper, D. (2004). *Animal Signals*. Oxford: Oxford University Press.

McDowell, J. (1984a). *De re* senses. In C. Wright (ed.), *Frege: Tradition and Influence*, pp. 98–109. Oxford: Blackwell.

(1984b). Wittgenstein on following a rule. *Synthese*, 58, 325–63.

(1991). Intentionality *de re*. In E. Lepore and R. Van Gulick (eds.), *John Searle and His Critics*, pp. 215–25. Oxford: Blackwell.

(1994). *Mind and World*. Cambridge, MA: Harvard University Press.

(1995). The content of perceptual experience. *Philosophical Quarterly*, 44, 190–205.

Merin, A. (1992). Permission sentences stand in the way of Boolean and other lattice-theoretic semantices. *Journal of Semantics*, 9, 95–162.

Mill, J. S. (1879). *A System of Logic* (10th edn). London: Longman, Green, and Co.

Moore, G. E. (1925). A defence of common sense. Reprinted in G. E. Moore, *Selected Writings*, ed. T. Baldwin, London: Routledge, 1993, pp. 106–33.

(1939). Proof of an external world. Reprinted in G. E. Moore, *Selected Writings*, ed. T. Baldwin, London: Routledge, 1993, pp. 147–70.

Murphy, G. L. (2002). *The Big Book of Concepts*. Cambridge, MA: MIT Press.

Pagin, P. (2004). Is assertion social? *Journal of Pragmatics*, 36, 833–59.

Perry, J. (1977). Frege on demonstratives. *Philosophical Review*, 89, 474–97.

(1979). The problem of the essential indexical. *Noûs*, 13, 3–21.

(2001). *Reference and Reflexivity*. Stanford, CA: CSLI Publications.

Perry, J., Israel, D., and Tutiya, S. (1993). Executions, motivations and accomplishments. *Philosophical Review*, 102, 515–40.

Petrie, M., Halliday, T. R., and Sanders, C. (1991). Peahens prefer males with elaborate trains. *Animal Behaviour*, 41, 323–31.

Pettit, P. (1990). The reality of rule-following. *Mind*, 99, 1–21.

Pinker, S. (1994). *The Language Instinct*. New York: W. Morrow and Co.

Plantinga, A. (1978). The Boethian compromise. *American Philosophical Quarterly*, 15, 129–38.

Poole, J. H. (1989). Announcing intent: the aggressive state of musth in African elephants. *Animal Behaviour*, 37, 140–52.

Portner, P. (2004). The semantics of imperatives within a theory of clause types. In R. B. Young (ed.), *Proceedings of Semantics and Linguistic Theory 14*. Ithaca, NY: Cornell Linguistics Circle Publications.

Prior, A. N. (1963). Thank goodness that's over. *Philosophy*, 34, 12–17. Reprinted in A. Prior, *Papers in Logic and Ethics*, London: Duckworth, 1976, pp. 78–84.

(1967). *Past, Present and Future*. Oxford: Clarendon Press.

(1968). *Papers on Time and Tense*. Oxford: Clarendon Press.

(1977), with K. Fine. *Worlds, Times and Selves*. London: Duckworth.

Putnam, H. (1962). It ain't necessarily so. *Journal of Philosophy*, 59, 658–71.

(1973). Meaning and reference. *Journal of Philosophy*, 70, 699–711.

(1981). *Reason, Truth, and History*. Cambridge: Cambridge University Press.

Pylyshyn, Z. (2002). Visual indexes, preconceptual objects, and situated vision. In B. Scholl (ed.), *Objects and Attention*, pp. 127–58. Cambridge, MA: MIT Press.

(2003). *Seeing and Visualizing*. Cambridge, MA: MIT Press.

Pylyshyn, Z. and Storm, R. (1988). Tracking multiple independent targets: evidence for a parallel tracking mechanism. *Spatial Vision*, 3, 179–97.

References

Recanati, F. (1981). *Les énoncés performatifs*. Paris: Éditions de Minuit.

  (1987). *Meaning and Force*. Cambridge: Cambridge University Press.

  (1996). Domains of discourse. *Linguistics and Philosophy*, 19, 445–75.

  (1997). The dynamics of situations. *European Review of Philosophy*, 2, 41–75.

  (1999). Situations and the structure of content. In K. Murasugi and R. Stainton (eds.), *Philosophy and Linguistics*, pp. 113–65. Boulder, CO: Westview Press.

  (2000). *Oratio Obliqua, Oratio Recta: An Essay on Metarepresentation*. Cambridge, MA: MIT Press.

  (forthcoming). *Perspectival Thought : A Plea for (Moderate) Relativism*. Oxford: Oxford University Press.

Reese, B. (2006). Negative polar interrogatives and bias. In T. Washio, A. Sakurai, K. Nakajima, H. Takeda, S. Tojo, and M. Yokoo (eds.), *New Frontiers in Artificial Intelligence: Joint JSAI 2005 Workshop Post-Proceedings*, pp. 85–92. Berlin: Springer.

Reichert, S. (1984). Games spiders play III: cues underlying context-associated changes in agonistic behaviour. *Animal Behaviour*, 32, 1–15.

Russell, B. ([1918] 1985). *The Philosophy of Logical Atomism*, ed. D. Pears. La Salle, IL: Open Court.

Searle, J. R. (1958). Proper names. *Mind*, 67, 166–73.

  (1967). Proper names and descriptions. In P. Edwards (ed.), *Encyclopedia of Philosophy*, vol. VI, pp. 487–91. New York: Macmillan.

  (1968). Austin on locutionary and illocutionary acts. *Philosophical Review*, 77, 405–24.

  (1969). *Speech Acts: An Essay in the Philosophy of Language*. Cambridge: Cambridge University Press.

  (1975a). A taxonomy of illocutionary acts. In K. Gunderson (ed.), *Language, Mind and Knowledge*, pp. 344–69. Minneapolis, MN: University of Minnesota Press.

  (1975b). Indirect speech acts. In J. L. Morgan and P. Cole (eds.), *Syntax and Semantics, 3: Speech Acts*, pp. 59–82. New York: Academic Press.

  (1979). *Expression and Meaning: Studies in the Theory of Speech Acts*. Cambridge: Cambridge University Press.

  (1980a). Minds, brains, and programs. *Behavioral and Brain Sciences*, 3, 417–24.

  (1980b). The background of meaning. In J. Searle, F. Kiefer, and M. Bierwisch (eds.), *Speech Act Theory and Pragmatics*, pp. 221–32. Dordrecht: Reidel.

  (1983). *Intentionality: An Essay in the Philosophy of Mind*. Cambridge: Cambridge University Press.

  (1989). How performatives work. *Linguistics and Philosophy*, 12, 535–58.

  (1991a). Perception and the satisfactions of intentionality. In E. Lepore and R. Van Gulick (eds.), *John Searle and his Critics*, pp. 181–92. Oxford: Blackwell.

  (1991b). Reference and intentionality. In E. Lepore and R. Van Gulick (eds.), *John Searle and his Critics*, pp. 227–41. Oxford: Blackwell.

  (1992). *The Rediscovery of the Mind*. Cambridge, MA: MIT Press.

  (1994). Intentionality (1). In S. Guttenplan (ed.), *A Companion to the Philosophy of Mind*, pp. 394–86. Oxford: Blackwell.

  (1995). *The Construction of Social Reality*. New York: The Free Press.

(1998). *Mind, Language and Society: Philosophy in the Real World*. New York: Basic Books.

(2001). *Rationality in Action*. Cambridge, MA: MIT Press.

(2002). *Consciousness and Language*. Cambridge: Cambridge University Press.

(2004). *Mind: A Brief Introduction*. Oxford: Oxford University Press.

Searle, J. R. and Vanderveken, D. (1985). *Foundations of Illocutionary Logic*. Cambridge: Cambridge University Press.

Soames, S. (2002). *Beyond Rigidity: The Unfinished Semantic Agenda of Naming and Necessity*. Oxford: Oxford University Press.

Soteriou, M. (2000). The particularity of visual perception. *European Journal of Philosophy*, 8, 173–89.

Sperber, D. (1982). Comments on Clark and Carlson's paper. In N. Smith (ed.), *Mutual Knowledge*, pp. 46–51. London: Academic Press.

Sperber, D. and Wilson, D. (1986). *Relevance: Communication and Cognition*. Oxford: Blackwell.

Stalnaker, R. (1972). Pragmatics. In G. Harman and D. Davidson (eds.), *Semantics of Natural Language*, pp. 380–97. Dordrecht: Reidel.

(1973). Presuppositions. *Journal of Philosophical Logic*, 2, 447–57.

(1974). Pragmatic presuppositions. In M. Munitz and P. Unger (eds.), *Semantics and Philosophy*, pp. 197–13. New York: New York University Press.

(1984). *Inquiry*. Cambridge, MA: MIT Press.

(1999). *Context and Content*. Oxford: Oxford University Press.

(2006). Saying and meaning, cheap talk and credibility. In A. Benz, C. Jager, and R. van Rooij (eds.), *Game Theory and Pragmatics*, pp. 83–100. London: Palgrave.

Stampe, D. (1975). Show and tell. In B. Freed, A. Marras, and P. Maynard (eds.), *Forms of Representation*, pp. 221–45. Amsterdam: North-Holland.

Strawson, P. F. (1950). On referring. *Mind*, 59, 320–44.

(1959). *Individuals: An Essay in Descriptive Metaphysics*. London: Methuen.

(1973). Austin and "locutionary meaning." In I. Berlin *et al.*, *Essays on J. L. Austin*, pp. 46–68. Oxford: Clarendon Press.

Thomason, R. (1990). Accommodation, meaning and implicature: interdisciplinary foundations for pragmatics. In P. R. Cohen, J. Morgan, and M. E. Pollock (eds.), *Intentions in Communication*, pp. 325–64. Cambridge, MA: MIT Press.

Txurruka, I. (2003). The natural language conjunction "and." *Linguistics and Philosophy*, 26, 255–85.

Valberg, J. J. (1992). *The Puzzle of Experience*. Oxford: Oxford University Press.

Van den Berg, M. (1996). Some Aspects of the Internal Structure of Discourse: The Dynamics of Nominal Anaphora. PhD Dissertation, University of Amsterdam.

Vanderveken, D. (1990). *Meaning and Speech Acts*, vol. I. Cambridge: Cambridge University Press.

Vauclair, J. (1996). *Animal Cognition: An Introduction to Modern Comparative Psychology*. Cambridge, MA: Harvard University Press.

Veltman, F. (1996). Defaults in update semantics. *Journal of Philosophical Logic*, 25, 221–61.

Wiggins, D. (1980). *Sameness and Substance*. Oxford: Blackwell.

Williams, B. (2002). *Truth and Truthfulness: An Essay in Genealogy*. Princeton, NJ: Princeton University Press.

Williams, M. (1999). Skepticism. In J. Greco and E. Sosa (eds.), *The Blackwell Guide to Epistemology*, pp. 35–69. Oxford: Blackwell.

Williamson, T. (1996). Knowing and asserting. *Philosophical Review*, 105, 489–523.

  (2000). *Knowledge and its Limits*. Oxford: Oxford University Press.

Wilson, G. M. (1994). Kripke on Wittgenstein and normativity. *Midwest Studies in Philosophy*, 19, 366–90.

Wittgenstein, L. (1922). *Tractatus Logico-Philosophicus*. London: Routledge and Kegan Paul.

  (1953). *Philosophical Investigations*, ed. G. E. M. Anscombe and R. Rhees, trans. G. E. M. Anscombe. Oxford: Blackwell.

Wright, C. (1984). Kripke's account of the argument against private language. *Journal of Philosophy*, 71, 759–78.

  (1992). *Truth and Objectivity*. Cambridge, MA: Harvard University Press.

Zahavi, Am. and Zahavi, Av. (1997). *The Handicap Principle: A Missing Piece of Darwin's Puzzle*. Oxford: Oxford University Press.

Zimmerman, E. (2000). Free choice disjunction and epistemic possibility. *Natural Language Semantics*, 8, 255–90.

Index

Index

dynamic semantics and discourse
representation theory 211–41

evaluative sentences 198–99
Evans, G. 58, 60, 68, 88, 106, 287
expression vs. representation 28–30, 269–70
expressivism 193–202

Fernandez, J. 63, 287
Fitch, T. 45, 287
Fodor, J. A. 25, 123, 136, 287
Foucault, M. 19
Frege, G. 11, 13, 15, 16, 33, 56, 68, 79, 80, 81,
     82, 83, 84, 88, 91, 92, 93, 95, 97, 98, 100,
     102, 105, 107, 109, 115, 123, 146, 153, 154,
     175, 190, 193, 199, 210, 249, 261, 262, 287

Gärdenfors, P. 135, 287
Gauker, C. 8–9, 142, 287, 289
Geach, P. T. 123, 175, 272, 287
generativity 18, 36
Gillies, A. 239, 287
Ginzburg, J. 242, 287
Goldman, A. I. 189, 288
Goodale, M. 99, 288
Green, M. 14, 277, 281, 283, 288
Grice, H. P. 38, 105, 130, 170, 171, 173–74,
     193, 264, 288
Groenendijk, J. 218, 241, 242, 288

Habermas, J. 19
Hamblin, C. 212, 216, 224, 288
Harper, D. 282, 289
Heal, J. 283, 288
Higginbotham, J. 56–58, 256, 288
Horty, J. 224, 241, 286
Horwich, D. 192, 289
Hume, D. 145

identity statements 105, 180–81, 184
illocutionary act classification 22–23, 258–65
illocutionary acts and norms 131–33, 140,
     272–79
illocutionary acts as expressions of mental
     states 22–23, 267–80
implicature 130, 170, 173, 234
indexicals and demonstratives 71, 88–96,
     106–07, 108, 111, 118–19, 170, 172, 173,
     179, 184, 188
intentionality, intrinsic vs. derived 19–37,
     126–33

irony 174, 208
isomorphism 43
Israel, D. 189, 290

James, W. 59, 289
Jeshion, R. 5, 6–7
Johnson-Laird, P. 282, 289

Kant, I. 23, 88
Kaplan, D. 92, 100, 118, 123, 138, 170,
     189, 289
Kölbel, M. 142, 289
Korta, K. 9–11, 170, 289
Krifka, M. 211, 213, 214, 216, 235, 289
Kripke, S. 9, 102, 105, 106, 115, 116, 117,
     118, 119, 122, 123, 143–66, 289
Kusch, M. 9, 143, 148, 159, 289

language and thought 19–37, 42, 125–41
language and society 18–19, 39–41, 43
language of thought 25, 135–37
Lascarides, A. 212, 219, 224, 231, 241,
     242, 285
Levinson, S. C. 137, 289
Lewis, D. 38, 192, 211, 274, 289
Loar, B. 162, 289
locutionary acts 169–86

Martin, M. 8–9, 63, 289
Mastop, R. 213, 241, 289
Maynard Smith, J. 282, 290
McDowell, J. 67, 68, 69, 71, 76, 100, 164, 290
meaning skepticism, see rule-following and
     skepticism
memory 56–57, 58–61
Merin, A. 213, 232, 290
metaphor 208
Mill, J. S. 102, 103, 105, 106, 118, 122, 290
Milner, D. 99, 288
Moore, G. E. 147, 163, 281, 290
Moore's Paradox 267, 268–69, 276, 278, 281
Murphy, G. L. 136, 290

orders 22, 49–50, 53–54, 86, 208–09, 280

Pagin, P. 190, 290
perceptual experience
     awareness of spatial locations in 83–84,
          88–98
     causal self-referentiality of 50–53, 66,
          68–77, 85–87

295

Index